ROUTLEDGE LIBRARY EDITIONS:
LEISURE STUDIES

Volume 2

THE PROBLEM OF LEISURE

THE PROBLEM OF LEISURE

HENRY DURANT

Taylor & Francis Group
LONDON AND NEW YORK

First published in 1938 by George Routledge & Sons Ltd.

This edition first published in 2019
by Routledge
2 Park Square, Milton Park, Abingdon, Oxon OX14 4RN

and by Routledge
52 Vanderbilt Avenue, New York, NY 10017

Routledge is an imprint of the Taylor & Francis Group, an informa business

© 1938 Henry Durant

All rights reserved. No part of this book may be reprinted or reproduced or utilised in any form or by any electronic, mechanical, or other means, now known or hereafter invented, including photocopying and recording, or in any information storage or retrieval system, without permission in writing from the publishers.

Trademark notice: Product or corporate names may be trademarks or registered trademarks, and are used only for identification and explanation without intent to infringe.

British Library Cataloguing in Publication Data
A catalogue record for this book is available from the British Library

ISBN: 978-0-367-11036-9 (Set)
ISBN: 978-0-429-24268-7 (Set) (ebk)
ISBN: 978-0-367-13300-9 (Volume 2) (hbk)
ISBN: 978-0-367-13307-8 (Volume 2) (pbk)
ISBN: 978-0-429-02578-5 (Volume 2) (ebk)

Publisher's Note
The publisher has gone to great lengths to ensure the quality of this reprint but points out that some imperfections in the original copies may be apparent.

Disclaimer
The publisher has made every effort to trace copyright holders and would welcome correspondence from those they have been unable to trace.

THE PROBLEM OF LEISURE

By

HENRY DURANT
B.Sc. Econ.

LONDON
GEORGE ROUTLEDGE & SONS LTD.
BROADWAY HOUSE: CARTER LANE, E.C.

First published 1938

Printed in Great Britain by T. and A. CONSTABLE LTD.
at the University Press, Edinburgh

TO
RUTH DURANT

CONTENTS

CHAP.	PAGE
I. LEISURE IN THE MACHINE AGE	1
II. LEISURE IN OUR SOCIETY	33
PART I. The Aristocracy	33
PART II. The Middle Classes	50
PART III. The Working Class	71
PART IV. The Unemployed	98
III. "THE MACHINERY OF AMUSEMENT"	109
PART I. The Cinema	109
PART II. Football	152
PART III. Racing and Gambling	158
IV. ORGANIZATIONS FOR LEISURE	189
PART I. Youth	189
PART II. Open Air Recreation	229
PART III. Broadcasting	233
PART IV. Organizations for Adults	236
V. THE OUTLOOK FOR LEISURE	249
BIBLIOGRAPHY	265
INDEX OF NAMES	272
INDEX OF SUBJECTS	274

ACKNOWLEDGEMENTS

To Mr. H. L. Beales my first thanks are due. The conventional phrase, "without whose assistance this work could not have been achieved," happens, in his case, to be literally true.

The Hon. Mary Best, Margaret C. Bottomley, Olive Durant, my sister, Molly Mortimer, Olga Servagnet, P. C. Branwhite, L. H. Bishop and A. C. Ellis, have each been exceedingly helpful in supplying material. My very grateful thanks go to them all.

Students at Toynbee Hall have given great assistance, not only by the discussions I have had with them, but in collecting valuable information. Other acknowledgements appear in the text, as showing the source of the facts cited.

The chief and largest debt remains: it is acknowledged in the dedication.

H. D.

CHAPTER I

LEISURE IN THE MACHINE AGE

THE sharp division which exists for the vast majority of people between their work and their leisure is the outstanding aspect of the problem as it presents itself to-day. This division is not given *a priori*: it has come about in the course of time and is the result of particular historical circumstances. Probably the concept of leisure as something apart from and opposed to work was unknown until there arose a group in society which did not need to labour in order to ensure its livelihood. And the evidence suggests that such groups have not existed in every society.[1] The changes which have occurred are brought out clearly by the author who wrote, "The distinction between work and release from work is thoroughly well recognized in a primitive community, but one activity may serve both purposes . . . one can hardly speak of a social function of amusements. . . . City life involves a formalizing and separation of the spheres of activity that set amusements apart in time and space and function from other activities."[2] Since the change can be found in rural areas, to refer simply to the growth of cities is not sufficient. Other factors, detailed in the following pages, have also to be taken into account

---

[1] It is significant that the Greeks did not evolve a separate and distinct term for leisure The word they used meant also school, an identity which throws a flood of light on their conception of living.
[2] "Amusements, Public," Ida Craven, *Encyclopædia of the Social Sciences*, London, 1931.

for a complete explanation. There is agreement, however, that at one time the present separation between work and leisure did not exist and that it has come about in the course of historical evolution. Like many other historical processes it is not complete. Even to-day difficulties often arise in trying to show the exact line of demarcation. Yet having stressed the existing division, it is equally necessary to underline that in fact work and leisure are closely related. As different aspects of a single whole, man's life in society, they are inseparably intertwined.

To-day leisure plays a greater rôle than at any previous time. On all sides educationalists and social workers say that the urgent questions are what people do with their spare time, how to guide their activities into the "right" channels and particularly how to tackle the juveniles in this context. The present attitude contrasts strangely with that of a few years ago. Little or no public discussion then took place.[1] The publications on leisure in Great Britain during the early post-war era have been meagre,[2] and whilst many countries in Western Europe, as well as America, were busily discussing and investigating the question of leisure there was no debate of any kind in England. Now all is changed. The difficulties and perplexities arising from a greater number of persons than ever before having means and energy at their disposal to

[1] Thus when in 1928 two sociologists from America came to England to investigate leisure they " hardly ever encountered any signs of a realization in any large bodies of public opinion of a problem of leisure occupation and its various dangers and possibilities." May, Herbert, and Petgen, Dorothy, *Leisure and Its Use*, New York.

[2] Spurr, Frederic C., *The Christian Use of Leisure* (London, 1928): Joad, C. E. M., *Diogenes or the Future of Leisure* (London, 1927): The Report of C.O.P.E.C. on *Leisure*, 1924: Boyd and Ogilvie, *The Challenge of Leisure* (London, 1936): C. Delisle Burns, *Leisure in the Modern World* (London, 1935): Eric Gill, *Work and Leisure* (London, 1935).

utilize during their free hours, are engaging the attention of educationalists, social workers and all those whose business it is to attend to the working of society.

Why should the opportunity for the vast majority of people to have time to spend, time to enjoy, time to develop their own private interests, be regarded as a problem, one almost said a danger? Usually the answer is given in terms of a faulty educational system. The remedy proposed, therefore, is to train the individual not for his work, which it is agreed makes little demands on his capacities, but for the business of living a rounded life. Little argument is necessary to show that such a diagnosis does not go to the root of the problem. The educational system in Great Britain is, as elsewhere, the reflection of deep social forces which determine its shape and condition its impact. If the education given is faulty then this fault must itself be explained in terms of other and more fundamental characteristics of our society. Accordingly it is to these that we must look.

Moreover, the evidence tends to suggest that, whatever the defects of the schooling, it does in fact turn out a product holding great promise. The children, however, rarely fulfil this promise. To walk through a poor urban district is at once a heartening and discouraging experience, to see the bright and eager faces of the children and to compare them with the faces of the adults, which portray nothing so much as dejection or indifference. Something has gone wrong between childhood and maturity. "Instead of the keen alive youth is now the rather sullen uninteresting boy or man . . . with the girl the result is more depressing. . . . It is one of the most disappointing facts to see boys and girls in the schools bright and intelligent . . . and then to note . . . the change that has taken place."[1]

This conclusion, that schooling tends to develop qualities which for the majority are lost as soon as it is necessary to earn a living, means that again our attention is directed to larger aspects outside of the educational system itself. The whole social and economic environment must be examined in order to grasp the essential characteristics of leisure in modern society.

The different strata in society give rise to different considerations. The analysis of the life of the unemployed in terms of leisure, which is so often made, must be rejected. The enjoyment of leisure is dependent on positive conditions, above all on social status and the possession of the means to participate in the activities and pursuits which are available. For the unemployed none of the necessary preconditions exist. He is condemned to a life of inaction and to talk of his having leisure is to mistake the desert created by the absence of work for the oasis of recreation.

Just as leisure is one of the crucial points at which many of the strains in our society converge, so the unemployed are the embodiment of these tensions. They are the tangible expression of a struggle which haunts most of their fellow-men. As children the unemployed were moulded and trained by their parents, teachers and club leaders, each of whom worked and earned his livelihood. Hence, for these

---

[1] Harris, Constance, *The Use of Leisure in Bethnal Green* (London, 1927), pp. 14 and 15. See also Paterson, Alexander, *Across the Bridges* (London, 1915), p. 79 : Freeman, Arnold, *Boy Life and Labour* (London, 1914), pp. 92 and 108, for the same conclusion.

children, heroes were people who secured recognition through their achievements in art, science, industry and the whole world of labour. Existence, therefore, meant to them work and work meant existence. Now grown up, they find themselves workless and unwanted. But, driven by want and by the standards they imbibed when young, they seek to secure work, the touchstone of their existence. To this demand society replies with Clubs, sports and handicrafts. Leisure is offered, not merely as a make-shift but as an ultimate good. The unemployed, however, cannot accept the substitution; both their need and the early training they received prevent their finding it satisfying. Hence the position of the unemployed in which, like condemned souls, they are unable to leave the old world of work or to enter into the new world of leisure.[1]

At the other end of society is another group which does not work. They are the fortunate persons who, through the possession of property, do not need to labour in order to live.[2] Occupying the leading social

[1] See Chapter II, Part IV, for an elaboration of this argument.
[2] It will be realized that the reference is mainly to the aristocracy in Great Britain. Such figures cannot be claimed as representative for the rest of Western Europe nor for America. Yet the striking fact remains that in all countries it is luxury, sport, recreation in general, which are set highest in the hierarchy of social values. Even in Fascist Germany, where the whole official emphasis is upon asceticism and self-denial, we find not only a marked emphasis upon sport, which can be explained perhaps by ulterior motives, but also that energetic steps are being taken through " Kraft durch Freude " to organize and provide leisure facilities for the workers.

Thus, while the leading figures in the other countries may be business men who are actively engaged in promoting their affairs, the aspect which tends to be stressed is not their work but their wealth, their ease and comfort which come from great possessions. And this after all is but different in degree from the position of the aristocracy in Great Britain. It must be remembered that they too are busily engaged in all shades of social and philanthropic activities which, if performed by other people, would be remunerated and called work. Yet it is as aristocrats *simple* that they are held up to the public gaze and esteem.

An interesting illustration of the increase in importance of leisure as

positions, they are at once the apex of society and the axis on which it revolves. Possessing riches, they are able to utilize all the multiform diversions and amusements which are so abundantly available. And, as the leading figures in innumerable philanthropic institutions, they are constantly before the eye of the public in a very favourable light. Their colour and brilliance radiate through every section of society, shedding brightness where otherwise would be nought but dull regimentation. Their impact is enormous and must be clearly envisaged since their norms of conduct and standards of value tend to be absorbed by the rest of the community.

Turning to these, the men and women who work, the best approach to understanding their leisure is through a discussion of the conditions of their labour, which are not merely particular forms of activity, but are their mode of existence itself.

In earlier days a handicraftsman, the typical labourer, received a certain satisfaction from the work he did. His efforts were mostly to his own immediate advantage. He saw the fruits of his work in the complete object he produced and, moreover, the making of this object often entailed calls upon his adaptability or inventiveness to overcome the difficulties which arose. In a real sense one can speak of his being educated by his labour. To-day all is changed. A standardized job is done in a standardized manner and a standardized time for a standardized wage. In place of the small forge

---

a status-giving function appears in *Middletown in Transition*, Lynd, Robert and Helen (London, 1937), p. 247. They describe the emergence, during the ten years which elapsed between their two surveys, of riding clubs exclusive to the younger members of the leading family in the town " to whom certain leisure activities have value not in relation to work, but quite independently as a symbol of status."

in the forest, with two or three men doing all the work, there are steel mills in which each man is engaged on only an infinitesimal portion of the whole process. He often has no knowledge of the beginning nor of the end, and he has no interests in making the discovery. He does not share in the ownership of the goods produced. His sole incentive is that at the end of the week he will be entitled to a certain wage. Not infrequently the nature of the work is in itself unpleasant, the conditions of work are trying, and only sheer necessity keeps the worker there. By chance the steel industry has been selected, almost any other would serve equally as an example. In each, the system of production is "roundabout"; in each, the processes are minutely subdivided; in each, the work is unpleasant, trying, boring; of none can it be said that they offer an immediate and urgent incentive to work. For the labourer, therefore, the world, viewed in terms of work, is a dull and senseless place.

Perhaps it will be argued that there is not the close connection, as alleged, between the nature of the employment and the attitude of the workman. The only real consideration, it might be said, is the size of the weekly wage. If this be such as to produce contentment, then all is well. Everyone is satisfied and no harm, psychological or otherwise, is experienced. But experiment shows that, *even at the expense of their wages*, workers "rebel" against employment which they find purposeless.

Thus, over a period of more than a year, various methods of payments were tried with a group of ten girls in order to ascertain which acted as the greatest incentive. The girls, working in pairs, did a different operation each day of the week, there being five operations altogether. After nineteen weeks it was found that one job, weighing the sweets in a tin, was no longer needed; enough had been packed to meet foreseeable needs. However, in order not to spoil the experiment, this operation was still continued. The girls quickly discovered that their work was useless, that the tins were merely being removed to another part of the factory and there unpacked again. Immediately *the output on this job fell*, irrespective of the girls at work on it and irrespective of the method of payment. "This is a silly business," and similar complaints were frequently heard. As the investigators themselves remark: "It is evident that, in the first place, the value attached to an operation may have an important effect on productive activity." This "effect on productive activity" is the result of a psychological change in the worker which must necessarily affect his whole attitude to life.

It should be remembered that these experiments were not made with people who had highly developed philosophies of life, and who might, therefore, be anticipated to react consciously to such a situation. The workers were factory girls of not more than fifteen or sixteen years of age.[1]

The same reactions are found amongst young boy workers. "The following views," writes an investigator, "are the result of observations made in the course of many years of close contact with hundreds of factory workers. . . . The chief complaint of the

[1] Medical Research Council, Industrial Health Research Board, Report No. 69.

worker is that his work lacks organic completeness. His labour is regulated by the hour and does not lead to any final result. . . . Even workers of little intelligence suffer from this situation although unconsciously. . . . It is simply the nature of his toil that makes life so hard for a young worker; there is also a moral, even a sentimental side of the question. He feels that a slight is being put on his dignity as a human being. He suffers because his existence seems of so little importance, the part he plays so insignificant . . . the apprentice (in bygone days) had certain compensations, he was master of a craft of which he could be proud as an art, he knew the value of that craft. . . . The factory lad who rarely sees the product to which he contributes despite his toil such a tiny fraction, whose relationship with the industry for which he works consists in a single movement repeated a given number of times in a specified number of hours, cannot acquire this sense of his personal importance—not even indirectly through the undertaking in which he works, for he often remains quite ignorant of its extent and ramifications." [1]

Before machine industry had scarcely been introduced Adam Smith realized the dangers entailed. He appreciated to the full its implications concerning the attitude that the worker would tend to adopt to matters lying

---

[1] Vajkai, J. F., *The Family and the Young Worker*, Studies and Reports, Series G. (Housing and Welfare), No. 4, I.L.O. (Geneva, 1936), p. 22. The argument applies with slight modification, if any, to those who earn their living by clerical work. Two concomitant changes have been occurring in the commercial world, the increase in centralization of authority and the spread of mechanization. In offices where there are recognized and fixed grades of work, *e.g.* the Civil Service, the same operation of work is being continually de-graded. The net result is that employees and salary earners are as vulnerable to the changes which are being discussed as are the more specifically manual workers.

outside the factory. One hundred and sixty years ago he wrote, with amazing insight:

"In the progress of the division of labour, the employment of the far greater part of those who live by labour, that is, of the great body of the people, comes to be confined to a very few simple operations, frequently to one or two. But the understanding of the greater part of men are necessarily formed by their ordinary employments. The man whose whole life is spent in performing simple operations of which the effects are perhaps always the same or nearly the same, has no occasion to exert his understanding or to exercise his invention, in finding out expedients for removing difficulties which never occur. He naturally . . . becomes as stupid and ignorant as it is possible for a human creature to become. The torpor of his mind renders him not only incapable of relishing or bearing a part in any rational conversation, but of conceiving any generous, noble, or tender sentiment, and, consequently, of providing any just judgment concerning many even of the ordinary duties of private life. . . ." [1]

Are we to explain, therefore, the problems of leisure solely in terms of depressing work and degrading environment? On the contrary, it seems that wretched conditions merely confirm men and women in their wretchedness by making them unaware of it; they produce "a population . . . leading a mere animal existence . . . without any . . . status whatever." [2] For them no problem exists except that of keeping alive.

But nowadays the hours of work have been shortened, wages have increased and the standard of housing has risen. These improvements brought with them the problems of leisure. The clear connection can be traced historically. Thus the Factory Act, 1833, was

[1] Smith, Adam, *Wealth of Nations*, 1776, Book V, Chapter I, 1st Edition, pp. 366-7.
[2] Second Report of Commissioners (Trades and Manufacturers). Employment of Children Commission, 1843, p. 158.

the first to be successful in regulating the hours of labour, and it was in the same year that the Government made its first grant towards public education. It was not till the Ten Hours Act of 1847 was on the Statute Book that attention began to be given to the provision of parks and open spaces.[1] Most of the present-day discussions are specifically put into the context of the 48 hours' week having been gained, with the possibility of its reduction to 40 hours. In other words, the relative improvement in general conditions, rather than their absolute badness, has brought the problem to the fore. But again a qualification has to be introduced. There is evidence to suggest that in earlier days the mere fact of people not being at work all day and every day did not in itself give rise to a problem of leisure.[2] Why then, with the increase in free time, do these difficulties and anxieties now appear? For the answer attention must be paid to the new rôle for leisure and the fresh circumstances of its enjoyment.

The new rôle for leisure is to be understood in terms of the changes in the relationship of the labourer to his work. The changes have occurred not only as the result of the rise of industrialism, but also during the evolution of industrialism itself. Machinery destroyed handicraft production and the attitudes which went with it. But early capitalism brought new incentives which played a large part in reconciling the factory workers to their lot. These incentives having disappeared in their turn, leisure must now function to fill the gap.

[1] Hammond, H. L. and B. J., *The Bleak Age* (London, 1935), Chapter V.
[2] See p. 82, where an account is given of miners who, working only six hours per day in 1741, instituted on their own initiative a circulating library.

Thus, whilst the onset of industrialism entailed poverty, misery and apathy for large numbers, one of the most potent influences in shaping the attitude of the more energetic and intelligent workmen was the possibility of prospering at their trade or business and reaching some state of affluence. There was a field-marshal's baton in every soldier's knapsack and a director's job in every workman's dinner pail. Samuel Smiles could write his *Lives of the Great Engineers* and show how diligence and honesty inevitably reaped their reward. If these virtues did not receive recognition in this country, there were always the New Lands in which fortune could be sought.[1]

But nowadays the possibility of starting with nothing and making a fortune is very slight. Emigration has practically ceased and even while it was allowed the emphasis has been, since the War, on the necessity of owning capital. At home, the growing stratifications and rigidity of the industrial system is best illustrated by the recent remark of Valentine Bell,[2] which is all the more enlightening because made incidentally. "The masters and foremen will be those who have been

---

[1] The extraordinary hold which emigration had on the imagination of workmen is shown by the following incident from *First Report, Midland Mining Commissioners*, 1843, p. cxd. "A miner whom I had seen before and who had been pointed out to me by a Methodist preacher as a very active person in distributing tracts, an intelligent man of his class, a remarkable workman, came to me with some papers which he said, as I was going to London, he wished to place in my hands. I found that they were testimonials to his character and skill as a miner from masters under whom he had worked and he said, as times were bad, he desired to engage himself to be sent abroad by some gentlemen in London. I asked who they were to whom he was willing to commit the fortunes of himself, his wife and his family. He replied he did not know, if I was going to London I should easily hear who the gentlemen were that were sending miners to America. I asked to what part of the U.S. of America men were being sent out? Whether to North or South America? He said he did not know and was not sure it was not Italy or China he meant!"

[2] Bell, Valentine, *Junior Instruction Centres and Their Future*, Report to the Carnegie Trust, U.K. (Edinburgh, 1934), p. 76.

educated in the Secondary ... and other schools providing higher education because the sorting out of ability, which was at one time done in industry, is now done in the schools." If we combine this with Carr-Saunders'[1] figure of 4·2 per 1000 for those children who, starting at an elementary school, finish their education at a University,[2] it will be clear that the prospect of a poor child eventually dying with considerable riches secured by his own efforts is mainly conjectural.

In passing, it should be noted that the personal relations between masters and craftsmen which were characteristic of handicraft and small scale production have also disappeared. The men have become mere "hands" and the masters, where they have not dissolved into anonymous shareholders, have turned into remote figures, aloof from those who labour for them. Earl Baldwin spoke admirable sociology when, in his maiden speech in the House of Commons, he said, "I belong to a class once called masters, then employers of labour and now capitalists, usually with an epithet in front of it."[3] That statement indeed summarizes the whole metamorphosis, which has had its counterpart in the destruction of close contacts between the workers themselves. Often the bond between them is literally only a moving belt whose speed is regulated from a distant control station: vast numbers of workers experience during their hours of toil nothing more personal than the machine they operate. They are

---

[1] Carr-Saunders and Jones, *A Survey of the Social Structure of England and Wales* (London, 1927), p. 128.
[2] On the opportunities for such children to secure any kind of higher education see the results of the enquiries by Gray, J. L., and Moshinsky, Pearl, in the *Sociological Review* of April and July, 1935.
[3] Hansard, 1908, vol. 190, 1433.

merely labour and to expect them to resume their individuality as soon as they leave the factory is to expect a miracle.

From this growing lack of mobility, with its consequent diminution of opportunity to seek a fortune, work has lost its thrill as the means to acquiring wealth and social position. As a result of the increasing depersonalization, work is losing any glow once derived from the contacts it involved.[1] It is now a necessary effort to continue existence, something to be repeated and forgotten each day afresh. But it is not easy for the majority of people to repress at will all thought of their work. In the world of to-day their constant dread is unemployment. Any job they may have, no matter what its character, is something to be guarded. It is their one link with society. Without it they are condemned to the ranks of the outcasts. Merely to say, therefore, that they loathe their work is to over-simplify the position. Desiring above all things to be rid of it, all their energies are devoted to keeping it.[2]

---

[1] That the individual tends to hate those with whom he works is one of the outstanding facts of to-day. It is found in factories and offices alike. A postman at the central buildings of the London postal service told the author that he changed the resort he had chosen for his annual holiday simply because he heard that another person from the building, with whom he had hardly ever had contact and whom, therefore, he had little specific reason to hate, would be there at the same time. Almost the first person he saw at the fresh place was a fellow postman, " and it completely spoiled my holiday ! "

[2] Plant, J. S., " Social Factors in Personality Integration," *American Journal of Psychiatry*, vol. ix, July 1929 : " Well may he (the psychiatrist) chuckle at our own fine theory of integrating the personality when success would land most of our patients in the poor-house " ; which expresses in picturesque phraseology the point that is being made. It is interesting to note that Plant's conclusions were reached as the result of six years' case study covering 2500 juveniles : some, delinquents and non-delinquents, came from industrial areas, others from the best residential districts.

One may well remark on the practically complete lack of study by psychoanalysts, psychiatrists and other psychologists of the place of work in the life of the individual. There is a psycho-analysis of the family, clothes,

It has been said that industrialism changed the nature of man's work and his attitude towards it. Not only this, industrialism has also stripped him of those social relationships which he possessed before the rise of factories. As a member of a family functioning as a unit, a member of a small community, and a member of a church, he was embedded in a network of relations which gave shape to his life. He was at no time completely dependent on his own resources for a design for living. The institutions surrounding him were so numerous and so closely knit that he could not "fall out of his world." What is the position now?

Apart from agricultural areas, the family has lost its identity as a producing unit and even its remaining functions are considerably attenuated.[1] Increasingly women are working, increasingly members of the family must live apart from home in order to obtain employment. The embracing character once belonging to family relationships is being lost. So far have they removed from central importance that Butler can remark ironically, "God chooses our family, but we choose our friends." And the position is little better if we examine the relations of the individual to those

---

sex, play, art, children, religion, politics, but almost none of work, the most important phenomenon of our society. The references to the topic in the writings of Freud are very few, three or four, and refer mainly to primitive society, yet it is clear that he is aware of the extreme importance of work to man, see, *e.g.*, *Civilization and Its Discontents* (London, 1930), p. 34, note: "It is not possible to discuss the significance of work for the economics of the libido adequately within the limits of a short survey. Laying stress upon importance of work has a greater effect than any other technique of living in the direction of binding the individual more closely to reality."

[1] For an authoritative statement on the changes in the family in the United States of America see *Recent Social Trends in the United States*, Report of the President's Committee on Social Trends, 1933, vol. 1, Committee Findings, pp. xiv and xv.

living around him. In what real sense can it be said that communities exist in urban areas, using community in the sense of a territorial group having a common way of life and some common objectives? The phrase, "lost in a crowd," expresses the actual condition of many people, and the fact of neighbours living together for years without being acquainted is notorious. Thus both community and family have declined in the part they play in fixing man in society [1] and in cementing his relationships to the larger group.

Does religion still act as an interpreter, supplying a meaning to experience and so a purpose to existence? Do the Churches as an institution continue to satisfy the needs they once served by forming a common meeting-ground? The evidence indicates that in neither the one respect nor in the other do they occupy the position they formerly held. As an interpretation of this life religion is now accepted by a relatively small proportion of people [2] and so, for the large remainder, one of the chief forces making for acquiescence with one's lot [3] no longer operates. Important for this argument is the fact that the historical alternative to religion, rationalism or materialism, also does not receive widespread acceptance to-day. Our age may be described as one of unbelief rather than disbelief. This absence of positive *Weltanschauung*, this hesitation between complete re-

---

[1] The meaning is better expressed by saying "fixing man into society." It is not argued that the family no longer plays its part in determining the status of a man in society, it is still the most important single factor in this respect. But as a framework and as a background to the actual business of living its significance has declined.

[2] If any confirmation be needed of this statement it is supplied by the campaign which the Anglican Church has been waging in the spring of 1937 to lead the people back to religion.

[3] It is true that religion has historically played other and important rôles, but it is not these aspects that concern us in the present context.

jection of religion and the drawing of all the implications of such a step, is a factor which is very relevant in understanding the present attitude to leisure.

A further aspect should also be noted. The relationship between religion and the rise of modern society is nowadays a familiar topic. One aspect of this relationship is the preaching by every denomination in Western Europe of the Gospel of Work.[1] Work was not only the means of subsistence in this world but also the hope of salvation in the next: the curse of Adam was transformed into a blessing. "Labour is a thing so good and god-like. . . . In the things of this life, the labourer is most like to God," preached Zwingli and his successors for more than three centuries; but can such teaching have relevance to-day, in a world with a permanent surplus of labour?

Thus work completely fails to supply to the workman the *rationale* of his existence. To the religion which formerly interpreted his world he remains indifferent: even if he responds he no longer hears a message justifying man's ways to man. The spontaneous relationships once assured to him by his family and the community in which he dwelt have all disappeared. He stands a lonely figure surrounded by his fellows, lacking contact with the world of things and the world of men. What must now suffice to link him with society?

The answer is the "machinery of amusement." Leisure as produced by the showman, the amusements caterer, the film magnate, must act as the substitute, filling the void which industrialism has entailed. And

---

[1] Laski, Harold J., *The Rise of European Liberalism* (1936), p. 34.

hence the new task for leisure. Hence, the fresh, outstanding, rôle it must play.[1] Living is no longer to be interpreted in terms of labour, but in terms of the hours spent away from the stool, the machine, and the plough.[2] Instead of being relaxation, leisure has become an effort to secure the meaning and justification of life itself.

The rise of the Gospel of Leisure cannot be explained simply by the necessity of replacing the Gospel of Work. Other developments also need to be considered for the proper understanding of why leisure has come to play its present rôle and why recreation activities have taken new forms. During the present century, and at an increasing tempo since the War, we have witnessed the growth of industries such as the popular Press, the cinema, advertising, all those agencies which mould public taste and opinion. *Pari passu* the aristocrats, the rich, the leisured, have come to occupy a more and more prominent position. It is their names which are most frequently heard, it is their faces which are most often seen, it is the record of their activities which occupy greater and greater space in the Press. This "high visibility," to use Lynd's phrase, is both a cause and effect. Granted the existing conditions of society, it is a necessary process of symbiosis. The leaders of society could not live in the glare of publicity without the agencies which have been enumerated. But these searchlights, once they have come into existence, will inevitably light up these leading figures,

---

[1] "Thus all the forces at work are combining to shift the main centre of a worker's life more and more from his daily work to his daily leisure." *New Survey of London Life and Labour*, vol. vii. (London, 1934), p. 36.
[2] Dean Inge has written : " The mind is dyed the colour of its thoughts—its leisure thoughts."

for in fact they constitute society, they are the fount of social virtue and norms.[1]

One of the most important agencies making for this change is the Press. With its motto, "Women is news," its increasing tendency to turn out a product more like a magazine than a newspaper, it necessarily shifts the emphasis away from the serious issues to lighter fare. What can be more entertaining, more thrilling than the lives and habits of those fortunate creatures who, having no need to earn their living, are able to indulge in all the fascinating pastimes which a richly endowed and highly organized society such as ours can offer?[2] And what can be more natural than that these people, being constantly depicted in the most favourable light, become the models for behaviour to the millions reading the popular Press?

More important even than the Press is the Cinema. It brings the inside of an expensively furnished home or the habits of the wealthy before the eyes of people who otherwise would have no conception of them. Opulence, power, leisure, it is true, are often presented on the screen in a manner calculated to show that they are merely glitter compared with the solid gold of virtues such as faithfulness or humility. Such lessons

[1] In *John Bull at Home* (London, 1931), Karl Silex brings out very clearly the overwhelming impact of "Society" on English life. All the social functions, the sporting events, the first nights and opera, are arranged for and patronized by the small coterie whose lives fluctuate between London, Scotland and the Riviera according to the time of the year. And yet he estimates that "Society" consists of not more than 2,000 persons and of these only 100 really count.

As an exact measurement his figures need not be considered, but the striking fact is, bearing in mind the great significance of the phenomena depicted, that a competent observer could even venture to put the figures so low.

[2] Mention should also be made of the large space allocated to sport and the importance which is given to reporting it. Current sporting items are front-page news. It is another aspect of the stress upon all facets of leisure.

in ethics perhaps produce their effect. It is not for them, however, that cinema-goers pay their money Their desire is to play a vicarious part in thrills, to experience luxury and romance even if at second hand. These aspects of films exercise a profound influence on the formation of value standards. Outward and visible signs of the impact are there to read: Greta Garbo changes the fashion of her hair and so do millions of girls. Clark Gable wears a particular type of coat and immediately it appears duly labelled in innumerable tailors' shops. In less obvious directions the cinema's influence is equally pervasive.

As a necessary result of the working of modern opinion-forming agencies, therefore, a much greater awareness now exists of the lives and activities of those in the upper social grades. But, on the other hand, the personal contacts of earlier times have declined. The change in the manner of life of the aristocracy has often involved selling the estate. If that has not occurred, at least the family seat is much less visited and lived in than formerly. The general loosening and in many cases the complete severance of the bonds between the owners and their estates, has been accompanied by a decline in their social obligations to the tenants and other workers living in the neighbourhood. "—— says he can't afford to live in his house and do his duty as a country gentleman," writes Earl Winterton, "yet he spends far more in giving lunches at the Ritz, dinners at Claridges and suppers at the Carlton than it would cost to keep his country home open through the year."[1]

A similar increase in social distance between em-

[1] *Pre-War* (London, 1932), p. 271.

ployers and employed has developed during the same period. In fact, such a separation was characteristic even in the comparatively early stages of industrialism. It frequently formed the subject of adverse comment by some of the more enlightened employers and by the gentry themselves.[1]

Thus, for the rest of the community, the rich, from being flesh of their flesh, have tended to become merely actors upon the public stage. Hence, the link which previously was one of common interests and participation, in however slight a degree, has changed into a one-way process of imitation. There is hardly a vogue in society which does not find its emulators amongst the less fortunate beings excluded from the charmed circle. And so the majority spend their days modelling themselves upon images which have almost shed their humanity.

The agencies which tend to create the atmosphere of a modern community and help to mould its standards of value combine in focussing attention on those aspects of our life which are divorced from work and on people who are significant, not in terms of what they have achieved, but in terms of having money and time to spend. The constant display of wealth and leisure as the desirable ends conditions those who witness it into accepting and embodying them into their own scheme of values. This process of absorption has been facilitated by the decline in spontaneous popular leisure, consequent upon institutional changes in the family and the community. The resulting gap has been filled by the "machinery of amusement," and we are so much

---

[1] See First Report, *Midland Mining Commission*, Appendix, Evidence of William Chance and John Kay Booth, 1843, vol. xiii, p. 3.

conditioned that consciousness of this substitution having occurred is lost to us. To children of our generation it is self-evident that, in order to achieve "a good time," it is necessary to spend money.[1] All forms of leisure have become commercialized, endless devices are offered to the idle person, each to be enjoyed only on condition that he has money to pay.[2] Without money he is condemned, unable to share in the pleasure and pastimes which press on him from all sides. But commercialization does not merely erect a gate through which only those with the necessary fee can pass. It has a profound effect also on the nature of the fare offered. The "machinery of amusement" is run by business men actuated by business motives. Their concern is not primarily with the character of the entertainment or amusement they provide, for it is merely a means to the end of making profits. For them good or bad means profitable or unprofitable. But profits can be secured only by attracting the greatest number. What is the common denominator to which they appeal?

Man has a fund of potential energy. The chief manifestation of this energy, the libido, is an urge to come into contact with the external world, which can be divided into two main aspects—the world of people and the world of things. The channels of expression of the libido may be diverted from the world of people to the world of things, or to a mixture of both in very

---

[1] Beveridge, Sir William, *Planning under Socialism* (London, 1936), p. 99: "Work is a means of making money. Leisure is a method of spending it."

[2] Balchin, Nigel, *Income and Outcome* (London, 1936), p. 171: "Whenever we are not actually working or calculatedly on holiday, most of us are amusing ourselves in ways, which, directly or indirectly, cost money."

different proportions, within very wide limits indeed.[1] For the majority the chief method of coming into contact with the world of things is undoubtedly work. When, however, work creates a relationship to things which is repellent and unsatisfying, then the way is left open for the other main avenue to be exploited. In other words, the emphasis will tend to shift from work to sex.[2] It is this situation which the "engineers of amusement" seize upon. In the absence of common interest in the world of things—all aspects of the production processes and culture—the common bond which remains is sex, in its widest sense. But it is given in the conditions in which this is exploited and the purpose for which the exploitation is carried out, that only its crudest manifestations will be developed. Our most successful theatre shows tend to be variations on one theme, "girl meets boy" is an indispensable ingredient in every film which is to pay for itself. Advertisement layouts excel each other in ingenious combinations of their goods with pictures of attractive girls. Newspapers and periodicals strive to fill their pages with pictures and accounts of the protagonists in the latest sex drama. The most successful of them have a circulation of 3,000,000.

The pre-eminence of sex is equalled perhaps only by drink, and the kind of society which emerges in the strata of big business, which is most typical for the dynamics at work, is vividly portrayed in John Dos

[1] Freud, Sigmund, *op. cit.*, p. 73 : " Since man has not an unlimited amount of mental energy at his disposal, he must accomplish his tasks by distributing his libido to the best advantage. What he employs for cultural purposes he withdraws to a great extent from women and his sexual life."

[2] It is noteworthy that, since the accession of Hitler to power, there is a greatly increased tendency in the German Press to exploit sex by pictures of bathing girls, alleged classical poses and so on ; cf. the *Berliner Illustrierte* of 1933 with the copies of to-day as one example of a general process.

Passos' latest book, *The Big Money*. Money, drink and sex are the sole values; intellectual questions are not once discussed and the only character who ever mentions art is last seen getting more pep and languor into a love scene for the movies. No one can read the book without the feeling that it is a portrait of a society which, although set in American terms, could be duplicated several times in Western Europe. It is a society which is perhaps more sex-conscious than any previously known: sex worship has moved from the temples into the market-place, the cinema and into the home on the printed page.[1]

In a world where relationships are in the main reduced to a cash nexus, the exploitation of leisure for profit is only to be expected. Nevertheless, it is often denied. We are told that the amusement industries offer the fare they do and continue to flourish only because they supply what is wanted. Therefore, to maintain that cinemas, racing, football matches, do not really meet the desires of the people is absurd.

Such a statement of the position is so simplified as to be almost meaningless. In the relationship of demand and supply the producer is the significant, determining factor, particularly in the sphere of amusements where propaganda plays so large a part.[2] One case might suffice to illustrate the point. Attempts, apparently successful, have been made to introduce baseball into England as a large-scale spectacle. How

---

[1] Bisland, Elizabeth, *The Life and Letters of Lafcadio Hearn* (London, 1906), vol. 2, p. 121: "The Western civilization is using all its arts, its sciences, its philosophy in stimulating and exacerbating the thought of sex." (Hearn in a letter to Ellwood Hendrick.)

[2] Loveday, A., *Britain and World Trade* (London, 1931), p. 93: ". . . a market which has in the first instance to be created by an elaborate advertisement campaign. . . ."

was it done? Paragraphs appeared in the newspapers lauding its attractions, picture strips were also shown dealing with various phases of the game, films were displayed which under the guise of entertainment gave instruction in understanding all the intricacies of baseball. An interest in and an appetite for baseball was thus artificially created. Are we, therefore, entitled to say, *ex post facto*, that baseball is "what the people want"?

The mistake must not be made of simplifying the problem from the other end. There is clearly a sense in which these amusements *are* "wanted" by their patrons, in the sense that it would now be very difficult, if not impossible, for propaganda to produce a general predisposition towards Bach instead of jazz, towards chess rather than bridge. In other words, the cinema, jazz, and the whole paraphernalia of modern amusements are widely accepted, whereas activities which for their enjoyment demand a greater effort and more sustained interest, receive scant support. In spite of this apparent correlation between what is wanted and what is given, however, there is indisputable evidence that the "machinery of amusement" fails in a very real and vital sense to meet the needs of the people. The restless changes which have taken place in the amusements offered—one can cite since the War the introduction of dirt-track racing, dog racing, ice hockey, all-in wrestling, pin tables, radio, yo-yo, cross-word competitions and football pools—were due primarily to profit-seeking. But that each innovation secures a clientele, that people already participating in leisure pursuits are ever ready to try something new, suggests that a search is being made, although the object of the search may be unknown and even the fact that a search is being made may not be present to consciousness. Apart from any questions of valuation, of whether the recreation pursuits of to-day are satisfactory, the conclusion seems justified that they do not wholly satisfy those who participate.

Failure to satisfy means that leisure fails to fulfil the function assigned to it, means that it does not prove adequate to its task of reconciling the people to their lot. Moreover, leisure is unable to do this. Some men and women achieve adjustment in spite of their surroundings and develop artistic or civic interests in their spare time. The majority are incapable of similarly defeating the dead weight of their circumstances. Engaged in monotonous, repetitive work, which makes no demands on their facilities,[1] they are everywhere enveloped in an environment which contains little or no stimulus to seek the more difficult adventures of life. Yet these very same conditions ensure that they shall be precluded from finding wholesome the easy substitute that is offered.

One important question, raised at the outset, remains only partly answered. What circumstances conspire to give leisure its present outstanding position? So far an answer has been given in terms of the demands which individuals make on leisure. It must supply the motive for their existence. But more must be said than this. Leisure is not merely a problem for the individual—it is a problem for society, just as, for instance, unemployment is a problem. It is something which those who are concerned to maintain

[1] "Ninety per cent. of the people are engaged in work which is far below their capacities." Captain Blakesley, National Institute of Industrial Psychology, at Conference on Leisure, London, 18th November 1937.

the social order are gravely anxious about. Why should this be?

The explanation is implicit in what has gone before. The continued existence of a deeply stratified community such as Great Britain is possible on one of three conditions, although, of course, at any one time all of them may be present in varying proportions. That those who fill the lower strata should be unconscious of the stratification. Unconscious, that is to say, in the sense of accepting it as in the natural order of things, just like the weather. That, for an important minority of those in the lower reaches, there should be the possibility of rising in the social scale. Thirdly, that, although everyone is conscious of the stratification, it should be accepted because the people's demands are met.

But Great Britain fits into none of these categories. Her development during the past decades has been one of increasing awareness and self-consciousness on the part of the majority of the people, a decline in the possibilities of improving one's status, and a growth in the demands made by the general population. The growth in wants and demands arises inevitably with the increase in production. In fact, it is deliberately stimulated for the purpose of trying to sell more goods. To some extent the demands have been met, witness the rise in the standard of living which has occurred for all except those facing or experiencing unemployment. But "man does not live by bread alone," and an increase in material comforts has been accompanied by a growth in "spiritual" demands. Men and women are no longer content to be a cog in a vast machine. They have evinced desires to develop their own personalities. Work offers no scope and they have turned to leisure for the purpose. This has also failed, but only recently has the failure loomed so large as to become an urgent social problem.

That the problem has arisen so late in Great Britain compared with, say, France and Germany, is not due to the individual idiosyncrasies of the British. The explanation lies in our peculiar history during the past two or three centuries and the resultant social structure, which is unlike that of any other country. A complete statement, would, therefore, involve an analysis of this history. This cannot be done here and only the most general aspects can be touched upon.[1]

Prior to factory production it was not a social problem how man spent his spare time, partly because he was surrounded by institutions which embraced all his life, partly because producing for himself, if he were a peasant, or for a master who conducted his business in an easy-going fashion, no difficulties arose if he were not regularly available for work. When, however, machines were introduced and profits now depended upon regularity and reliability of production, the conduct of labour had to become predictable and controllable. All things needed to be subordinated to the demands of work. Interferences arising from leisure pursuits had, therefore, to be eliminated as far as possible. Thus, holidays and saints' days, which in mediaeval days had numbered nearly 120 in the year, were drastically reduced. Drunkenness had been a besetting sin in England from time immemorial, but it was not till the after effects of alcohol conflicted with the needs of organized production that, in 1830, a

[1] For further elaboration, see The Aristocracy, Chapter II.

temperance movement started in the highly industrialized portions of Lancashire and Yorkshire.

But the onset of industrialism in Great Britain resulted, more than in any other country, in the destruction of institutions such as the family and the community, and little was evolved to replace them. The institutional poverty of the people less than one hundred years ago comes out only too clearly in contemporary accounts such as the Commissioners' Reports on the Employment of Women and Children, 1843. The difficulties and dangers to society arising from the mass of the people leading lives under conditions which left them absolutely purposeless, without integration into the social structure, were clearly recognized. Religion was to be the cement binding together the human bricks. Ure,[1] writing in 1835, could observe:

"National bankruptcy and beggary with a dismantled army and navy would be the result of any great convulsion among our factory population. This catastrophe should be deprecated with the most solemn adjuration by every patriot and counteracted *in ovo*. . . . I indeed apprehend no such result because I believe there is an abundant increase of intelligence and moral sentiment springing up amongst the factories, the fruits of Sunday School and other philanthropic establishments. It is, therefore, excessively the interest of every mill-owner to organize his moral machinery on equally sound principles with his mechanical. . . . There is in fact no case to which the Gospel truth 'Godliness is great gain' is more applicable than to the administration of an extensive factory."

The hold of religion has seriously declined and the institutional poverty has not been remedied. Even of London, which is not the result of rapid industrialization, Paterson has written "little provision is made for

---

[1] Ure, Andrew, *Philosophy of Manufactures* (London, 1835), pp. 407 and 416.

the reasonable and innocent enjoyment of the adults' spare hours."[1] The same point clearly emerges from a perusal of the volume entitled *London Life and Leisure*, in the *New Survey of London*. The continued prosperity of Britain has in the past, however, served the purpose of binding the people to their lot. But since the War, and more especially since the economic depression of 1931-32, with its vast unemployment and its severe jolt to all social institutions, all the bareness of our institutional life has become visible.[2] Those concerned to maintain the structure of society perceived the lack and its consequent perils.

But unable to provide work or to alter the conditions of existing work, it was inevitable that to them the problem should present itself in terms of leisure. Hence all the discussion which has arisen, all the anxious endeavours to provide further amenities for recreation and all the attention which has been focussed on the age-group, 14-18. It is at this point, where the influence of school and family ceases and industry has not yet had time to condition the labourer into acquiescence, that the stresses and strains are most clearly evident.

Thus leisure has a twofold aspect. To individuals it indicates the difficulties which they experience in attempting to wrest from life a meaning and purpose. They live an unmotivated social life. That is to say, no religious and no rational principle has appointed them to their given place. The society they live in becomes ever more rigid. But their status, fixed by

---

[1] Paterson, *op. cit.*, p. 213.
[2] Crucial instances of this state of affairs may be found in the New Housing Estates, often as big as large towns, where the newly arrived inhabitants have lost even those social contacts and institutions which they had in the old milieu.

the work they do, leaves them unsatisfied: it determines decisively the shallowness, the incomprehensibility of their lives. They have one hope, their spare time. It should provide the reason for their existence and the satisfaction they are seeking. But their leisure is conditioned by the same society which conditions their work, which means that whilst their leisure should be a catharsis, it must also complete the industrial training of turning actors into spectators. Hence the "machinery of amusement," visualized day-dreams of a fully leisured, unproductive life are presented, and for the public which watches, leisure becomes the ultimate good.

But it is unobtainable, because those who have just learned the lesson in the cinema, have to return to the factory and the office. The work seems more dreary after the leisure hour, and the leisure hour is no climax to their work. It is a vicious circle, completed by the "engineers of amusement." Concerned with their financial profit, they seize upon the already blunted tastes of their patrons and proceed still further to debase them.

This struggle is the reflection of a similar conflict in our society. Work is its foundation. Hence, the value of work should be its basic ethic. But, because the dominating values arise from people who need not toil and because a substitute for integration by labour must be given to the millions who know work only as an evil necessity, leisure is offered as the supreme goal. Leisure, therefore, attempts to supplant work. Only when this division ceases, when leisure is complementary and not opposed to work, can its problems, as we know them, be solved.

CHAPTER II

LEISURE IN OUR SOCIETY

PART I

THE ARISTOCRACY

"EVERY Englishman loves a lord." The aristocracy are admired and envied; they are fully leisured and, moreover, are nowadays admired because they are fully leisured.

The position they occupy to-day is one inherited through many centuries. Since the Wars of the Roses, which eliminated most of the feudal barons, England's only experience of fighting on her own soil has been the Civil War. Even the changes which this struggle entailed were largely eliminated before the end of the seventeenth century.[1] Thus almost without a break national development has evolved during the past five hundred years till the present day. And this continuity is embodied visibly in the unbroken dominance of the aristocracy.

Moreover, the large degree of subjection into which the nobility were forced during the reigns of the Tudors gradually passed away. Their triumph was signalized by the deposing of James II. By the middle of the

[1] The effacement of the changes wrought during the period is shown interestingly by the facts that the *Statutes of the Realm* does not contain any of the Acts passed during Cromwell's time, and that the first Statutes of Charles II are not numbered 1 Car. but 12 Car., as though he had ascended the throne immediately after Charles I was executed. The Glorious Revolution of 1688 completed the restoration of the large landowners, which is shown by the fact that the first measure passed through the 1689 Parliament was for the protection of corn.

eighteenth century their position had developed so far that except for foreign affairs they were rulers, as Justices of the Peace, of almost completely autonomous districts. The early and gradual industrialization of England, with its consequent amassing of great wealth, enabled the aristocracy to adapt themselves to the new social order. "The country is much indebted to gentlemen of large landed property for . . . entering into the commercial concerns of a bank." [1]

These same gentlemen also adapted the new social order to themselves. The rising industrialists and merchants were assimilated, preventing the splitting of the English people into sharply opposed groups. At the same time, by mingling with the new ruling class the old retained its influence. The first Reform Bill of 1832 implied that the self-made men were admitted to the seats of power. They, having grown up largely under the influence of feudal ideas, themselves tended to adopt a feudal mode of life, in conformity with their upbringing and the model which was set for them by their social superiors. They did not consider their careers finished if they had not acquired land, perhaps a title, and the social habits of the previous owner of their country seat. Thus they helped largely to preserve the values of the old order whilst supplying it with a new basis. "Practically anyone with sufficient money can get into society," writes a member of the Peerage, "and we have to-day far more of a plutocracy than an aristocracy. . . ." [2]

But the workers on the soil were driven into the towns, deprived under the Enclosure Acts of their strips

---

[1] *The Utility of Country Banks Considered*, 1802, quoted, Halévy, Élie, *A History of the English People in 1815* (London, 1924), vol. i. p. 298, note.
[2] Gorell, Lord, *Evening Standard*, 11th October 1928.

of land which they had owned as long as the open field system had endured. They were crowded together under conditions which represented a complete break with their past. Their only incentive to continue an existence the reason for which they no longer understood, was the urge for money, so that, if they were successful they could return whence they had come, to the country-side. Thus, all groups in society had as their model the county and the squire.

The aristocracy having lost some of their former spheres of action, were soon invited from many quarters to contribute their prestige, their influence and their abilities. They provided business, as we have seen, with titles, administration and philanthropy with a never failing supply of unpaid servants, to the envy of the world. Hence the tradition that those who have time at their disposal undertake "good works" of some kind has become firmly enrooted in English social life, and has assisted till to-day in maintaining popular sympathy for the aristocracy. The tradition has, in fact, survived from the time when, as Justices of the Peace, the nobility and gentry ruled what were almost autonomous districts. All initiative was in their hands, and if a project were to succeed it needed the support of prominent members of the county. The common people became used to things being done for them. During the first half of the nineteenth century they tended to produce their own leaders, for instance, the Chartists, but gradually it became once more the practice to rely upon guidance and assistance from the rich and the aristocratic.

The nobility being thus sanctioned by their philanthropy, their other attributes were also deemed admirable and desirable. Their sport, entertaining, travelling, were accepted as the proper expressions of a civilized life. The more so since aristocratic institutions, above all the Public Schools, preached and perpetuated this idea of the identity of good manners and active sports with goodness itself. Leisure and the social ideal became firmly equated and for many it was a natural identification. The Dowager Duchess of Chevron, that forthright old lady in Sackville West's *The Edwardians*, had no doubts on the point. "What would happen to the country, I should like to know, if the people at the top enjoyed no leisure. Besides, the country likes it. Don't you make any mistake about that. People must have something to look up to. It's good for 'em: gives 'em an ideal."

The aristocracy, therefore, set the tone and their values were accepted everywhere, the kind of recreation they thought desirable was desired. Until recently, however, it was not possible to imitate the upper stratum. The majority had little time and little money. The main forms of leisure, hunting and shooting, were completely beyond their compass. Moreover, personal relationships between the rich and the poor had tended to disappear. The more industrialization advanced the rarer became direct contacts between individuals of greatly different economic status, and the process has not yet ended. Dwelling in isolation, the poor of the new towns had no other source of information on the life of dukes and lords than hearsay stories. They hardly even saw anyone belonging to the fortunate circle. The exclusiveness of the aristocracy, particularly during their pastimes, prevented any onlookers until the modern agencies of propaganda appeared. The Press, the cinema, even the advertisements, have turned their searchlights on to the leisured, and now the multitude watches.

To-day the rich are very visible and mostly so during their recreation. Indeed, although the English leisured class are distinguished by the public services they perform, their impact tends more and more to be in their capacity as leisured people, not as the occupiers of public offices.

Two major reasons account for this shift of emphasis. On the one hand, the modern agencies of propaganda distribute throughout the country only those pictures and items of news which are interesting and saleable. "Interest" in this context must be interpreted as "Human Interest," and this frantic search for H.I. conditions the approach adopted towards the leisured class. To report that Lord —— spent the day as Chairman of the Quarter Sessions has little or no news value, but to show a picture of the same lord riding his horse to victory in a point-to-point is very much better for newspaper making. Very seldom does the cinema portray a member of the aristocracy as the director of a company, the chairman of the Board of Governors of a hospital, or the indefatigable president of a charitable association. His rôle is that of the idle man about town, immaculately clothed; and the constant repetition of this theme, in every conceivable variation, inevitably produced the effect that, to the majority of people, the possession of riches, membership of the aristocracy, moving amongst the social élite, are all synonymous with leading a completely leisured life.

Secondly, there has occurred in a double sense the

"democratization of leisure." The forms of leisure for the rich have been altered by the introduction of the motor car, tennis, golf and easier foreign travel: the former predominance of shooting and hunting have gone.[1] For our purpose this change is important because the new pastimes were, and are, within the reach of those possessing little money. During the same period the possibility of free time has become a reality for many: working hours have been reduced, real wages have increased, and so the opportunity for imitation of the favoured few has been presented to millions. The precepts which they had been absorbing from the Press and the cinema could now be put into practice. "The appetite grows with what it feeds on," and their interest, aroused by direct participation in varied leisure pursuits, was both satisfied and further stimulated by the panorama of the rich often engaged in those games and activities which they themselves could play or watch during the evenings or on Saturday afternoons. Thus a considerable degree of formal similarity has developed in the leisure sphere between the activities of the rich and those of the remainder of society.

The tendency for a section of the population in Britain to imitate those above is very strong indeed, owing to the characteristics in our history which have been discussed in the foregoing pages. But these characteristics tend to give merely the special shape to a general form which is determined by its being an industrialized, competitive, society. Competition motivates modern industrialism and permeates each

[1] For the impact on the habits of the aristocracy produced by these changes, which seem to have occurred in the early years of King George V's reign, see an account in *Pre-War*, Earl Winterton (1932), p. 270.

aspect of social life. But when competition exists within a hierarchy it is accompanied by its opposite, emulation. Thus each person competes with those in the same rank and emulates those above him; even the people whose business it is to stimulate the struggle find the forces at work too strong for them and they become their unwilling captives.[1] Competitive emulation is a necessary feature where social status is primarily determined by the capacity to consume, in other words, the amount of wealth possessed. If social prestige is to be secured and kept, it is necessary to shine in the leisure sphere,[2] to stand out by a display of clothes, servants, wine, furniture and cars which compares favourably with that of those on the same social rung and if possible surpasses it. This rule holds good from the highest to the lowest. Carnegie had four chauffeurs in order to compete with Astor, living across the way, who had only three; and both, together with others of equal footing in the social hierarchy, would act as models to the remainder, making it imperative for those who harboured social aspirations also to have a chauffeur. In this country there is but one behaviour-pattern for the vast majority of the population, and this one is determined by the

[1] Lynd, *op. cit.*, p. 257, note, quotes the following to illustrate how motor-car manufacturers, unwilling to make drastic changes in their models, were nevertheless forced to do so because, in the hopes of stealing a march on their rivals, one or two producers altered their designs for the coming year. " *Several manufacturers thought they had done enough to make the prospects dissatisfied with their present cars and planned to bring out new models with noticeable but unimportant changes.* But competition, and the increasing necessity of turning the last penny . . . are forcing last minute shifts. So the new models will have the traditionally radical differences. . . . And one may add, the consumer will pay most of the bill." " Detroit Spends to Save." Business Week, 10th November 1934.
[2] " Membership of the ' right ' golf club would perhaps still be accepted as one of the most important indices of status in the social scale." Lundbergh, G. A., *Leisure* (New York, 1934), p. 65.

aristocracy: the supreme value is money plus a title. It is thus the impact of the aristocracy which gives English society its peculiar timbre. They are the pivot and the pillar of the whole structure.[1]

In other countries the prevalence of a naked commercial ethic with little veneer of aristocratic tradition and breeding, and the growing feeling that the world is moving to a catastrophic change, have produced important reactions amongst those sections which had already developed their own specific outlook and behaviour-patterns. The intellectual ferment amongst the French *bourgeoisie*, the upheavals there amongst the workers which, interestingly enough, have been followed by the appointment of a Minister of Leisure, the considerable growth in the United States of a virile literature which explicitly or implicitly sets out the authors' critical valuation of their society, the immense struggles which have occurred in the field of American labour, are some indications of the social movements abroad. In England the aristocracy have not only given grace to the social order, but by their absorbing or embracing all contiguous groups have largely avoided any considerable effort to discuss or to alter it.

The native lack of concern for matters of the intellect is both cause and effect of a more tangible impact of the English aristocratic tradition. Having their life centred in the country, the landed nobility naturally developed their country house at the expense of their

---

[1] "A wedding between the ducal houses of Douglas and Percy is another episode in which democracy responds to the glamour of old romance. Centuries have passed since the historic Border rivalry surrendered the last of its pangs, but the magic of its poetry has never weakened, and the Englishman or Scotsman who does not feel some individual inheritance in the memories of 'Chevy Chase' is rather less than a 'first-class citizen.'" *The Observer*, quoted, *New Statesman*, 18th December 1937.

residence in town. ". . . Englishmen made more of their country house than their town house," writes Hammond, quoting a German of the eighteenth century. He comments: "Now this attractive country life with its beauty, culture, pleasure, and state was open to all who made their way into the aristocracy, to men whom success in business, their own or their fathers', brought into this world. The governing class drew into its orbit almost all those who acquired wealth, setting the standard, mode and plan of life. Hence the invested wealth of the Industrial Revolution was largely used for creating new territorial families with mansions and estates in the country."[1] As a result, the people who in other countries developed a philosophy, an art, a literature and social rules of their own, the rising industrialists and traders, were in England dreaming only of acceptance by the county. Even the working class symbolized its adherence to aristocratic forms of life by insisting on living in houses rather than flats and thus giving English cities their characteristic sprawling aspect. The Cinderellas of English social life have been the towns.

Unlike the other great Western democracies, England has scarcely known a rich urban culture and an intelligentsia which could pride itself on an independent social status. Dr. Johnson's famous letter to Lord Chesterfield reveals the position which existed during his time and also marks the beginning of a period, the end of the eighteenth and the early part of the nineteenth century, when this country approached nearest to a situation of writers, poets, artists and actors, forming an important and relatively autonomous

[1] Hammond, J. L., and B., *The Bleak Age* (London, 1935), p. 128.

section of society. But learning and education have been but little desired for their own sake by any broad section of the English; from the time of Poggio, the Italian Humanist of the fourteenth century, till the present day, it is possible to find representative foreigners commenting upon our lack of interest in learning. It is even recognized by prominent members of the aristocracy themselves. "The British worship of aristocracy," writes a well-known peer, "demands some popular sporting peer—preferably known by his tie, button-hole or cigar—as its hero."[1] And the apex of the British educational system, the Public Schools, particularly the dozen most exclusive, exist to educate its members in ease of right manners and efficacy in sport. They are designed to inculcate those qualities which are expressed, not in intellectual capacity, but in the ability to handle persons and situations. It is difficult not to be reminded of Oscar Wilde's remark: "If you are a gentleman, then you know enough. If you are not a gentleman, then it is hopeless to know anything at all." A recent indication that there is no alteration in this attitude is the change made in May, 1937, of the importance attached to the interview in the Civil Service Administrative Grade Examination, which is designed to attract the élite from the Universities. Previously the interview counted for 300 out of a total of 1800 marks; it now counts for 300 out of only 1200, which means that since an interview reveals the attitude and general ability of the interviewee more

---

[1] Winterton, Earl, *op. cit.*, p. 20. This section of the book contains an interesting and revealing discussion of the difficulties which arose for A. J. Balfour, when he was Prime Minister, because he habitually moved amongst a small group who were concerned with matters of the intellect. Hence they were naturally suspect for a large section of his followers.

than his intellectual capacity, these qualities will have greater weight in the final result.

Although the growth of an independent urban culture has been inhibited, the centre of English social life has now shifted away from the country on to London. Many causes contributed to the increasing unattractiveness of holding rural land as a source of income and as a place of residence.[1] The decreased rents for farms which had to be accepted for many years from 1873 onwards, the impact of death duties and the growing competition of other forms of investments, the greater length of the Sessions of Parliament, particularly in the autumn, which involved staying longer in town, the higher speed of travel which made possible even short week-end visits to the country, the growth of new forms of leisure, which has been commented upon, all contributed to this movement to the capital. But the development has occurred almost, if not quite, too late, for the absence of a vigorous culture centred in the towns has seriously enhanced the magnitude of the leisure problem for Britain. It implies that few artistic and intellectual interests, with their corresponding institutions, have been created to fill the leisure of the people. Comparatively small sections of the English middle and working classes are actively concerned with literature and art or with the affairs of the outside world; they have no coffee-houses, hardly any open-air cafés, few social institutions such as the German *Verein* and *Stammtisch*,[2]

---

[1] See Durant, "The Developments in Landownership since 1873," *Sociological Review*, January, 1936.

[2] *Verein*—Union or Association: "When two Germans meet they form a *Verein*." The term covers a large variety of types of organized meetings consisting of people having a common interest in things from skittles to the theatre, or merely an interest in meeting.

Stammtisch—a regular meeting of a few people at reserved tables in a restaurant for social purposes.

no people's theatre where they can make easy and varied social contacts. Of all the major European Powers, Britain is alone in having no State or Municipal Opera.

It is even not fanciful to suggest that a partial cause of the difficulties with which the British film industry has been struggling is the overshadowing of the rest of the community by the aristocracy. The raw material for the cinema must be the social life surrounding it. But if only one section of society is of importance, and this the one which offers least scope as a background for striving and success, their battles having already been won, the poor producer must needs have recourse to the rather fatuous story which has come to be characteristic of the majority of British films. At least one leading figure in the British cinema industry appreciates that this is the position. "British film producers," writes Hitchcock, perhaps the best of our native film producers, "know only two strata of English existence, the poor and the rich. On these they base the plots of their films. Forgotten are the men who leap on buses, the girls who pack in the tube, the commercial traveller ... the people in the charabancs, on the beaches. ... In them lies the spirit of England that, for some unknown reason, is almost entirely ignored on the screen. The higher you run your finger up the British social scale, the faster the drama dies." [1]

Whilst the impact of the aristocracy has, therefore, been to retard the growth of an urban and folk culture with its spontaneous leisure pursuits and institutions,

---

[1] Hitchcock, Alfred, *Kine Weekly*, Annual Number, 1937, quoted, *World Film News*, January 1937.

THE ARISTOCRACY

those organizations which do exist are mostly maintained by aristocratic patronage. Many of the boys' clubs and girls' clubs have such an origin and are dependent upon such sources for the bulk of their income. Most of the Settlements to be found in London, which are active centres of learning and social life, owe their existence to aristocratic or upper middle-class initiative in the last decades of the nineteenth century.

The American sociologists, May and Petgen, who investigated the English use of leisure were much struck by this phenomenon, recording that "since a great part of the provision existing has definitely philanthropic origin it is very apt to appear superimposed and thus to eliminate or fail to attract large portions of the population who could greatly benefit by it. This perhaps accounts for the fact that it was possible to spend two months in England, with the utmost attentiveness, without ever being made aware of the people as a force in the leisure problem."[1]

The special characteristics of English social life will appear more clearly if the development of England, as sketched, is compared with the history of Germany, prior to Hitler. Industrialism came comparatively late to Germany. It was not till about 1870 that really rapid progress was made and by this date there were enormous advances to be made if England were to be equalled. Moreover, Germany itself was poor in raw materials and did not possess an Empire which could function as a source of supply and as a market. Hence, industrialization took place under conditions of difficulty, enormous stresses developed and the society

[1] *Op. cit.*, p. xii.

divided into sharply opposed camps. The unbroken tradition of England was absent. Its great wealth was also absent. There was nothing to bridge the gap, with the result that the workers and labourers were organized into a political party with an independent *Weltanschauung*, having little or no relation with the rest of society. The Social Democratic Party and the German Trades Unions accordingly did not stop short at dealing merely with wages and working conditions. Their concern was with every aspect of their members' lives and, especially after the Great War, much attention was paid to people's recreation. They provided every imaginable facility—schools, theatres, sports clubs, even inns.[1] Nor were they alone in making such provision. Weimarian Germany, consequently, presented the spectacle of the people split up and segregated into a number of organizations each providing for its own leisure. On the one hand, this meant a lack of contact and often hostility between the groups, on the other, that the people themselves were responsible for and provided their own means and instruments of organized leisure, they were not erected for them as in England. The aristocracy, the landed proprietors, played a very small part in forming the patterns of behaviour for society as a whole: their modes of conduct remained isolated and uncopied. The other members of society who were significant in terms of their possessions and their leisure, the industrialists and professional men of all kinds, reflected very accurately in their recreation the curiously indeterminate, unstable character of post-War Germany. They maintained the tradition of their own culture

[1] May and Petgen, *op. cit.*, p. 152.

and interest in the arts, based on liberalism and cosmopolitanism (*Weltbürgertum*), they were very susceptible to foreign influence and even to currents emanating from sections lower in the social scale. Thus it was fashionable to patronize the Socialist theatres, film shows and concerts.

This practice was directly connected with another aspect of German society which sharply differentiated it from its British counterpart, the conspicuous position occupied by the intellectuals. Since the death of A. B. Walkley, it is difficult to find in England an art critic who has played an important social rôle, but in many large German newspapers their theatre critic occupied much of the limelight. The representative people at a first night in England would be members of the aristocracy, a few of the better known racehorse owners, the most recent successful airman or better still airwoman; an actor or actress is to be found here and there. In Weimarian Germany, however, it was the artistes and their critics who were the guests of honour, and whose presence was essential if the opening were to be successful.

Thus the difference between the two countries was that in Germany a number of groups existed each with its own standards of value, with its own ideals to be served in leisure or, as in the case of the middle classes, they were even open to influences originating in sections beneath them in the social scale. In England these differentiations can scarcely be discovered, and certainly the imitation is only one-way. There is, one can say, a hierarchy with the few at the apex as the model for the vast majority. A single thread runs through the whole of society.

The long continued aristocratic tradition of Britain has had three main results in relation to leisure. The centre of social gravity being not in the towns but in the country has retarded the appearance of spontaneous self-supporting institutions for recreation, and has also discouraged the emergence of popular artistic and intellectual pursuits. These two aspects need to be stressed, since from them arise many of the immediate difficulties which confront this country in relation to leisure. The nobility have, on the other hand, created patronized organizations for leisure and have determined the popular attitude to recreation, causing it to be regarded as the end of existence.[1]

Thus arises one of the aspects of the problem of leisure which is present in an acute form in Great Britain. Work is a necessity imposed upon all but a few. The cult of leisure, therefore, is bound to have important and unfortunate repercussions. A divergence arises between the conditions of existence imposed by the need to earn a livelihood and the kind of life which is held out as desirable. On the one hand, the message society has to preach is

---

Because leisured people are accepted as models it follows not only that what they do becomes valuable but reciprocally that if they do it well their prestige is enhanced in all directions. Thus one of the most prominent figures in the sporting world happened to be the possessor of the horse which won last year's Derby. On the next Sunday a full-page article appeared over his name in a newspaper, entitled, "If I were Dictator." Clearly his views were now considered to be worth listening to. It is not an isolated instance. A sportsman whose ill-luck in the Derby is notorious had the good fortune to win one of the other classic races. His wife, who represents a constituency in Parliament, immediately told him that if only the race his horse had won had been the Derby she would never need fight her seat again. (*Daily Telegraph*, 25th June 1936.) The implications are clear : leisure activities are rated so highly that excellence in them is the unfailing passport to popular favour. Thus both for the people who participate and for those who merely watch they have an importance extending far beyond their own sphere.

that the end of life is idleness and enjoyment; on the other, the people having absorbed the message must return to the factory, the workshop and the office, in order to earn the money without which they cannot live.

Part II

THE MIDDLE CLASSES[1]

OXFORD STREET on a fine afternoon: it is crowded, particularly the north side, with those who buy and those who are merely window shopping. At least 80 per cent. of them are women: many are really well dressed, none are poorly clad, and all seem to have one characteristic in common, time to spend, to shop, to drink tea and gossip. And Oxford Street is merely one instance of a scene which is repeated daily in every town throughout Western Europe and America: the middle-class housewife passing the hours till the return of her husband to the home in the evening. The telephone and the tin-opener, the vacuum cleaner and contraceptives, have all combined to remove the burdens which once condemned her to a life of unremitting duties. Nowadays, increased division of labour has taken a vast number of operations out of the home to be performed by people specializing in them—cooking, laundering, dressmaking, to quote three examples. Those that remain have been immeasurably lightened by the technical advances in even that least rationalized of occupations—housekeeping. And because it is fashionable, where a man has the money, to keep his wife in idleness and as an ornament, it is true that even if the women desired to secure work there is little now available—the person whose day

---

[1] For further discussion of the leisure of independent business men, artists, and professional people, see Chapter V, p. 249.

was once fully occupied and who was never at a loss for some employment is now the one upon whom leisure is forced.

A statesman of the last century described the middle classes as "those natural representatives of the human race," and to-day it can be claimed not unfairly that the middle-class woman epitomizes the difficulties and problems which appear when the spending of free time is considered.

The place of leisure is interstitial. For the people we are discussing, however, it is often their only motive in life. A similar position exists for the aristocracy: the difference is that in the one case there is sufficient wealth available to make a life of constant movement and variety possible; new faces are met, new places are seen and a stream of change suffices to hide from those concerned the real lack of content. They feel important and justified in their existence, particularly since they occupy the leading social positions. For those less fortunately endowed the possibility of incessant variety does not exist and the emptiness of their days is hard to escape.

A middle-class woman has few children, the average number for all sections has nearly halved during the past seventy years, having fallen from 4·8 to 2·7.[1] The decline, moreover, has been greatest amongst the well-to-do. If the children are young, caring for them occupies her time.[2] If they are older, then they are

[1] Glass, David, *Eugenics Review*, April, 1937, p. 40.
[2] Lynd, R. and M., *Middletown* (London, 1930), p. 147, suggests that perhaps the time now spent by some middle-class mothers with their children is greater than the time similarly spent thirty years ago by mothers in the same social grade. The conclusion is based on a small sample only and is advanced very tentatively. An important relevant difference is that in Britain many more children are sent to a boarding-school as compared with the United States.

away from home at school and may be completely absent by living there. For the rest of the housework a maid may be available. Visits to the hairdresser, perhaps the beauty specialist and dressmaker, will take up some of her mornings after she has attended to household questions: shopping and committee meetings will occupy others. The afternoons will ring the changes on paying or receiving calls, golf, bridge and a visit to a cinema or theatre. Her time is filled with a number of activities, all of them trivial, none can stand as valuable in itself. As a result, standards of value become so attenuated that one investigator was told by a woman: "Yes, I think it is very important to do something with leisure time so I go to the movies every day."[1] And, quoting from the same source, what could appear more depressing than the following description of "the big social event of the week" by a member of the exclusive Country Club in New York's "best suburb"? "The 'young marrieds' usually get mildly drunk to feel gay and to make themselves think they are having a good time. The older people sit around and discuss each others' manners, morals, and clothes. At two, three o'clock in the morning they all go home to sleep off the effects of the good time and get in trim for golf or tennis on the following morning."[2]

The picture is drawn from America but, perhaps with some modification, it is also applicable to every industrial country. Whilst each displays unique features, to be explained in terms of its own history,

---

[1] Quoted, Lundbergh, George A., and others, *Leisure: A Suburban Study* (New York, 1934), p. 290.
[2] *Op. cit.*, p. 163. See also Hergesheimer's *The Party Dress*, for a description of the lives led by a group of well-to-do business people in an American provincial town.

an underlying unity characterizes them all. The unity arises from their bases being identical. In each the people secure their living either by owning the factories, plant and land, or by working for these owners. Each is in much the same stage of technical development; production in all of them is for profit, and thus not only are the types of work very similar but their systems of social relationships bear a very marked resemblance to each other. Hence, it is not surprising that the attitudes, interests and behaviour to be discovered in one such country are repeated amongst the comparable strata of the others. That the identity is real and not fancied is testified by the American investigators who made a leisure survey of Europe, and to whom reference has already been made. "Whether one attempts to compare European leisure occupation with the American," write May and Petgen, "or to compare with one another the countries of Europe, it must not be forgotten that similar classes will be found to have practically similar ways of life everywhere, and, in similar environments with similar facilities, different peoples will be found exercising fairly similar choices."[1] It should be remembered that this conclusion was reached after a visit to most countries in Europe for the purpose of comparing methods of spending leisure.

The similarity in the case of the middle-class women in the different countries is that the main integrating force, work, is mostly absent from their lives. For the majority in this country their education has not been firmly enough grounded to imbue them with intellectual interests sufficiently robust to survive after

[1] *Op. cit.*, p. 17.

they leave school or college. In America, it is true, the pattern is a little different, partly because a much larger number of women go to the Universities and partly because of the greater emphasis in the social tradition, as contrasted with England, on the importance of intellectual activities. As a result, we often find women's clubs with a formidable programme of papers and discussions on subjects ranging over a very wide field of knowledge. Their level of performance is perhaps not commensurate with the programmes as drawn up, yet it would be a remarkable phenomenon in England if social clubs for women even attempted to arrange regular discussions on Keats' poetry or the customs of the Eskimos; lecture programmes or discussion groups do not figure prominently in their list of activities.

The general description which has been given of the middle-class woman is in many instances aggravated by conditions peculiar to the situation which arises when they marry. Formerly they were employed and were used to travelling to work each day, they had friends there and were at least sustained by the necessities of the daily routine. Now there is a change to a fresh neighbourhood, for often of deliberate policy they move from their old home district in order not to be near their parents. They have no children. In their new setting they have hardly any acquaintances, it is not easy to find friends and often it is not considered desirable to make the effort to secure them from amongst the people living near by.

That the situation depicted is a common one, little investigation is needed to discover and is well illustrated by the following case taken from *The Case for Action*.¹ "A young woman complained that she was suffering from 'neurasthenia.' She had been married four years. At the time of her marriage she came to live the other side of London. This meant that she was cut off from her own home and from the many friends she had made before marriage, for formerly she had been a keen swimmer and belonged to a women's swimming club.

"The woman's mental condition was bad. She was diffident, depressed. . . . She was unoccupied all day, except for the brief period taken up by the shopping necessary for herself and her husband. There were five families living in the same house as she and her husband, but owing to social and moral distinctions between herself and the other families she 'kept herself to herself.' This resulted in her being literally friendless. . . ."

Except that this woman lived in a flat, her condition is typical.

Special reference should be made to the districts where recently private builders have erected new houses and where there has not yet been time to develop the institutions usually available for recreation. The areas concerned are large, 2,120,000 ² houses have been built through private enterprise since 1919; the major portion during the last seven or eight years, the era of cheap money. Of these houses 80 per cent., approximately, are occupied by clerical and professional workers, busi-

---

[1] Pearse, Innes H., and Williamson, G. Scott, who worked at The Pioneer Health Centre, Peckham.
[2] Ministry of Health Report, 1936, Cmd. 5237, p. 84.

ness men and, in general, members of the middle classes.[1]

These estates illustrate the difficulties in achieving satisfactory leisure. All the inhabitants must simultaneously strive to adjust themselves to a neighbourhood where there are no traditions and no corporate life, where each home tends to be and to remain an isolated unit. Purchasing the house, as the great majority have done, has often proved a greater financial burden than was anticipated. After the necessary items of expenditure have been met, even these often have to be curtailed, little money remains, therefore, to develop varied interests. And this poverty of the pocket reacts with especial force upon the women, for owing to the need to save money in travelling literally every service that can be transported is available at the door of the home. Even the hairdresser makes regular visits throughout many of these estates. The result is that the opportunities for the housewife to go abroad, to shop and to deal with affairs outside the home is reduced to a minimum. She remains the prisoner of her narrow environment, her daily horizon scarcely varying, bounded by the vicarious catching of the 8.25 a.m. and the prompt arrival of the 6.15 p.m.

"Keeping one's self to one's self" and the lack of money are factors which need elaborating. The one is connected with the other. Perhaps the relation

---

[1] Ministry of Health Report, 1934, Cmd. 4664, p. 151. A sample enquiry showed that artisans and skilled labourers occupied 30 per cent. of the new houses privately erected during the preceding six months. This figure is certain to be lower in respect of all the houses erected since the Armistice, for only during the past six or seven years, since house purchasing facilities have increased, have the purchasers belonged in any significant numbers to the working class.

becomes clear if they are re-expressed as the insistence upon social stratification and competitive consumption. England is *par excellence* the land of castes within castes, and this phenomenon is found in particular amongst the middle classes and those sections of the skilled workers who aspire socially. An incident will illustrate this state of mind. On one occasion a fellow-traveller on a train journey proved to be a linotyper employed by a London daily newspaper. On my questioning him concerning an historic occasion, when a portion of the staff refused to allow publication, he replied, "Oh, that was the act of the labouring masses." It is no exaggeration to say that he himself was dressed like an eccentric tramp.

Observers, trained to record social events and attitudes, emphasize this aspect of our society. "I believe the first of these ultra-English characteristics was an inspissated class-consciousness," writes Vincent Sheean, who has had excellent opportunities for comparing different countries. "Their divisions," he continues, "are far more numerous, more rigid and more irrational than anything known to the rest of the world."[1] A fellow-countryman of Sheean, Negley Farson, equally experienced in the world, comments that "the class system was so rigid that the average Englishman had no hopes of breaking out of it. Therefore he accepted his status as a *fait accompli* and resolved to make the best of it." He remarks that the works manager spoke of the directors as though they were a different species of mankind, and "in fact this class concept began to frighten me."[2]

[1] *In Search of History* (London, 1934), p. 167.
[2] *The Way of a Transgressor*, pp. 107-115.

From English writings an author might be quoted who, judging by the title he chose for his work and the pseudonym under which he sheltered, felt that he was competent to diagnose the nature of the social system. We are told by "The Man in the Club Window": "The different members of these professions (the Army, the Church, higher reaches in the medical world), their wives and families, are fit for any society . . . provided they are well bred and agreeable. The literary man, if a gentleman by education and manners, is always an agreeable addition: and the highest in rank have in this country set the example of inviting artists, architects and sculptors, but not always their families, to their tables." [1]

The insistence upon divisions and sub-divisions, even upon distinctions between members of the same family, means that the sphere of possible acquaintances and of associations to join is greatly restricted. Each person tends to move in a small circle, all the time insistent upon the status which he or she believes is due. But it is combined, as has been suggested, with competition and emulation in the consumption sphere. Probably this is the most important aspect of the leisure of the majority of the middle classes. To many of them it is essential in earning their living, to use their leisure to make useful contacts and to achieve a distinctive mark upon their social world. They must join the proper associations; they must join the right club; they must pay visits; they must

---

[1] *The Habits of Good Society* (1890), p. 324. Although this was written nearly fifty years ago it is still a sufficiently faithful picture of England. More than one recent case is on record of a local authority allowing a claim for a reduction in rating value of the house on the grounds that the property has deteriorated through a man in uniform, *e.g.* a 'bus driver, coming to live near by and walking along the street.

entertain whether they wish to or not. And even if the compulsion does not arise from their business needs, then the universally existing stimulus to emulation of the appearance, habits and manners displayed by people higher in the social ladder will force them to spend more money than they can really afford on clothes, motor cars, keeping a maid and all the other devices whereby one's social status is confirmed to the world. The phenomenon is by no means confined to England. On the contrary, it is found amongst the corresponding strata in all industrialized centres in Western Europe and also in America. "Nothing is more arresting," says a doctor who, through his treatment of their maladjusted children, has had exceptional opportunities to study the conditions of American middle-class families, "than the realization of the intensity of the struggle to 'keep up' in these neighbourhoods which so seem to radiate comfort." [1]

In this strata income more and more is being derived from work and not from the ownership of property. Hence, there is a growing absence of the sense of security which the possession of property gives. Concomitantly has come an increase in the need for assertion and reassurance in the social sphere, the need for giving the children the best possible education so that they may retain or improve on the family's present social position. But all of this is difficult, it all costs money, of which there is often not a great abundance. Illness or a turn in the tide of trade will wreak havoc with the carefully balanced budget. Blindfolded they must walk both a financial and social tight-rope without the comfort of a safety net. All the doubts about their

[1] Plant, Dr. J. S., as quoted by Lundbergh, *op. cit.*, p. 64.

position in the world will be introjected and will in turn be reflected in their behaviour. The general state of mind produced is not far to seek. It will be marked by timidity from fear of falling into the social abyss, and by conformity, because from the same fear of falling their gaze is directed only upwards, in order to ensure that they are following the proper pattern. The activities which they follow in leisure and the attitude they bring to bear on it are as a result profoundly influenced.

That their social circle will tend to be restricted has already been observed, and that, even within this circumscribed area the contacts they make will tend to be superficial and the pursuits they indulge in will be cautiously chosen, is the implication of their timidity and conformity. They must "keep up" and, above all, they must not "let themselves down." Hence, activities which open a vista of really investigating the nature of the economic and social world, with the untold dangers that that may uncover, tend to be left on one side. Activities which may involve becoming really intimate with others, who will thus be given an opportunity of seeing how thin the social pretence is, must be avoided. Refuge can and is taken in card-playing, the significance of which is brilliantly analysed by the Lynds in their new study of *Middletown,* in tennis and golf, where everyone meets at the club-house and all are extraverts together. In many cases everything is sacrificed to getting and running a motor car which, when used as the main mode of recreation, is the ideal form of challenging one's neighbours and at the same time maintaining one's privacy.

Particularly for the young women it is extremely

difficult to break this circle. They are reared in a male dominated society with its resultant handicaps against their leading an independent and full existence. Moreover, it is assumed that their object in life will be the securing of a husband. Hence, for those to whom this is not the sole purpose, a serious division often arises. Unless they are fortunate enough to meet a man who is agreeable to their devoting themselves to a profession, to cultural or intellectual objects, they must envisage the prospect of marriage only at the price of abandoning their chief interests. And their chances of meeting a suitable man are correspondingly reduced by the restricted social contacts open to the majority of the women. Thus one can see contra-selection often at work, and those who by all tests are eminently fitted to be the mothers of the coming generation remain unmarried.

But this is not all. The choice of an occupation for a woman is in fact severely limited. Unless she is willing to become a teacher there are few opportunities open to her. Whilst the opportunities in the professions are *de jure* equal for both sexes, in fact the scales are heavily weighted against women, as statistics of the membership of women amongst lawyers, dentists, doctors and other professions conclusively show.[1]

[1] Census figures for Great Britain, 1931.

	Men	Women
Religious Orders	38,684	9,368
Judges, stipendiary magistrates, barristers	3,291	80
Solicitors	19,081	133
Physicians, surgeons	30,057	3,331
Veterinary surgeons and practitioners	2,456	86
Professional engineers	38,829	209
Architects	10,154	111
Ship designers, surveyors, naval architects	1,165	80
Dental practitioners	12,434	469
Total	156,151	13,867

Because of these meagre opportunities the education of a woman is often a thing not considered worth making sacrifices for, the girls are treated less generously so that the boys may enter the Army and the Church.[1] And because of this comparative lack of education the opportunities cannot be seized even if they come their way. They must fill in as best they may that awkward period between leaving school and setting up their own home. For the majority, some form of clerical work forms the stop-gap. "Clerks are very mixed in origin," is the conclusion reached after one of the largest social surveys undertaken in England. "A few boys and a much larger number of girls come from the professional classes. This can be explained by the fact," continues the same authority, "that there is little work of any other kind for girls of this class who are anxious to earn their own living during the few years between the time they leave school and marriage." [2]

Those who have never experienced clerical work have no conception of its dullness, of the enervation it produces, of the monotony which characterizes a life dedicated to double entry book-keeping, to dictating or typing each day "We are in receipt of . . ." A new typewriter or calculating machine is a major event. It is not surprising that when a hundred clerks and typists were questioned on whether they considered that the term "work" necessarily had an unpleasant connotation, ninety-eight answered "Yes" without

---

[1] The total number of University students in Great Britain has risen steadily since 1929. The number of girl undergraduates, however, has, during this period, shown a consistent decline. See the Annual Reports, University Grants Committee.

[2] *Survey of Merseyside*, vol. ii. p. 335.

hesitation, although the conditions under which they worked were comparatively favourable.[1] There is ample justification for the man who remarked that a person who manages to keep out of an office need not count his life a failure, in the fact that those clerks and typists who take their work seriously often have boring personalities, with few interests outside their daily occupations.

This arises from two factors. Concentrating on success in commercial work means paying attention almost exclusively to a small section of the whole economic process. Perhaps it is banking, insurance, or even the commercial side of an industry. Whatever the particular work may be, absorption in it usually involves a failure to comprehend that it forms only a segment of a much wider field. Its relations to the other parts are not realized, and this intellectual myopia is carried over into other aspects of living. In addition, success is achieved by competing with fellow-workers. Frequently the conditions entail that, in striving for success, the qualities required are not intelligence, sympathy and broadmindedness. On the contrary, beyond virtues such as the capacity for hard work, there is demanded a restriction of sympathy and a pliancy towards those above, surpassed only by the firmness displayed towards equals or people lower in the hierarchy of the firm.

The existence of competition and stratification in the commercial world, together with the uninteresting character of the work, has other relevant results. These factors must, for instance, be taken into account

[1] The enquiry was made by the writer amongst the employees in a large insurance company.

when explaining the almost universal failure, comparatively speaking, of the attempts by firms and offices to provide leisure facilities for their employees. Even a slight experience of trying to organize sports clubs and recreation activities in an office is enough to convince one of the difficulty in evoking any response, though the facilities are often provided very cheaply and perhaps free of charge. Work is unpleasant or dull. Therefore all associations with it are to be avoided, if possible. Work is bound up with a hierarchical order amongst the staff. Therefore once more associations with it are to be avoided, for with all the goodwill which may exist this same hierarchical order is carried over into the leisure sphere. Thus, a large manufacturing firm which has many thousands of employees provides excellent recreation facilities for them, including a dramatic society. In theory, membership of the society is open to each employee, but only those with university degrees, and these form no more than a minute proportion of the whole, are found as members.[1]

Secondly, many cases occur where attaching importance to work is presented as an alternative to cultivating free time pursuits. A choice is involved because often success in an office is dependent upon being prepared to work any number of hours overtime when required; often years of study in the evenings must be devoted to obtaining a professional qualification; the employee must secure a reputation for soundness, and any out-of-the-way interest may damage this reputation. In other words, a successful black-coated worker must

[1] See also in this connection, Dreyfus, Carl, *Beruf und Ideologie der Angestellten* (Munich, 1933), pp. 194-197.

be absolutely "available," in the American sense of the term; he must conform completely. Many such workers realize only dimly if at all that a choice is, in fact, presented to them. The direction of their interests, however, is shown by the impatience with which the week-end is awaited and by the literal counting of the days until the arrival of Easter, then Whitsun, then the annual holidays. What happens, in effect, is that the whole level of feeling and perception tends to be lowered so that the uninteresting work causes little repugnance. But the price which has to be paid for thus accommodating themselves is a lack of initiative and individuality in the hours spent outside the office. Where the choice has to be made, embracing hopes of success at work involves submerging the more attractive side of their life and their personality, whilst deciding to develop tastes and interests lying outside the office usually results in their being indifferent and lackadaisical when they should be immersed in their job. The conflict is never resolved for some, and just this fact indicates that they were the people with the greatest potentialities for leading a unified life.

So far stress has been laid upon the element of competition in the commercial world and its effect upon the employees concerned. Many large offices and services, however, are now completely rationalized. That is to say, a man joining such a staff will know with a considerable degree of confidence what he will be doing and earning during the next ten, twenty, perhaps thirty years. Where such a bureaucracy exists, the tendencies which have been discussed can be observed still more clearly in relation to the attitude that is brought to leisure and free time. Thus, of nearly five hundred persons who completed a questionnaire issued by the writer, most of them being employed in very large offices,[1] only one replied, in answer to the question "Please describe a typical Sunday spent by you," that he had no typical mode of passing Sunday. As is remarked in the following quotation, routine work produces routine leisure or results in attempts to readjust the balance, often ending in overcompensation. "The bureaucrat," writes Karl Mannheim, "must carry out tasks forming only a part of a whole which mostly they are unable to survey. . . . The lack of sense or purpose in his work produces certain mental patterns which are either reinforced in his spare time, for instance, by day-dreaming in the inn, or . . . which engenders the desire to obtain from leisure all that which is denied in the working hours. . . . For the second type of reaction is true what Charles Louis Philippe wrote of love, 'L'amour, c'est tout ce que l'on n'a pas.'"[2] The first mode of reaction is symbolized by a recent cartoon. It depicted a man in bathing costume, obviously a clerk, who, with a vacant expression on his face, was sitting on the sands. The caption read, "Waiting for lunch time." The second is typified by the many young men who speed about in sports cars or on motor cycles, who actively organize each week-end as an expedition to the country or the seaside. A few obtain their

---

[1] The forms were issued mainly to employees in insurance offices and public services and to adult evening students. They were, therefore, a selected rather than a representative group, and the basis of selection was such as to suggest that they would include the more active and intelligent people, as well as those working under favourable conditions.

[2] "Der Sinn des wirtschaftlichen Erfolgstrebens," *Archiv für Sozialwissenschaft*, vol. 63, pp. 501-2.

compensation by devoting their free time to serious study.

The problem of leisure is present in an acute form in the middle classes [1] owing to the possession of time, energy and some cash after the work is done and after necessities have been met. Many of its aspects are illuminated by the autobiographical note which follows. It was submitted amongst others, from people who had filled in the questionnaire forms referred to above, by a man who is employed in a secure post. As he himself describes, his work is not fatiguing nor are the hours long. But the apparent purposelessness of the tasks he must perform render the pleasures of recreation largely nugatory.

It should be stressed that the only terms of reference given were, "Please write about your leisure."

"My unbalanced conscious life is divided into two sections. It is said that in the one I do what I like and that in the other I ought to do what somebody else, my employer, likes. If this description were true I should have simply to enjoy my work in order to sleep untroubled. As it is, however, I have no chance of putting this statement to the test of experience, my employer's idea of what I ought to do failing to coincide with my own.

After several years of inefficiency caused in the main by adolescent day-dreaming, surreptitious reading and jobs for which I had no aptitude, I tired of the humiliations inflicted on me by the senior staff, some of whom I regarded as the merest ticks, and managed, finally, to sever my waking moments into disjointed sections. First of all I tried to work sufficiently well to escape censure; and so a desire to soar in the cloudy reaches of the young mind was subordinated to a growing

---

[1] That the problem is felt by the people themselves is shown by the large number who added some discussion on their free time to the questionnaire forms which they completed.

sense of dignity and, in working better than before, I did what I liked to the extent of avoiding rebuke. Later I attained that frame of mind in which I could look upon the completion of each duty as an absolute finality. By this attainment I was enabled to get some satisfaction from the competent performance of those parts of the work which passed through my hands.

I am still at this stage and am likely to remain so, unless I absorb the outlook of my employers; for, to my mind, the work in which I collaborate is a colossal banditry. This point of view robs me of that pride in social endeavour which is enjoyable.

My sense of isolation during work-hours, however, is not entirely due to disagreement with my employer's motives and distaste for particular duties. The performance of a task efficiently breeds in the performer an appreciation of efficiency, and so the incompetence of some of my overseers is a constant irritation. Hence there is a cleft in my life incompatible with psychic health. I do a job well and so assist an agency I dislike, and I dislike those who hinder that agency by inefficiency; though purposive sabotage I might admire. Furthermore, I cannot call a senior fool a fool, without rendering myself liable to persecution where I am most vulnerable.

The way out of the dilemma is to forget it; and I do turn my mind from it when I can. This way out, of course, is no true exit.

It must be obvious that I leave the office each day without regret and often with relief; drawing, as I step across the official threshold, shutters across that part of my mind which operates from nine to four. And then comes the time when I can do what I like; or, to be more realistic, then comes the time when the patterns imposed on my conduct are more elastic than the office ties. Then it is practicable to expand one's personality by a variety of contacts impossible in the working-day; but one is constantly driven back upon oneself by the tenuousness of any moral tradition. One can so easily be lonely in the crowd to-day; like the damned souls in Beckford's Hell, each with its hand on its own tortured heart.

I do not believe that this feeling of isolation would be so emphatic during periods of leisure were they times of relaxation from a work in which one participated as something better than a mere operative. But today I leave the office trying to forget, and, being a conservative creature, fill in my leisure with a round become habit. Let me outline what I do, during the winter, after work is done.

On Monday I go to a public library and read, usually some sober journal, until nearly six, when I go to the swimming-baths with a friend. At eight we meet a mutual pal in a pub and drink, joke, laugh and dispute (about gods, white-slave traffic, evolution, etc.) until closing time. On the following three days I swim during the lunch hour, so that the evenings can be free from athleticism. On Tuesday, save for an occasional attendance at a lecture, I spend the evening in the company of my parents. They often wonder, and sometimes express their regret, at the gulf which separates them from me; for although we roughly agree about many major things, we find it easier to establish contact with our contemporaries, however intellectually antagonistic they are to us, than with each other. Nevertheless my parents are hurt if I am away from home for too many evenings at a stretch. I talk very little. We sit round the fire and read or listen to the wireless; but the latter occupation is often irksome to me, as I like to listen to talks and music without an accompanying discourse upon neighbours, the sins of shopkeepers, and other suburban trivia. Fortunately we all listen to the comic programmes. Wednesday evening passes in the company of friends, sometimes met privately and sometimes accompanied to lectures, concerts, or the cinema. Thursday is kept vacant for any chance engagements which may turn up; so it often passes as a duplicate of Tuesday. On Friday I visit the library again and afterwards spend a couple of hours at an evening class, in which I take philosophy in a very easy-going way. The week-end goes in gardening, an occupation forced on me as my parents aged, but which I have come to enjoy; in walking in the remnants of the neighbouring rurality; in odd jobs about the house, which I still dislike doing; in reading; in trying to listen-in; and in meditation which shades either into vacuity or melancholy.

I have outlined the regular round. It is sometimes broken into by week-ends in the country, where, if alone, I can fall by simple contemplation into a sort of nirvana, from which I emerge refreshed but a little sad with nostalgia. I also love to visit prehistoric monuments; from them I obtain a feeling of fellowship with my kind and an appreciation of its roots.

I like to collect recollections of them and take a pride in increasing my bag.

Yet man of habit as I am, I know that it is habit alone which binds my interests together. All my leisure is selfish indulgence, save for the a-penny-for-the-blind-man type of charity, the easy generosity of those with a little to spare, and those acts which follow a reluctance to increase pain where it is observable.

I change over a period of years by exercising my body; by filling my mind; by refining my sensibilities; by achieving contacts with friends; with works of art and science; with nature and with old stones and ancient earthworks. But all my activities, in a way which I cannot adequately describe, seem stunted by the limitations of a non-purposive life. When the stimulation obtained from a concert or landscape has subsided, one feels an enrichment which is only wasted, like coming into money on a desert island; and what is there left for one to do but to repeat the experience? And so the goods of life become opiates; but fortunately some are so good that they will last out a man's life without palling."

Part III

THE WORKING CLASS

THE problems which confront the working class are not primarily those relating to leisure. They arise from low wages, unemployment, insecurity, long hours of work, in many cases monotonous and fatiguing jobs, bad housing and poor health. When these evils are remedied the conditions in which leisure can be enjoyed will have been provided and it will then be possible to tackle its specific problems.

Much has been said concerning the increase in the time free from work which has occurred during the past decades. The *New Survey of London* estimates that during the past forty years the average free time available has increased by 15 per cent.[1] The *Merseyside Survey* shows that all sections of the population enjoy approximately six hours' leisure daily, including time for meals. The sample on which these results were obtained was small and its representative character is almost entirely vitiated by the questionnaires having been completed only by persons who were already members of societies. Thus, as the *Survey* points out, much selection had occurred. The figures must, therefore, be used with caution. Apart from this evidence, however, there are the statistics of changes in the recognized hours of work since 1914, as given in the Abstract of Statistics published by the Ministry of Labour. The main industries are covered and the

[1] Vol. ix. p. 3.

position is stated as at July, 1914, as at 31st December, 1922-25, and finally as at 31st December, 1926-36. Comparison of the first two periods shows that in all industries there had been a drop of 4 to $7\frac{1}{2}$ hours in the "recognized normal weekly hours of labour." The position, however, remained practically stationary from 1925 onwards. Only three changes are recorded. Surface workers in the coal-mining industry now work from 44 to 49 hours a week: previously their week was fixed at $46\frac{1}{2}$ hours. The workers in the boot and shoe manufacturing trade experienced a further drop of 2 hours in their working week, whilst the hours for the building trade were, if anything slightly increased.[1]

That hours of work have varied very little on the average during the past seventeen years is confirmed by another Table in the same Abstract. This records the "Estimated Weekly Amount of Change in Hours of Labour." The figures are given for 1915 onwards. Up till 1920 substantial reductions were granted, totalling approximately $43\frac{1}{2}$ million hours per week in the aggregate. Since that date, however, the changes recorded actually show an *increase*, in the aggregate, of slightly more than 1 million hours per week.[2]

These two official Tables show, therefore, that

[1] Twenty-second Abstract of Labour Statistics of the U.K. (1922-1936). Cmd. 5556, p. 87. Shop assistants, domestic servants, clerks and Government employees are excluded from the Table.

[2] *Ibid.*, p. 100, corrected, by means of the *Ministry of Labour Gazette*, till November, 1937. The Table excludes agricultural labourers, Government employees, domestic servants, shop assistants and clerks. All these groups of employees tend to work the same hours per week from year to year. Accordingly their exclusion has little effect on the total. The new factories which are opened will, of course, affect the existing average number of hours worked over the whole field of labour according as the hours of work for their employees are higher or lower than that average. The Table given does not reflect any such changes. Since, however, the new industries rely predominantly on juvenile or female labour, whose organization in

reductions in working hours occurred during the years immediately following the War, but since then, apart from the definite advance of the regulation of young persons' hours in shops, there has been no net movement in that direction. Such a conclusion confirms the analysis given earlier [1] that the discussion which has arisen in Great Britain on the problems of leisure is due, not so much to the increase in free time, but to changes occurring in the socio-economic situation, mainly as a result of the economic depression of 1931 onwards.

The question remains of the actual number of hours worked during the week. "Young persons" may not work more than 48 hours a week if engaged in a shop, not more than $55\frac{1}{2}$ hours in a textile factory, or 60 hours in any other factory or workshop, excluding meal times. But "a number of occupations are still unregulated," runs the Annual Report of the National Association of Boys' Clubs for 1934-35, "and Club Leaders frequently find that boys are working an average of more than twelve hours a day for six days a week." Women's hours of work are similarly regulated except in a shop, where no legal limit exists. For men, *i.e.* males eighteen years of age or over, hours of work are in no way restricted. For most of the industries where Trades Unions exist amongst the employees, the working hours are normally 45 to 48 per week, subject to the demands of overtime. The enquiry by the Ministry of Labour, referred to above, showed

Trades Unions is very undeveloped, it is unlikely that the hours of work in such factories are less than those in the old-established industries. It follows, therefore, that if the Table were composed to reflect changes in the aggregate of the hours of work due to the opening of new factories, there would probably be no improvement in the picture presented.

[1] See Chapter I, p. 30.

that in the industries covered the average number of hours actually worked during one week of October, 1935, fluctuated around a mean of 48. This figure is an average over men, women, young persons and juveniles. It conceals the fact that in the building trade one-quarter of all the employees worked more than 48 hours, in the cement manufacturing industry the working hours of nearly one-third exceeded 48, whilst in other large industries, such as woodworking and food, drink and tobacco, the proportion so affected was nearly 1 in 7.

Trades Union agreements do not cover each industry. Particularly is this the case in just those trades and industries, employing ever-increasing numbers, which are excluded from the statistics quoted above: shop assistants, clerks, domestic servants. It is impossible to give exact figures of their hours of employment. Assistants in co-operative societies' shops are restricted to 48 hours a week. For private shops the figure varies considerably: it may be as low as an average of $45\frac{1}{2}$ hours per week, excluding overtime, it may be as high as 70 hours per week in such shops as tobacconists. The hours of work for clerks differ enormously. Some are employed for only 30 to 35 hours per week: these, however, would not be included in the working class. Others, attached to shops and factories, have very much longer hours, 45 to 55 a week.

The following Table briefly summarises the various aspects of the hours of work per week. Meal times are excluded from the total of hours given: the exclusion is important since in the textile factories, for instance, the legal limit for young persons and

HOURS OF WORK PER WEEK
[EXCLUDING MEAL TIME]

	Type of Employee.	Shops.	Textile Factories.	Other Factories and Workshops; Transport.	Clerical Establishments.	Other Commercial Establishments.
Legal Limits	Young persons	48 [longer in certain trades]	55½	60	None	None[1]
	Women	None	55½	60	None	None
	Men	None	None	None	None	None
Normal recognized[2]	All	48	48	Mainly 47–48	Various [little regulated]	Various [little regulated]
Actually worked [excluding overtime]	Young persons	45–48	48	46–60	Black-coated workers from 30–40; others 45–55	Varies greatly: may be 70 or more even for "young persons."[3]
	Women	45–65				
	Men					

[1] Local authorities would have powers to adopt by-laws regulating the hours of work for van boys provided that an Order has been issued by the Secretary of State under Section 19 (3) Employment of Children and Young Persons Act, 1933. No such Order has yet been issued: the question is being considered at the present time.

[2] "Normal Recognized" means the usual terms of agreement between employers' and employees' organizations.

[3] See the Annual Reports, Chief Inspector of Factories and Workshops, for accounts of such cases. See also the recent Report of the Departmental Committee on the Employment of Young Persons in Unregulated Trades.

women would be increased to 66½ hours by their inclusion.

Apart from the length of the working week the actual incidence of the working time is important in relation to leisure. Where shift work or spells of night work are the rule, then any planning of spare time for the purpose of joining associations is almost completely eliminated. A high proportion of workers are subject to such changes in their hours of work. The position is not improved by the passing, in 1936, of an Act allowing the Secretary of State to grant a permit for the employment of women and young persons on shifts between 6 a.m. and 10 p.m.[1] In many large stores the hour of ceasing work is 6 p.m. in one week, 7 p.m. in the next; the assistants are thus unable to enter into any regular leisure engagements, such as clubs or classes, unless these start well after 7 p.m.: the later hour governs their organized activities. A recent investigator into the position of Girls' Clubs writes, "The returns from Club leaders on the question of hours of work of Club members show, in the great majority of cases, that shop assistants and domestic workers are the two groups most often prevented from attending regularly or punctually. Maids seem to be unfortunate in many cases, since they are liable to have their 'evening out' changed at short notice and they are prevented from going to their Club on the usual night." Seasonal rushes, involving overtime, also play havoc with regular, planned recreation, not only obviating the benefit to be derived therefrom, but also inculcating "a restlessness of spirit which penetrates

[1] See the comments in the *Annual Survey of English Law* (1936), pp. 239-240.

his (the worker's) whole life and he finds it increasingly difficult to concentrate on any activity which requires thought." [1]

To give a full analysis of the amount of poverty and of the level of wages amongst the working class would be to go beyond the scope of the present work. Nevertheless, the subject is important since, as has been stressed, participation in leisure pursuits to-day is so much a question of possessing money. The extent of poverty is shown by the results of the Social Surveys which during the past few years have been conducted in various parts of the country. The percentage of working-class families on or below the poverty line, as variously defined but always so as to include only a bare minimum necessary to existence, ranged from 21 per cent. in Southampton, 18·9 per cent. in Sheffield, 17·3 per cent. in Liverpool, to 9·1 per cent. in London.[2] The *Merseyside Survey* comments, "It is an ironical reflection that . . . in one of the most important areas in England . . . some 3000 families out of a random sample of 7000 . . . failed to secure what Rowntree termed 'the bare essentials of a civilized life.'" And, referring to these "bare essentials," it further adds, ". . . anyone unacquainted with Mr. Rowntree's book will be astonished to discover how narrow a margin is allowed over and

---

[1] Rooff, Madeline, *op. cit.*, pp. 75-76.
[2] Ford, P., *Work and Wealth in a Modern Port* (London, 1934), p. 118. The actual findings were as follows : ". . . the numbers of working-class families beneath the standard was between 25·8 per cent. and 17·2 per cent., and was probably between 22·5 per cent. and 20·6 per cent." It will be seen that the mean of the last two figures has been taken ; Owen, A. D. K., *A Survey of the Standard of Living in Sheffield*, 1933 (pamphlet) ; *Survey of Merseyside*, vol. i. p. 153 ; *New Survey of London*, vol. vi. p. 87. See also Bowley and Hogg, *Has Poverty Diminished?* London, 1925, for statistics resulting from somewhat earlier enquiries.

above the absolute essentials of existence."[1] Whilst, therefore, a great improvement has been recorded since the 1880's when Charles Booth made his Survey of London, a considerable increase in the standard of living is necessary before the claim can be made that poverty is abolished. This becomes clearer when it is considered that a large proportion of the families, more than 20 per cent. in some cases, were less than 50 per cent. above the poverty line.

Unfortunately, of the many published budgets of working-class families none distinguish in detail the various items comprised in "Miscellaneous." It is impossible to tell, therefore, what is the average proportion that is spent on amusements and recreation of all kinds. Two things are certain. Youths and girls of the working class tend to spend more on the cinema, dances[2] and clothes, than seems to be compatible with the small total sum they earn.[3] Secondly, the amount expended on amusements rapidly decreases as they grow older, especially when they marry and have children. Thus an enquiry made in Germany shows that in families with an income of between RM. 3000 and 3600 per annum, savings was the only item in the

---

[1] Vol. i. pp. 155-156.

[2] Perhaps it should be noted that a decline in dancing is recorded in Liverpool, and that, although in some cases the entrance fee is only 3d., the decline was explained to the investigators in terms of poverty. *Survey of Merseyside*, vol. iii. p. 287.

[3] A sample enquiry of actual earnings was conducted by the Ministry of Labour in October, 1935. Separate statistics are given for men, women, youths and girls. "Youths and Boys (under 21 years)" in only two industries earned more than 26s. per week, the highest figure being 28s. 3d. per week. Their earnings in the majority of the other industries were between 22s. and 24s. per week. "Girls (under 18 years)" nowhere earned more than 17s. 11d. per week, the mean fluctuated around 16s. per week. These figures exclude the Government Industrial Establishments, where comparatively few youths and girls are employed: earnings in these Establishments were approximately 1s. 6d. per week higher.

budget which, as children were born, declined more quickly than the amount spent on recreation.[1]

Another general factor to be taken into account is the lack of energy after the day's work is done. In spite of the generally decreased working day, this factor is still important when discussing leisure in relation to the working class. The Peckham Health Centre, where the unit of membership is the family, finds it extremely difficult to secure the co-operation and attendance of the men. The reason mainly given for failure to attend is tiredness. The Centre offers many attractions for men and, therefore, the explanation seems to be genuine.

The position varies from industry to industry: dock labourers are exhausted after a full day's work, light machine tenders have energy left, especially since they are usually young people.[2] This is clearly a question on which exact information is difficult to obtain: probably if hours of work do not decrease then the importance of the factor of tiredness is likely to increase as a result of the continually growing speed of work in workshops, in factories, in transport and even in offices. Home is also becoming further and further separated from work. Time is taken by the travelling thus involved and energy is absorbed by it. The remedy is undoubtedly the shortening of the hours of work.

Apart from the general conditions of their lives so far discussed, are there any problems relating specifically to the leisure of labourers and unskilled workers in general? What was the attitude of the workers to

[1] Quoted Halbwachs, M., *L'Évolution des Besoins dans les classes ouvrières* (Paris, 1933), p. 54.
[2] But even with young people the position is not very satisfactory. "Club Leaders and Heads of Evening Institutes report that many of their members are too tired to take part in the evening's activities." *The Coming of Leisure*, New Education Fellowship, 1935 (pamphlet).

leisure before their working hours were reduced? What did they desire to do with the free time which they hoped to get?

Partial answers to these questions are available as the result of an enquiry made in Germany prior to the granting of the 10-hour day. For four years, from 1907-11, the investigator collected questionnaires and replies by correspondence and interviews from 5,040 workers, of whom 2,084 were miners, 1,153 textile workers and 1,803 metal workers.[1] Their hours were long, often 12 or 13 a day, their wages varied, but in the main were low, the textile workers being paid on the average less than those in the other two industries.

They were asked, "If you had the necessary money, what would you buy?" The following Table gives the first choice named, often many desires were expressed in the full answers. The percentages are calculated on the number who replied to that question, which in the case of both this and the following questions was high, sometimes being equal to the total number who returned the questionnaires.

Industry.	Good Clothes.	Enough to Eat.	A Better Home.	A Piece of Land.	Books.	Miscellaneous.
	Per Cent.	Per Cent.	Per Cent.	Per Cent.	Per Cent.	Per Cent.
Textile Workers	17	17	14	17	7	28
Miners	15	15	18	—	9	43
Metal Workers	9	4	12	22	22	31

Comparison of the percentages in the first two

[1] Levenstein, Adolf, *Die Arbeiterfrage*, Munich, 1912. The men were secured as to the first thousand through their being members of Trades Unions and political parties. They were each given several forms and asked to distribute all but the one for themselves amongst their acquaintances. Thus it was not a true random sample; at the same time the selection exercised was not great since a high proportion of all the forms issued were returned and most of them (seven-eighths) had been given to random acquaintances of the original one thousand men.

columns shows that of the poorest paid, the textile workers, those wanting clothes and enough to eat were a higher percentage than of the miners, and that in their turn more of these made such first choices than of the metal workers, the highest paid of all three. The last column shows that with the drop in these choices, so there is a striking increase in the proportion wanting books, from 7 per cent. textile workers, to 22 per cent. metal workers. This suggestion of active intellectual interest is confirmed by the answers to the next question, "If you had the necessary time what would you do?"

Industry.	Enough Sleep.	With Family.	Walk in the Country.	Political Work.	Painting (Pictures).	Further Education.	Miscellaneous.
	Per Cent.	Per Cent.	Per Cent.	Per Cent.	Per Cent.	Per Cent.	Per Cent.
Textile Workers	—	13	19	10	9	32	17
Miners . .	7	16	12	11	—	21	33
Metal Workers	—	26	8	11	7	30	18

The proportion desiring to improve their education was in no case lower than 1 in 5 and reached almost 1 in 3 of the textile and metal workers. The combined percentages for those desiring to do political work, to paint or to improve their education, *i.e.* some form of intellectual or creative work, were 51 per cent. for textile workers, 32 per cent. for miners, and 48 per cent. for metal workers. The figures do not reflect the men's interest in and attachment to painting. Many wrote that they already painted as often as they could. It is to be understood as the easiest expression of their creative urge, having the additional advantage that at the same time they could be in the open air.

This evidence of intellectual interest amongst the workers is by no means confined to Germany. The history of the Mechanics' Institutes in this country in the middle of last century, the large sale of cheap scientific, political and economic books during the same period, the fact that when, for instance, the Birmingham museums were opened in the evenings they were immediately crowded by people who had previously never had an opportunity of visiting them,[1] all are proof of the thirst for knowledge and the willingness after the day's work was done to spend time to acquire it. Perhaps the most striking evidence, referring as it does to 1741, comes from Scotland. It is to be found in *The Second Report on Trades and Manufactures*, 1843.[2] "Leadhills is remarkable for the institution, by its mining work people, in 1741, of a library of circulating, the first established by mechanics in Scotland and apparently the first in the whole Kingdom. It was instituted entirely by the miners themselves and wholly at their own suggestion. They then worked only 6 hours a day, had much spare time on their hands. . . ."

This same library consisted in 1835 of 1,633 volumes, classified as follows: divinity 471, history 324, voyages and travels 177, arts and sciences 177, philosophy and letters 87, poetry 47, novels and romances 212, miscellaneous 138. Fiction thus accounted for less than 13 per cent. of the total.

The question will be asked, "Why has this intellectual curiosity and interest failed to develop and expand with

---

[1] Speech by Jesse Collings, On the resolution to open the Public Art Gallery and Free Reference Library on Sunday, 1872. (Published National Sunday League.)
[2] Vol. xiii, p. 167.

the increased provision of adult education, libraries, radio and cheap books?" Answers must be sought in various directions. The intellectual ferment which existed in this country throughout most of the last century, as evidenced in the vast interest in science and the struggles over evolution and religion, tended to die down in the last decade, and unfortunately has scarcely been revived. The time when famous scientists, writers and educationalists felt it a duty to explain the nature of the world, natural and social, to working-class audiences has almost completely passed away. Secondly, the nature of work has changed so that its effects are mainly soporific. Highly paid experts have the express job of saving the workers thought in their daily toil. The division of labour has proceeded to the extent of an almost complete divorce between manual and brain work. Thirdly, there are other highly paid experts employed by enterprises such as newspapers, cinema circuits and advertising firms, who justify the salary they receive by their ability to purvey their wares. Formerly those who sought out the poor did so for the purposes of charity or to educate them. Now it is to secure their money by diverting their attention to the cinema, to football and to all the other spectacles.

Moreover, all the conditions of life of an unskilled workman are against his developing fixed and strong interests. Apart from his work three main agencies might inculcate interests into him: the family, the school and social organizations. Teachers often strive devotedly at their task, in spite of all the handicaps under which they labour, and the boy when he leaves at fourteen years of age is full of zest and curiosity.

But the conditions he meets outside serve effectively to dampen his energy and his spirits. The social organizations which are available are discussed in Chapter IV, and so the question will not be pursued here.

The first agency, the family, it is necessary to discuss in some little detail. Nearly 20 per cent. of the German workmen, already quoted, gave as their first wish to be more with their family. Thus they showed considerable evidence of family feeling. Yet all observers have commented that for the working-class boy the family ceases to be important as soon as he leaves school.[1] Evidence on this point may be gathered from accounts of their spare time activities which were collected by the author from twenty boys employed in a large distributive stores. Their ages ranged from 15 to 17; they lived mainly in East London. They recounted with a wealth of detail, which was sometimes embarrassing, how they spent their free time with girls, with their "pals," with their "bikes," playing football or cricket, going to the cinema: one went to a Club. Not one of them said anything of activities connected with the family apart from the boy who wrote, "On the Sabath day, I am unlike most animals, I do not lay in bed from morn till night, semiquaver! I take my parants a cup of tea. . . ."[2]

---

[1] See, for example, Freeman, Arnold, *Boy Life and Labour* (1913), p. 124. " With the bulk of the boys we are considering the Home provides practically nothing for those needs of the adolescent. . . . It is a conclusion which apparently all investigators have reached, that the home may be almost left out of account as a positive influence in the life of the boys of this class."

[2] The whole of this boy's paper is given below since the variety of his recreations is so exceptional. He was astonishingly stupid at class work, being genuinely suspicious when it was suggested to him that two and two

This was the sole mention of the existence of any relatives: for these youths home seems to serve as a place to sleep, to secure their meals, occasionally to read a book, " I read *The Scalp Hunters* and *The Coral Island* which I have found are very good," but more often to clean their bicycle. After his two-years' study of the New Housing Estates at Becontree or Dagenham, Terence Young writes that it is difficult to say where the 18 to 24 years old young people spend their spare time, but "they certainly attend cinemas, and they most certainly do not stay at home if they can possibly help it." [1]

make four, yet, as will be seen, he was so immersed in music that instead of ordinary punctuation he resorted to musical terms. It is not surprising that he writes of " hell . . . work . . . that hatred, or wreched, debt (he means ' department ') the Grocery."

My Leisure Time

On the Sabath day, I am unlike most animals, I do not lay in bed from morn till night, semiquaver ! I take my parants a cup of tea, and take my fellow animal, the dog, for a stroll and a swim in the balmy waters of Wanstead Flats pond. I then have breakfast and traverse to church. After dinner, I sleep till tea-time, then I practise on my viola with pianoforte accompanyment.

On Monday I get up at seven o'clock and tone up my muscles for work, with aid of chest-expanders, springs. I then breakfast, and go to hell—in other words—to work. I work in that hatred, or wreched, debt—the Grocery. Monday night's I go to night school.

On Tuesday night's I go to Band Practise, because am in the (Y.M.C.A.) intermediate string orchestra. On Wednesday night's I go to Gymnasium to learn gymnastics and acrobatics. Thursdays I go swimming with the swimming club.

Friday night I do my night-school homework, which takes me about 3 hrs instead of 1 hr, because as far as arithmetic is concerned my name is, (dense).

Saturday night I go to music lessons, unless I have a (date) with my viola, or violin.

My favourite hobbies are music, which I spent all my money on, and put my heart and sole to.

Also Gymnasium, swimming, and reading English Litterature. Altogether, my full repertwar of hobbies is :—football, which I play for the league on Thursday afternoon's. Also Boxing and acrobatics, arts and crafts and reading, music and gymnastics, are my hobbies.

Semibreve—
full stop.

[1] Young, Terence, *Becontree and Dagenham* (London, 1934), p. 224.

Why, although the parents are anxious to spend time with their family, do they play such a small part in the lives of their sons? Space at home is limited and, therefore, since the boys are noisy and often quarrelsome the street must be their playground. Since this is a male-dominated society, which means in the present case that little assistance is demanded from the boys for housework, they have most of their time out of school to themselves, and thus, because the home mainly lacks positive attractions, the tendency for them to prefer the street is strengthened. As soon as they earn money they become independent. Their earnings form a welcome addition to the slender family budget. Accordingly, they must not be driven away and the best method of keeping them is to leave them alone to do as they wish. They are at once freed from the restriction of school and any slight influence which the home till then had exercised. Thus, even if they wish to mould their sons, parents have little opportunity of so doing. Unless the sons come into contact with outside organizations, their interests are derived solely from the world of sport and amusement.

The girls are differently affected. To understand their position it is necessary to realize the rôle of the mother in working-class families.[1] She holds the key

[1] The conditions of working-class family life, with special reference to the mode of life of factory girls and its mental consequences, are perhaps best shown in a German study. Its author, Lisbeth Franzen Hellersberg, a sociologist and psychologist, for six years lived and worked under varying conditions with young factory girls in order to ascertain whether such circumstances produce a specific type, the young working woman, and if so, what are her characteristics. Her book appeared in 1932, *Die jugendliche Arbeiterin: ihre Arbeitsweise u. Lebensform. Ein Versuch Sozialpsychologischer Forschung zum Zweck der Umwertung proletarischer Tatbestände.* (The young working woman, her conditions of work and her way of life. An attempt at social-psychological research for the purpose of re-valuing judgments concerning the working class.) No corresponding study of English conditions seems to be available, although perhaps Paterson's

position. But in spite of that, the general tendency in working-class families is rather to neglect than to esteem the women. That the housework is done, that the children are looked after, that gaps in the budget are made as invisible to other members of the family as possible, is the responsibility of the mother; it does not follow that she is respected for doing it. Much more it implies that it is the women's lot to do all this work; the men have some time to themselves, the women hardly ever. The mother is, if necessary, both wage-earner and housekeeper. "Even though she may not do so much baking and washing as formerly," writes a keen observer of English life, "the Lancashire mother who divides herself between the weaving shed and the home still has a busy time of it. Her eight-hour day at the mill will mean starting at 7.15 in the morning and returning home at 6. Then she must see to the arranging, the cleaning, the cooking, the nursing, perhaps even the washing. The woman whose husband is an ordinary mill-hand has no money for work to be done, and the ordinary mill-hand takes it that woman's work is woman's work. . . ."[1]

And the heavy task is taken over by the daughters; while, as has been said, the boys are usually allowed to play, the girls must assist in running the home, looking after children, going errands, any of the multitudinous jobs which need to be done.[2] All over

---

chapter on Family Life in *Across the Bridges* should be mentioned, but there is every reason to believe that her findings are valid for the industrial conditions of the whole of Western Europe. Those who are acquainted with the work will appreciate the ample use which, in the following pages, has been made of her findings.

[1] Nevinson, H. W., *The English* (1929), pp. 54-55.
[2] Mess, Henry A., *The Facts of Poverty* (London, 1920), p. 115. " Girls, in particular, have to do an immense amount of home drudgery. They often drag about younger brothers and sisters and lift babies whose weight

the country educationalists complain that owing to the calls of housework girls' attendance at school drop from the time they are ten or eleven onwards. They are subordinate to their brothers, they are treated as their inferiors. From early childhood their dependence on and subjection to a patriarchal society is imposed on them. They are faithful replicas of their mothers, who have always "the air of trying to catch up with the work; always the incessant certainty that it is impossible." [1] They experience, too, the same neglect. Living in a constant hurry, there is little time or opportunity for the parents to develop understanding and patience towards the children. "Love needs time and time is money." Often the mother will try to be kindly and loving, but if the child cries or disobeys is it not easiest to leave it or to punish it? Hence the girls' desire for affection is never satisfied, and this lack is carried over into the time they become adolescents.

Moreover, poor children, and particularly the girls, have comparatively slight opportunities for play. Yet play is essential if they are to gain self-confidence and real self-discipline. That they seem so realistic in their behaviour is because "They have learned to put up with things, to avoid them. . . . But this attitude which is forced upon them, should not be confused with self-

---

is too heavy for them . . . and they may have to spend their holidays cleaning. Visitors for the Children's Country Holiday Fund find that mothers are less willing to allow girls to go away than boys because the girls are so useful at home."

Similarly, a small girl of ten years of age, in a south-east London school, was recently in trouble with her teacher over her arithmetic. She was completely unable to do it. Her mother came to defend her and said in the course of the interview, " She's ever such a good girl at home. Every night she scrubs and dusts a room for me."

[1] Nevinson, H. W., *op. cit.*, pp. 54-55.

discipline."[1] They have scarcely realized that there are demands which they might legitimately make for their own lives, for the handicaps from which they suffer both in the home and at school impress upon them a sense of inferiority. The subordination their mothers endured is continued; because of it and because of their narrow lives, the girls' imaginations tend to centre around the three things which experience has taught them are valuable—money, frocks and boys.

In the factory these interests are reinforced. Just as in the family, so in the factory, the males dominate; the immediate superior may be a woman, but all those jobs requiring skill and technique, such as maintenance of machines, are in male hands, and inevitably the person with whom the last word rests is a male. Hence the dependency which has already been noted is re-emphasized.

Even apart from this atmosphere of male domination, the girls are prevented from reaching self-confidence and achieving a status in their own eyes. They must earn wages as early as possible. Without any future they have no idea of the desirability of training, but they grasp clearly the desirability of money. For them the only means to satisfaction is the greatest exploitation of the immediate moment. The nature of the work they do re-emphasizes this escape into the present. The operations to be performed are usually trivial, the whole process whereby the article is completed often remains a mystery to them, and why should they find out? Their jobs are suitable for "headless" people, as the following incident, recounted by an American psychiatrist, vividly illustrates. "One

[1] Hellersberg, *op. cit.*, p. 46.

day last fall I examined a feeble-minded 18-year-old girl. Edna had been working at a punch press for six months. At seeing that all her ten fingers were intact I could not hide my surprise. Her reply was as spontaneous as it was profound—" 'It's only them that thinks that loses their fingers.' " [1]

The girls become stupefied with the boredom their work requires.[2] When it is not heavy but merely repetitive, they are given endless opportunities to day-dream. "We like this work," the author was told by girls operating light, simple machines in a biscuit factory. "We can think of something else all the time." Often the work demands a physical endurance which young women do not possess as a result of the early overtaxing of their strength. Hence they become indifferent and inefficient.[3] A thing of the moment, their work is something to be forgotten as soon as done, to be ignored, rather than to be incorporated into a plan of life.[4]

Not only are they indifferent to their work, there is lack of unity and organization amongst the girls. This lack is a necessary implication of the specifically

---

[1] Plant, Dr. J. S., *American Journal of Psychiatry*, vol. viii. The dangers of employing intelligent girls are consciously avoided by some employers. ". . . there were firms in London . . . who made a point of employing mentally defective girls," it was reported at the National Special Schools Union Conference, 1937. " Mentally deficient girls make steady employees in a monotonous job and employers are glad to have them."

[2] Hellersberg, *op. cit.*, p. 33, reports that of even educated women, after a period of assimilation, 70 to 80 per cent. come to like repetitive, unskilled work.

[3] It is clear that special circumstances produce this inefficiency. It is an accepted fact that trained and educated women in posts which involve responsibility or application are, as a rule, more conscientious and dependable than men.

Perhaps because of this absence of close bonds between the factory girl and her work, welfare schemes have tended to develop in those firms where large numbers of girl employees are to be found.

[4] " We have no profession, we have work," was the reply given by young factory girls. Hellersberg, *op. cit.*, p. 34.

feminine attitude forced upon them from all their values arising out of their being girls, and in turn emphasizing the fact. In an environment in which their colleagues are women but their foremen and managers are men, their desire is orientated towards gaining the recognition of the men. The achievement of this often involves sacrificing the interests of the other workers and of themselves. The men, of course, exploit this tendency. "The factory managers are as good practical psychologists in relation to their factory girls as the hotel porter is towards his guests." [1]

Because they have no interest in unity they tend not to be members of Trades Unions, and hence the demands on their spare time which would arise from such activities are absent. Thus they escape their educative effect and they have the hours away from the factory free for amusing themselves.

That they are subordinated to the male is the constant lesson of the factory, and the attitude engendered is inevitably carried outside.[2] They can hope in turn to dominate the male, only during leisure. Thus every influence bearing on the girls tends to shift the centre of their lives to the hours after 7 o'clock. Hence the emphasized erotic attitude of the factory girls, their display of finery, their love of dancing and cinemas, their loud shrieks of laughter in the streets which serve to draw attention to themselves, their competitive boasting of wild adventures on Monday morning.

Could not this vitality in their leisure hours prevent

---

[1] Hellersberg, *op. cit.*, p. 31.
[2] Medical Research Council, Report No. 69, p. 35. "The general behaviour of the operatives employed was also related to the type of work . . . *there is little doubt that continued exposure to industrial conditions may have an effect on feelings and behaviour which is by no means confined to the hours of work*" (italics added).

the deterioration which monotonous work inevitably entails? But, for just those things which seem to them to be valuable,[1] philandering, their amusements, their pathetic attempts at elegance, they are rebuked by the world outside the factory. The schools they have recently left, their parents, the officials they encounter, have little to offer but condemnation of their only quality: that they are girls and nothing but girls. Yet the films, the theatres, the music halls, the sporting events, cheap books almost always dealing with love, the gossip columns of the Press, the whole "machinery of amusement" glorify the people who in effect form their prototype. The girls read of the rich whose lives seem nothing but amusement, they see on the screen the well-groomed, the ideal people,[2] for whom work seems to play but little part. Thus is the justification to the factory girl provided.

However, it is not complete. It is a tussle, for in the films the people are not so adventurous, nor so amorous, that they destroy the standards which condemn flirting, adventuring and idling. Some *deus ex machina*, a rich father, a handsome detective, a woman's true love, rescues them and the social norms are preserved. Thus the characters in filmland escape social condemnation or, if they are really bad, then a terrible punishment awaits them. Either the standards which the audience learned at school are upheld or

[1] Commenting on the records of *The Southwark Diocesan for Moral Welfare* for the past thirty years the writer of *The New Survey of London Life and Labour*, vol. ix. p. 435, states, " Those ' wilful girls ' of 1900 who left home owing to their ' uncontrolled passion ' are probably not unlike ones now described as having no healthy outlet for their energies and no interests in which to express themselves."

[2] " The West End prefers spectacular films. Working-class audiences are more interested in society dramas, which profess to portray the lives of the rich." *The Film in National Life* (London, 1932), p. 82.

their breach involves destruction. And so the ambivalent, conflicting, codes are preserved by the amusements industry and the mental disturbance of the onlooker is completed. This inescapable conflict in standards of value prevents even those with great potentialities from developing a new form and justification of their life. The only reason which has been left to them for self-appraisal is also a continual reason for guilt feelings. They receive from the Press and the cinema a constant vindication of their determination to amuse themselves, to leave all else on one side. But from the same source they are continually given reminders that there is more in life than mere pleasure and enjoyment, that serious, solid, virtues count. To which message are they to listen? Is it not inevitable that they should be disturbed and bewildered?[1]

It is not merely that the conflict of values is enhanced, sometimes the effect of the amusements industry is actively to promote mischief or delinquency. Factory girls usually have no contact with the rich. They live amongst people of their own kind; they go with youths and men who are members of their own milieu and, therefore, they are seldom ambitious to rise socially by having rich friends. They know the fate of prostitutes from its darkest side. As a result, domestic servants, waitresses, shopgirls, clerks and typists are found much more in the ranks of the prostitute; these are in contact with people of a higher social grade and can, therefore, watch longingly their ease and comfort. Mainly through the medium of the films factory girls are also brought into contact with other modes of living and

[1] See Chapter III, Part I, " The Cinema," for further discussion of this point.

discover their appeal. They witness the rise of girls who achieve comfort by being betrothed to their employers—or almost betrothed. These *fata morgana* become the day-dream of the factory girl.[1]

Between Wales and the North on the one hand, and the South of England on the other, there are differences in working-class leisure. The people in Durham, Lancashire, South Wales and Yorkshire have grown up mainly amongst neighbours of their own social standing. Complementary to this is the fact that the division between the directors and employers on the one hand, and the employees on the other, is sharply marked. Outside the factory the line of demarcation is much less blurred than in the South where a host of officials and commercial employees of indefinite status serve as a bridge from the one social rank to the other. Moreover, at least till the War, since then to a decreasing extent, religion, nearly always some branch of Nonconformity, has been a unifying bond. At the same time these areas have been the strongholds of Trade Unionism.

All factors have been favourable, therefore, to spontaneous social and cultural organizations being erected, outside of the world of commercial amusements. Used to managing their own affairs in the chapels and their Trades Union, the miners and steel

---

[1] At a Conference of experienced workers amongst girls and women, quoted in *The New Survey of London Life and Labour*, vol. ix. p. 434, one of the chief reasons for promiscuity was agreed as follows : " Dire poverty is less often a reason for such behaviour than is the desire of girls earning a moderate wage to have a good time and to dress in the prevailing fashion." The Secretary of the Police Court Mission states, *ibid.*, p. 437 : " A notable change is evident in the age of sex-delinquents. There are far more young women and even girls of 15 and 16 years of age coming into this category . . . their chief desire has been to earn extra pocket money or ' to have a good time ' going to a show and having supper with a man, etc."

workers have also organized their own choral societies, brass bands, orchestras, dramatic societies, educational courses and institutes for recreation. That they have kept alive their intellectual interests even to-day is shown by Swansea, with a population of only 180,000, having more manual workers who are members of Three-Year University Tutorial Classes, the most disciplined form of Extra-Mural Education, than are to be found in the whole of London.[1] Unfortunately, with the advent of the omnibus even their partial isolation has tended to break down. Moreover, just these districts have been most blighted by unemployment and have become the centres of much philanthropic social effort, while the press of commercial amusements becomes ever stronger. These regional differences, therefore, are tending to be ironed out,[2] but nevertheless their existence is a testimony to the creative impulses which are discoverable in the working people.

All over the country one institution plays a large rôle in the leisure of the poor people, the public-house. Often it has been commented that only in Britain are the existing social gradations perpetuated by dividing the public-houses into separate compartments where different prices are charged. It is true and, unfortunately, is evidence of the divisions and subdivisions which exist. But the other side of the picture is that the "pub" is essentially a social institution. Previously the English workers were

[1] Central Joint Advisory Committee on Tutorial Classes, 27th Annual Report, p. 42.
[2] See the chapter "Leisure," in *Portrait of a Mining Town*, Philip Massey, 1937, for an account of the decline in organized recreation from the causes mentioned.

notorious for their drunkenness, a habit to be explained in terms of their miserable existence and lack of amenities. Drinking was "the quickest way out of Whitechapel." Drunkenness and the incidence of drink have declined, but much the same amount of money *per capita* is spent on beer and spirits. The *New Survey of London* shows that out of an average family income of 75s. per week, not less than 10s. 6d. per week goes in drink.[1]

Why should the "pub" remain the outstanding social institution? Its informality has enormous appeal. You come when you like, you go when you like. It is a matter for choice whether you keep on your working clothes. It is the only place you can stay as long as you like without being pestered to spend more money. It is near home, and when you get there no demands are made to be active mentally or physically. It is as though you are at home except that you are in the company of other people, and just this is the important difference. The beer is an attraction, but so also are all the associations with which it is surrounded.

The attitude of the unemployed brings out very clearly the social status of "pubs." They "regard the public-houses as closed to them," writes the investigator in the *New Survey of London*, "and in conversation will admit to being afraid someone will stand them a drink they can't return. The activities discussed in the bar," he continues, "will in any case be mainly closed to them, and the feeling of most of them appears to be that they would be both embarrassed and a source of embarrassment even if they could raise the price of a drink."[2]

[1] Vol. ix., chapter "Drinking."   [2] Vol. ix. p. 254.

Public-houses continue their popularity in spite of the fact that an unfortunate combination of brewers' interests and temperance ethics keeps them to outward seeming very unattractive places. The brewers have little interest in providing amenities because they know that if music, games, comfortable chairs, are provided, their clientele will certainly stay longer but will spend no more. The licensing authorities only reluctantly grant permits for providing attractions other than beer, even in many cases discouraging darts or shove-halfpenny, because they fear that if the public-houses become more than a place for getting a drink they will exercise additional attractions, especially for the young persons. But since the people go to the public-houses in any case, and since in their present condition they are regarded as an evil to be abolished, two main courses for improvement seem available. On the one hand, the Carlisle scheme should be extended throughout the country so that the drive in public-houses is behind the sale of things other than drink. At the same time amenities could be introduced and restrictions removed so that the public-houses become places for real pleasure and recreation. On the other hand, and this is by no means an alternative but an additional policy to the first, new social and recreational institutions need to be created which will attract the working men. Although the wives are not well catered for, they are richer than their husbands in this respect. For the majority of the men, unless they are members of a church or chapel or of a Trade Union, the meetings of which they regularly attend, their horizon is limited by their labour, their home and their public-house.

Part IV

THE UNEMPLOYED

WHILST the aristocracy presents features peculiar to English history, the leisure problem for the unemployed has aspects common to all industrial countries. The unemployed have free time, but have they leisure? Why are the social services for them mainly providing organized leisure activities but not work?[1] Why do the unemployed feel themselves to be "misfits" in society?

In trying to tackle these questions one answer immediately suggests itself; to have leisure alone, to have nothing but free time, means to have no contacts, no friends, no money, no justification for existence, and last, but not least, to have no leisure. Why is it true to say that to be without work is to be without reason for existence?[2] Has it not been said that it is just the task of leisure to provide the reason for

---

[1] Concerning the provision of training for unemployed in Great Britain see the summary in *Unemployment, An International Problem*, a report by a Study Group of Members of the Royal Institute of International Affairs, pp. 420-423.

[2] "To an extent which is very hard to estimate, but is certainly not negligible, the character and atmosphere of industrial life as at present ordered are affected by the fact and character of unemployment. Over a great multitude of employed men hangs the menace of that hideous possibility. Through no fault of his own a man may at a week's notice be out of work. Then, unless he is fortunate enough quickly to find work again, he loses his skill; he loses the activity which has become the stimulus to his mental processes; he loses his familiar social intercourse; he is cut off from his friends; he becomes desperate and discontented. Even in his home, perhaps, an unwelcome intruder, outside it an unwanted idler." Dr. Temple, Archbishop of York, *The Times*, 5th February 1935.

existence? But up to this point it has not been possible to state definitely whether modern leisure really fulfils that task.

In observing the unemployed it becomes quite clear that the ethics of work are still dominant even though they are directly threatened by the competition of the ethics of amusement. It also becomes clear how inextricably the two are interwoven. "Most of all I'd like to work so as to pass the time,"[1] said one Viennese unemployed youth when he discussed with an investigator about what he would best like to do. "I'll get a permanent girl only when I have some permanent work," said another when he talked of his relationship to girls. For unemployed youths, whose lives most clearly present the "human aspects" of unemployment,[2] the chief merit of work seems to be to provide money; to work or to have money are for them interchangeable terms. If they have no money they are only tolerated at home, they are treated very indifferently by the girls, for they cannot take them to the cinema or to dances, they have no prospects what-

---

[1] Reported by Gau in his thesis on *Die Einstellung des Jugendlichen zu sienem Beruf*, quoted in *Children and Unemployment*, The Save the Children Fund (Geneva, 1933), p. 130, note.

[2] Instead of an analysis of the mental make-up of long term unemployed men an analysis of the juvenile unemployed is substituted. Several reasons are responsible for that shift of emphasis. We find that those traits which are most significant in the mentality of unemployed people, *i.e.*, those which distinguish most clearly workless from working people, are very conspicuously present in unemployed juveniles. In their stage of development the absence of work has most disastrous consequences. Older people have gone through the school of employment, they have established contacts and interests and hence, when they become unemployed, there is something to remember, their mode of life might become distorted but not completely destroyed. Hence, the rôle which work really plays in the existence of modern men can best be understood by watching the effects which its absence exercises on the young. If we see that youths fail to develop social relationships and interests because they have no work, we infer that it is the same force, in the case of the older men, which turns their interests into apathy, causes them to drop their friends and robs them of all that gave colour and shape to life.

ever of establishing their own households. The only companions they can find are young unemployed like themselves who at first stand aimlessly at the corners of the streets and later develop more definite purposes.[1] Why are not all these young people in opposition and rebellion? Very rarely does it become visible that they are in fact embittered. But it is everywhere visible that they are ashamed of their situation. It is true, there are obvious reasons for their being ashamed, as has just been said; having no money, or girl friend, being hardly tolerated by the family, having nowhere to belong. But if we consider that the unemployed reaches that situation through no fault of his own, and if he himself would also quite clearly realize that, instead of shame he would probably feel opposition. There would not be such widespread feelings of guilt amongst unemployed if they did not regard unemployment as a vice rather than as a fate.

Moreover, this feeling of guilt through being unemployed gives rise to actual asocial behaviour of all degrees: waywardness, delinquency, vagrancy. "In many criminals, especially youthful ones, it is possible to detect a very powerful sense of guilt which existed before the crime and is not, therefore, the result of it but its motive. It is as if it had been a relief to be able to fasten this sense of guilt on to something real and immediate."[2] This explanation of many types of

---

[1] Those purposes vary according to whether these youths find any other vents for their vitality and according to the degree of vitality they have been able to preserve. Some engage in pure mischief such as is usual with adolescents, some develop more or less delinquent tendencies. But it has to be kept in mind that the gangs they thus form are, so to say, inter-murally social, they are the form of social organization appropriate to the circumstances of their members. See Thrasher, *The Gang*, Chicago, 1926, *passim*.

[2] Sigmund Freud, *op. cit.*, p. 76.

delinquency has been widely accepted. Less known is the answer to the question as to why unemployment produces guilt feelings.

This seems to be the process in the light of psychoanalysis. The two main principles controlling man's behaviour are the super-ego and the reality principle.[1] The formation of the super-ego comes about mainly by identification with the father, but also by identification with heroes in literature, with teachers, in other words, with the whole set of surrounding value standards.[2] This formation although complete, normal and healthy, might in later life bring the individual into conflict with his environment. A change of social standards between childhood and adult life, a change to which the super-ego cannot adjust itself, may perhaps provoke the trouble, either because a strand in the character which is now required is lacking, or one is present, inherited from childhood, which is incompatible with the existing environment. In such cases the young person is delinquent or asocial only by definition in terms of his present situation, he may have no neurosis. The trouble arises solely from the change in the external situation, and adjustment to this change is difficult or perhaps even impossible.

And we see at once that unemployment might easily give rise to such a position; the new social adaptation required from the juvenile out-of-work might not be compatible with his super-ego, derived from his working father, his working teacher, the active heroes of the

[1] Freud, *op. cit.*, p. 69 : " It (the super-ego) is a memorial of the former weakness, and dependence of the ego and the mature ego remains subject to its domination. As the child was once compelled to obey its parents, so the ego submits to the categorical imperative pronounced by its super-ego."
[2] See Aichhorn, August, *Wayward Youth* (London, 1936), p. 221.

literature which he read. The super-ego might require the proof that he works because work is a moral demand, but the unemployed cannot obtain work and, therefore, cannot supply the proof.[1] The voice of conscience becomes stronger, it has, therefore, to be suppressed; guilt feelings develop, these have to be affirmed, and hence the performance of asocial actions, the realization of the desire to be punished which is really nothing but the desire to work, to obey the super-ego. "The delinquents of this type are the victims of their own morality. They try to withdraw themselves from the too severe demands of the ego-ideal and are punished for so doing." [2] The divergence between the impulses of the unemployed and the possibilities presented by his environment might lead to serious difficulties, and after a comparison of the relevant data from the different countries it seems to be the source of much of the trouble amongst the juvenile unemployed.

The unemployed's consciousness of being a misfit in society has already been mentioned. Quite clearly it is derived from his actual state of worklessness clashing with the moral standards of his super-ego. And, strikingly enough, reports of guilt feelings and its often disastrous consequences for the unemployed come mainly from those countries which had no unemployment insurance, only charity, an especially painful and

---

[1] Aichhorn, *op. cit.*, p. 229 : " If there is no contradiction between what the ego-ideal (the super-ego) dictates and what the ego carries out, thinks or feels as an impulse, if the ego and the ego-ideal are agreed, then no conflict arises. But it is otherwise when the ego-ideal sits in judgment on the ego. This is perceived in the ego as a feeling of guilt. It is easy to understand that the ego thus falls into a conflict, the severity of which varies with the insistence of the demands of the ego-ideal for the fulfilment of its claims. The more the conscience warns and threatens, the more painful are the guilt feelings which emerge into consciousness. The conflict would be over at once if the ego gave in to the demands of the ego-ideal."

[2] Aichhorn, *op. cit.*, p. 232.

humiliating experience.[1] Thus the great bulk of American juvenile vagrancy has been traced by many observers to arise from feelings of shame.[2]

The reality principle, complementary to the super-ego, is the name given to an individual's process of assessment of the pleasure-pain involved in alternative modes of conduct open to him. The method of assessing the alternatives is dependent upon the education received.[3] Work is the necessary completion of education into a social being, and hence on the existence of work depends the successful creation of the reality principle. If an individual has no work, not only is his adjustment to reality and hence to society arrested,

---

[1] *I.e.*, United States of America, the Scandinavian countries. See The Save the Children International Union, *Children and Young People and Unemployment* (Geneva, 1933), p. 84, quoted : " The man (the unemployed) begins to think of himself as cut off from the family and friends. He is unable to justify to himself his reason for being alive, and often he seeks relief from this feeling of guilt in illness or drink." Professor Williams, quoted, *op. cit.*, p. 281 : " The feeling of inferiority aggravated by the consciousness of being ill-clad and obliged to accept public or private relief, makes the unemployed believe that he is good-for-nothing. He feels, therefore, that he is justified—or almost—in doing something wrong, and in letting himself go morally. ' When you believe you will never have a regular job, and that you'll never get to be like the others, you feel that others look upon you as an inferior kind of humanity,' said one young unemployed during a discussion."

[2] *Children and Unemployment*, p. 91 : " On the road are many boys too proud to remain in the community where, for the first time, and inconceivably to them, their families are reduced to accepting charity. . . . Social workers, police and railroad men, who are in constant touch with these boys assert their belief that the overwhelming majority of them are young men who would normally be in school or at work ; that they are ' on the road ' because there is nothing else to do—sometimes because sheer pride will not permit them to sit idle at home, sometimes because support for the whole family came from a relief agency . . . that they are, on the whole, not of the habitual hobo or criminal types."

[3] Aichhorn, *op. cit.*, p. 199 : " We have learned that the first adaptations to reality are biologically determined and that their expression is influenced by the circumstances in the outer world. This is the primitive adjustment to reality. Further development toward social adaptability is achieved through education. Thus the individual becomes capable of recognizing and submitting to the demands of society, and of co-operating in the maintenance and the advance of civilization. . . . By social adaptation we mean the expansion of our first primitive adjustments to the stage of our present civilization."

but he finds himself in an environment of so much pain arising from the demands of his super-ego that his old pleasure economics are no longer employable; the only source of pleasure is now opposition to reality.[1] But even if his reality principle has already been completely formed it is unable to provide him with a guide to keeping a balance midst the painfulness of unemployment.

Here the reintegrating function of leisure might start. Cannot leisure provide the satisfaction which unemployment withholds? But there is hardly any leisure, open to those who are no longer children, for which they do not have to pay. The unemployed have no money. The few leisure pursuits for which no cash is required depend on interests, ambitions or fitness. The unemployed are not fit. And as to the direction which interests and ambitions take they depend on an already existent social status, on the character of man's whole relationship to his environment, they cannot grow *ad hoc*.[2] Thus the Viennese clubs, "Youth in Need," attracted the unemployed mainly on those days when they knew that there were no

---

[1] Aichhorn, *op. cit.*, p. 197: "If the child suffers too much from punishment or severity and is not compensated for this by the parents' love, he is forced into opposition and has no further incentive to submit to their demands and thus to subject himself to the reality principle. His main object is to resist authority. Rebellion against his parents, teachers and society—and the assertion of his ego against them—becomes just as great a source of pleasure to him as the gratification of his instincts."

[2] *Children, Young People and Unemployment*, p. 130: "It has often been asked, in connection with the problem of unemployed youth, whether this leisure-time could not be usefully employed in furthering their general education. An affirmative answer seems to us to leave entirely out of account the fact of their resignation. An apathetic mind cannot apply itself to purposeless studies. Only those whose faith in life remained whole can do so. As a matter of fact, the way the young unemployed fill in their time is perhaps the most significant, and the most easily apprehended, expression of their resignation. In the great majority of cases they do absolutely nothing." See also *Die Arbeitslosen von Marienthal*, Leipzig, 1933.

talks and no special programme, the days of card-playing and nothing else.

Recreation cannot supply all the pleasure which the absence of work denies. "The leisure of the unemployed is not normal leisure but tormented leisure."[1] Leisure is pleasant only if a man is already assured of the reason for existence.[2] In spite of that, there is undoubtedly special stress laid on the recreational activities of unemployed,[3] but it could be argued they are actually fostering the tendency of the juvenile unemployed to regress into infantility. The centre of a child's life is play. If leisure is pushed into the centre of the lives of young people who have not yet developed, they adapt themselves mainly by lapsing into childishness. The new manifestations of this old behaviour pattern, however, are usually not called infantile, but delinquent or asocial.

Hence, the social maladjustment of the unemployed is not subject to their being deprived of leisure but to their being deprived of work.[4] But to provide work for them is not just a simple administrative

[1] This is a statement by Dr. Henry Mess, Reader in Sociology in the University of London, *Birmingham Daily Mail*, 26th October 1935.

[2] " Instead of time to enjoy life, unemployment means enforced idleness. The enjoyment of true leisure depends not only upon having a job but also upon an adequate income from work, upon a sense of security in the occupation. . . . Accordingly the unemployed do not have true leisure unless they have sufficient income without work. . . ." Neumeyer, M. H. and E. S., *Leisure and Recreation*, p. 21.

[3] *E.g.* holiday camps, social clubs, classes, drama, etc. See *Unemployment, an International Problem*, pp. 407-417. " Part of our problem is converting unemployment into leisure," said Dr. Temple, the Archbishop of York, at a meeting of the York Rotary Club. Reported by *Unemployment, an International Problem*.

[4] It is now agreed that leisure activities for the unemployed do not really tackle their specific problems, *e.g.*, Valentine A. Bell says in *Juvenile Instruction Centres* (Edinburgh, 1934), p. 103 : " It is by now realized that solely vocational training or entertainment in clubs is utterly insufficient." The *Chatham House Report*, p. 423, says : " It is too easily assumed that recreational facilities meet the needs of leisure ; active minds and bodies demand real work."

measure: "The provision of occupation in camps or training centres presents certain difficulties. It must not be competitive, and it is so difficult to find non-competitive occupations which are useful, and unless they are useful there is little interest in pursuing them. The dilemma is an old one, which has confounded, in another connection, prison and poor-law authorities in the past."[1] A partial way is found in "amenity" construction which would not otherwise be undertaken; but not all unemployed are fit for outdoor occupation, especially in winter. Hence, the statutory and voluntary services for the unemployed are not concerned so much with eliminating the cause of unemployment as with attempting to remedy its effects.[2]

Leisure facilities alone, if they are especially provided for the unemployed, are found, however, to segregate them and so to enhance their consciousness of being "misfits" in society.[3] And if not mere entertainment is offered to them, but useless work or work under conditions which mark them off, the effect is the same,

---

[1] *Unemployment, an International Problem*, op. cit., p. 419.

[2] There have been attempts in England, just as there were in Germany, to introduce work courses for unemployed at their social centres. It was assumed that it would help the young unemployed if they learned a craft and experienced the pleasure of creativeness. This assumption would probably have been fully substantiated if the intentions could have been realized. But if the unemployed learn cobbling, the cobblers protest; if they learn cabinet-making, the cabinet-makers likewise protest. It is literally impossible to find any work which does not interfere with the normal economic process. If the unemployed work without receiving wages they create unemployment. There are only two possible ways out of that situation, either to organize some " arty" work, but this does not have the desired educative effect, or to proceed with some project the execution of which serves the common interest but could not be undertaken in the normal course, *e.g.*, a playing-field, which the local authority is too poor to afford. But there can be only few such cases; the benefit cannot be extended to a great number of the unemployed.

[3] The 13th Annual Report of the National Council of Social Service emphasizes the undesirability of segregating the unemployed in special clubs and classes.

THE UNEMPLOYED

the unemployed feel themselves to be workless outsiders and disturbers.[1] Both leisure and work substitutes are incapable of making any real impact upon the long-term unemployed. Hence, in Bulgaria and Germany, for instance, such social services have become controlled by political parties, with the result that their effect upon the lives of the unemployed has certainly been more far-reaching.[2] In labour camps the unemployed are offered a new philosophy of life and they are drilled to become the soldiers of party struggles.[3] Thus, finally,

[1] " On the other hand . . . communal work (*e.g.* construction of Club-Huts, Nursery Schools, etc.) has been found to give to those who engage in it an ultimate satisfaction which perhaps none of other activities already described can give. For it does more than release initiative and individuality; it restores to men their social importance and their place in the community, giving them respectability and an honourable and honoured function. It is as restoring as compulsory relief work is degrading." A. D. Lindsay, quoted, *Unemployment, an International Problem*, p. 413.

Ibid., p. 434 : " A man's self-respect requires that he should do something which he regards as justifying his continued existence and which gives him satisfaction. Nothing but work on an ordinary economic basis will meet his (the unemployed) moral requirements fully."

Unemployment among Young Persons, Report to the International Labour Conference (Geneva, 1935), pp. 65, 137 and 177 : " Whatever their value, measures for the general and vocational education of young unemployed persons and their temporary occupation in labour centres are, after all, mere palliatives, and when all is said and done reincorporation in normal employment is the only lasting solution of the problem of unemployment."

[2] Dr. Zeitler, a German Civil Servant, wrote in a paper read at the Third International Conference for Social Work, London, 1936 : ". . . The less the thought (of the unemployed) was trained, the less he was able to survey the economic position, the more easily he followed attractive promises which had far greater importance for him than for those in a secure economic position. Inherent in this attitude is the possibility of gaining the support of such people for the political ends of the State. . . ."

[3] *Unemployment, an International Problem*, p. 419 : " The camps do not solve the problem, since the young men must eventually be placed in employment, and there is as yet not sufficient evidence to show whether the prospects of eventual employment are improved or not. Apart from the question of compulsion, a reasonable fear exists that the drafting into camps of unemployed persons, especially of young people, may be accompanied by efforts on the part of the camp authorities to inculcate the political opinions of the ruling classes. In countries where propaganda is a recognized function of Government this is in fact an important element in camp training."

The only way by which educative results from labour-camps can be reached is by safeguarding the principle of voluntary recruitment and of

as the case of the unemployed shows, if leisure is not an organic function of a man's work it is apt to be forced upon him as a function of other people's politics.

instruction : then, the unemployed know that they are not competing but learning in order to increase their chances of re-employment.

CHAPTER III

THE MACHINERY OF AMUSEMENT

PART I

THE CINEMA

"THE state of isolation in which the artisans of big cities dwell seems to have received but little attention. So complete is it that when faced with some quandary or difficulty there is literally no one to whom he can turn for information. . . . The isolation in which he is compelled to live is a specific source of disease, physical, psychological and social alike." This striking statement is made by two doctors who worked in one of the poorer districts in South-East London in order to conduct an extraordinarily interesting experiment—providing for the purpose unique facilities for the spending of family leisure.[1] From their own account the conclusion is all the more significant since it seems to have been reached slowly, to have been forced on them by their experiences of the people with whom they had to deal. When we remember that these are representative of the vast majority in Great Britain, the magnitude of the problem becomes apparent.

Faced with such loneliness, how do people spend their free time? Living under conditions which ensure that most know and are known to but few of their fellows, what serves as a bond to unite those who live in great cities? What is the purpose for which

[1] Pearse, Innes H., and Williamson, G. Scott, *The Case for Action* (London, 1931), p. 43.

great crowds gather and peacefully disperse again, a phenomenon which prior to modern days was almost unknown. What is the most general topic of conversation amongst people who are thrown together in the factory, office, public-house, perhaps even the home? The answer to all these questions is the "machinery of amusement," one or other aspect of those multitudinous undertakings, whether theatres or cinemas, tennis or cricket or football matches, motor-car or dog racing. These are the things that the people have in common.

When work lacks interest, it is discussed in their free hours only to be complained of or it is ignored altogether. Paterson brings this out very clearly when he says, "The boy never thinks of his work as a feature of his life . . . it is a dull thing . . . and no conversation can live which begins from this starting point. No group of lads talking at the corner on a summer evening would ever be found to be speaking of work."[1] That complaints about work is the main conversational approach to the subject is disclosed in the Report of the Medical Research Council, to which reference has already been made. Over a period of twelve weeks the subjects of conversation during working hours were noted: of the thirty-seven occasions on which the conditions of work were broached only five were for the purpose of favourable comments, complaints were the topic on the other thirty-two.[2]

---

[1] Paterson, Alexander, *op. cit.*, p. 90.
[2] Medical Research Council Report, No. 69, p. 48. It is not clear how the investigators defined " a conversation " nor whether all the girls were observed all the time. In spite of these difficulties the trend is so marked as to be unmistakable, especially as care had been taken to provide favourable conditions in order to retain the girls at least until the end of the experiment, *i.e.*, over a period of more than one year

Nowadays it is a damaging indictment of a person to be told that he can never forget his work. To talk "shop" is the height of bad taste in many social circles.

How potent a link amusements can be is shown illuminatingly in the following incident. Two years ago the author met in Czecho-Slovakia a young native boy, fifteen years of age, who came from a small out-of-the-way village. I imagined there would be nothing to say except to ask the usual conventional questions. But as soon as he discovered that I was English he started a keen cross-examination on my knowledge of the English Association footballers. "Who is the best goalkeeper in the First Division of the League?" Since the little interest I take nowadays in football is confined to mere Rugby I had to hunt for the name of any soccer player. "Bastin," I replied. His scorn was immense since Bastin proved to be a wing forward. "Who were members of the English team which visited Prague during the summer of last year?" After long cogitation I suggested Bastin again, but this time with considerably less assurance. As it happened, and to my surprise, he had been a member. I was assured that this boy was scarcely an exception in the interest he took in the subject, which went so far as to include keeping a fully documented note-book of the results not only for England but the Continent, together with the names of the outstanding players.

But, more than any incident, statistics can show what place the "machinery of amusement" occupies in people's lives.

In Great Britain, with a population of little more

than 45 millions, there were, in 1934, approximately 963 million admissions to the cinemas—at the rate of 18·5 millions per week.[1] The gross box-office receipts were more than £41 millions. (The expenditure on education by the Central Authority, in 1934, was £43½ millions.) The average price of a seat was just over 10d., the most frequent prices being 6d. and 7d.; nearly four out of every five persons going to the cinema paid not more than 1s. (including duty) for admission. It is thus essentially an industry dependent on people who do not spend at any one time a large sum for their entertainment.

Its rapid growth in London is shown by the following Table [2]—which also brings out that so far as London is concerned this growth has scarcely been at the expense of the theatre and music hall.

	1891		1911		1929	
	No.	Seating Accommodation.	No.	Seating Accommodation.	No.	Seating Accommodation.
Theatres	49	65,550	54	67,187	87	127,000
Music Halls	42	50,000	50	73,670		
Cinemas	—	—	94	55,149	257	344,000 [3]
TOTAL	91	115,550	198	196,006	344	471,000

[1] Unless otherwise stated, the statistics for cinemas are taken from Rowson, S., "A Statistical Survey of the Cinema Industry in Great Britain in 1934," *Journal of the Roy. Stats. Society*, vol. xcix. Rowson estimated, when speaking at the Cinema Exhibitors' Association Conference, in 1936, that during the previous year the weekly attendance had increased to approximately 19·5 millions, representing roughly 14 million persons.

[2] *New Survey of London Life and Labour*, vol. ix. p. 295.

[3] This figure is for 1934, the number of cinemas having remained stationary from 1929-34.

It will be seen that whilst the seating accommodation in theatres and music halls has only slightly increased over the whole period, and the number of halls has actually declined, there has been in the case of cinemas what must be called the startling rise from none in 1891, to 257 less than forty years later.

Liverpool also illustrates this rapid rise of the cinema. During the period 1913 to 1930 cinemas increased from 32 to 69, with a total seating accommodation of 72,000. It is estimated that there are on the average 576,000 admissions each week, a figure equal to two-thirds of the population of that city.[1]

In 1934, there were in the whole of Great Britain 4,305 cinemas,[2] with an estimated seating accommodation of 3,872,000. It is calculated that at least 1,200 were built during the seven years from 1925 to 1932.[3] During the five years ended October 1937, approximately 890 cinemas were built, with seating accommodation of nearly 1,000,000.[4]

In the United States of America at the peak of the industry (1930), there were more than 22,700 cinemas, with a weekly attendance estimated between 100 and 115 million persons who paid, in round figures, $1½ billion (thousand million) for admission throughout the year. Dale, who has conducted a large-scale enquiry into cinema attendances in the United States, gives a more conservative estimate of the total yearly attendance at 77 millions.[5] The admissions were nearly trebled in the eight years from 1922. The

---

[1] Jones, D. Caradog, *Survey of Merseyside*, vol. iii. p. 278.
[2] This figure is given as 5,006 for 1932 in *The Film in National Life*, Commission on Cultural and Educational Films (1932), p. 43.
[3] *Ibid.*   [4] *The Cinema*, 1934-1938.
[5] Dale, Edgar, *Children's Attendance at Cinemas* (New York, 1935), p. 43.

capital investment is estimated to be in the neighbourhood of \$2½ billions,[1] which ranks fourth in the list of American industries arranged according to their amount of capitalization. On a production-cost basis the films produced in 1929 were valued at more than \$184 millions.[2]

Finally, in the whole world there are between 60,000 and 65,000 cinemas, the majority of which are wired for sound, and estimates of the world attendance vary between 20 millions each day and 250 millions each week.

Who attends the cinemas — children or adults, labourers or professional people? What influence does the cinema exert on those who attend? As soon as these questions are raised we move into much more debatable fields.

Firstly, as regards those who attend. Somewhat surprisingly Rowson, who is regarded as the statistician of the cinema trade in Great Britain, assumes that children under fifteen years of age do not attend in proportion to their numbers in the population: according to him, "they represent a relatively small fraction only of the total cinema patrons." The evidence available does not support this.[3] Confining ourselves to the larger enquiries, we find in Liverpool "that working-class children, it appears, nearly all attend the cinema at least once weekly," and the conclusion

---

[1] Neumeyer, *op. cit.*, p. 224.
[2] U.S., Census of Distribution, Wholesale. *Motion Picture Films* (1932), pp. 3-4.
[3] It is probable that Rowson is basing himself upon the enquiry made by Dr. J. L. Holmes, the results of which support the conclusion quoted. See " Crime and the Press," *Journal of Criminal Law and Criminology*, vol. xx. Nos. 1 and 2, May and August, 1929. Very good reasons are present, however, for believing that Dr. Holmes' enquiry is not sufficiently representative to serve as a basis for wide generalization. See Dale, *op. cit.*, pp. 65-67.

is drawn that "the young—even the selected class who belong to clubs and societies and are therefore less likely than others to go to pictures—attend in greater numbers than the population as a whole."[1] An enquiry was conducted by the London County Council at 29 schools into the facts of children's attendance at cinemas. The selection of the areas of enquiry was such that it is probable that the facts are representative not only of London conditions, but also of those obtaining in most very large English towns.[2] There were 21,280 children concerned, and throughout 1931 their average cinema attendances numbered 32. As in the case of most averages this is not very meaningful. It is significant, however, that for the whole population the similar figure is only 21 attendances.

The details of the children's attendance divided on the basis of age groups reveals how very young the cinema habit is formed.

Age Group.	Percentage of Children attending once or twice a week.
11–14 years	40·9
8–10 ,,	41·1
5–7 ,,	36·5
under 5 ,,	30·0

By including all who go only occasionally it is found that the last figure of 30 per cent., in respect of those under 5 years of age, is increased to no less than 63 per cent.

[1] *Survey of Merseyside*, op. cit., p. 281.
[2] *School Children and the Cinema*, 1932, London County Council, No. 2890.

In the total of more than 21,000 children there were only just over 900, of 7 years of age or older, who never went to the cinema. If it be remembered that the sample included children whose parents were unemployed, who would, therefore, be too poor to see any films, it will be realized that, granted the opportunity of going, the cinema habit amongst the young is practically universal.

From America comes the same kind of evidence. Of 10,052 children studied in Chicago only two failed to go because they did not like the cinema, and those who stayed away for other reasons amounted to no more than 168: 1·7 per cent of the sample.[1] Dale, in his investigation in Columbus, Ohio, supports the findings of the Chicago enquiry. Minors between 5 years and 20 years of age form 31·5 per cent. of the population of America but are 37 per cent. of the cinema audiences, a total weekly attendance on their part of more than 28 million.[2] Even those under 7 years of age form 3 per cent. of the American audiences, which represents, on Dale's basis, a total weekly attendance by such children totalling nearly 2 million. From the Tables on p. 119 it will be seen that cinema attendance declines consistently with age, even amongst the adult population.

Just as would be expected, if the analysis given of the working-class family be correct, boys tend to go to the motion pictures much more than girls. This is stated both in the London County Council's Report, already quoted, and by Alice Mitchell.[3] Dale finds

---

[1] Mitchell, Alice M., *Children and Movies*, University of Chicago Press (1929), p. 18: "The majority of the 168 who did not go to the movies gave religious restrictions as the reason."

[2] Dale, *op. cit.*, p. 61.   [3] Mitchell, *op. cit.*, p. 21.

that of the children attending who are between 7 and 13 years of age 64·4 per cent. are boys; the percentage for boys between 14 and 20 years of age is slightly lower at 57·2 per cent., but nevertheless they continue to exceed the number of girls of comparable ages who visit the cinema. "Expressed in average attendances per year, the average girl (8 to 19) goes 46 times and the average boy (of the same ages) 57 times." [1]

Does the same difference exist between the sexes amongst the adults? The evidence is not so clear. In the *New Survey of London* we are told, "It is estimated that 70 per cent. of the weekly audiences consists of women and girls," [2] but the basis of calculation is not given. The *Merseyside Survey* states: "Of the married, women go more often than their husbands," [3] whilst it is recorded that "the audiences during the depression" of a cinema in *Middletown*, "are estimated by its owner to have consisted of 60 per cent. women over sixteen, 30 per cent. males over sixteen and 10 per cent. children." [4] It is suggested by Lynd that *Middletown* "is probably representative of other localities" in this respect.

On the other hand, the most comprehensive investigation made into the question reveals that even in the age group, 21 years and over, men formed 59·3 per cent. and women only 40·7 per cent. [5] Since these figures are based upon observations extending over three months and relate to 67,000 admissions at fifteen cinemas, their representative character seems difficult

---

[1] Dale, *op. cit.*, p. 37. See also pp. 42 and 43 where he tabulates the results of all the known enquiries conducted in America into the attendance of children at the motion pictures. In all cases where comparable figures are available it emerges that boys attend more than girls.
[2] *Op. cit.*, vol. ix. p. 45.   [3] *Op. cit.*, vol. iii. p. 281.
[4] Lynd, *op. cit.*, p. 263, note.   [5] Dale, *op. cit.*, p. 64.

to question. At the same time it is not certain that Columbus, capital of Ohio, the *locus* of the enquiry, is a sufficiently representative town for its results to be able to stand as a true sample for the rest of the country.

A recent enquiry in Great Britain, however, tends to confirm the findings of Dale's enquiry. The investigation was carried out in January, 1938, by the British Institute of Public Opinion,[1] in four widely separated areas. The districts were chosen because various tests indicated that they were representative of the country as a whole. Interviewers then covered these areas, questioning as representative a cross-section of the adult inhabitants as possible concerning their cinema-going habits. The total number questioned was 700. The two questions asked were designed to give results which could be checked against each other. It will be seen from the following Tables that in fact the answers show consistently a more recent last attendance by the men than by the women, and that the men also reported a greater average attendance. Moreover, a greater percentage of women than of men have never been to the cinema. For both sexes the latter figure is strikingly high. These results are so much at variance with the popular conception, that women go to the cinema more frequently than men, that the question deserves further investigation.

Ascertaining the sex composition of cinema audiences would become extremely important if it were considered that it is this factor which determines the *contents* of films. It does not seem necessary to make this assump-

---

[1] The Institute is an affiliate of the American Institute of Public Opinion, whose Director, Dr. George Gallup, has very kindly allowed me to use this material.

CINEMA ATTENDANCES ANALYSED ACCORDING TO SEX AND AGE

Length of time elapsed since the last visit to cinema?	3 Days.	1 Week.	2 Weeks.	3 Weeks.	1 Month.	More than 1, less than 6 Months.	More than 6 Months.	Never.	Total.
	Per Cent.	Per Cent.	Per Cent.	Per Cent.	Per Cent.	Per Cent.	Per Cent.	Per Cent.	Per Cent.
TOTAL	15	38	9	2	9	6	8	13	100
MEN	14	38	12	3	9	7	6	11	100
WOMEN	16	37	6	1	9	5	10	16	100
21–30 years of age	29	49	5	2	2	3	4	6	100
30–50 years	12	38	10	2	12	7	7	12	100
Over 50 years	10	20	12	2	5	9	15	27	100

Average number of visits to cinema during one month?	Less than 1 Visit.	1 Visit.	2 Visits.	3 Visits.	4 Visits.	5 to 7 Visits.	8 and more Visits.	Never.	Total.
	Per Cent.	Per Cent.	Per Cent.	Per Cent.	Per Cent.	Per Cent.	Per Cent.	Per Cent.	Per Cent.
TOTAL	15	14	15	3	30	4	6	13	100
MEN	13	14	18	4	30	4	6	11	100
WOMEN	17	14	11	2	30	4	6	16	100
21–30 years	8	6	13	2	47	7	11	6	100
30–50 years	16	15	17	3	29	3	5	12	100
Over 50 years	22	15	10	6	13	3	4	27	100

tion. Even accepting that men are in the majority, it is primarily with a view to attracting the women that motion pictures are designed. "As for being thrilled by love scenes, oh goodness! I can picture John Gilbert and Greta Garbo rehearsing a love scene right now, but in my mind it isn't Greta Garbo—it's me!"[1] writes a young American girl, and this process of identification seems to be very much more common with women than with men. Thus, in the same enquiry, twice as many girls as men admitted that they had day-dreamed of playing opposite the actor or actress in love pictures.[2] The males seem much more to secure a vicarious satisfaction in having witnessed someone being brave, dashing or amorous. The same difference in reaction can be discovered in even small children.[3] Whilst a strong case could be submitted for suggesting that the difference is not inherent but arises from social conditioning, this does not disprove its existence—on the contrary. It is taken into account by the producers of motion pictures, who, in their turn, tend to define it still more clearly. Women like to see themselves and the men like to see the women, and this is the starting-point for most film scenarios. But before dealing further with the contents of films there is one more question to discuss concerning the composition of cinema audiences.

What social group or groups are most attracted to the films? The statistics which have already been given suggest that all strata of society attend the cinema,

---

[1] Blumer, Herbert, *Movies and Conduct* (New York, 1935), p. 68.
[2] *Ibid.*, p. 65.
[3] See the L.C.C. Report already quoted, No. 2890. The material collected by Funk, A., in *Film und Jugend*, Munich, 1934, points to the same conclusion in the case of adolescents.

but the question arises, do the members of some go more frequently than those of others? Evidence comes from America for believing that typical members of the professional class go much less frequently than people of a lower social status. Thus, in a budget enquiry conducted in San Francisco it was found that whilst for a member of the professional class earning $6,085 per annum, $11 was a sufficient average allocation for movie-going, twice as much had to be allocated for the same purpose in the budget of a worker. And this increase from $11 to $23 is found in spite of the fact that the one is earning $6,085 per annum and the other not much more than a quarter of this sum, *i.e.*, $1,632. The same enquiry revealed that a clerk, earning $2,175 per year, also spent $23 on going to the cinema.[1] If, moreover, the reasonable assumption be made that on the average the worker pays much less for a seat than does the professional person, it becomes clear that he not only spends in the aggregate twice as much but also that he goes far more than twice as frequently.[2]

An enquiry was conducted in New York during 1931-33, for the Y.W.C.A., into the leisure-time habits of 550 girls during these two years.[3] Both Y.W.C.A. and non-Y.W.C.A. groups were included, although in the

[1] Heller Committee, University of California, under Dr. Jessica B. Peixotto, quoted, *Recent Social Trends*, p. 895. The budget approach to this problem is one of the most promising avenues open, and it is much to be regretted that similar enquiries do not differentiate the items of miscellaneous expenditure

[2] A point on which unfortunately no information is available, concerns the possibility of the age structure of cinema audiences of one social stratum being different from that of another. It is possible, for instance, that proportionately more adult males of the middle classes go to movies than of the working classes.

[3] The enquiry was under the control of Dr. Janet Fowler Nelson, by whose kindness I am able to quote the results.

presentation of the results this division was abandoned since no material differences emerged. The girls were classified into business employees—secretaries, clerks, telephone operators, etc., and professional workers—teachers, research assistants, librarians, etc. The average wage difference between the two groups was approximately $7 a week to the advantage of the professional group. Each group was asked to indicate in respect of a long list of possible activities whether they were interested in and whether they actually participated in each item enumerated. For the cinema nearly 75 per cent. of the business girls indicated a high degree of interest compared with less than 60 per cent. of the professional group who so indicated. Also it emerged that nearly 7 per cent. more of the business girls actually went to the cinema compared with the corresponding figure for the professional workers.

From Germany comes much the same evidence, that the greater the training the lower is the attendance at the cinema. The Director of a Berufschule (where attendance was obligatory in Weimarian Germany for all those who left school at 14 years of age) investigated the attendance at the movies of all such pupils in Essen. There was a definite correlation between the nature of the occupation and the percentage who went regularly to the cinema. The barber, the painter, the baker, the labourer went more often than any other: the trained carpenter and locksmith went very seldom, and the skilled handicraftsman went least of all.[1]

Turning to Great Britain, mention should be made of the statement in the *Survey of Merseyside*[2] that

[1] Quoted, Funk, A., *op. cit.*, p. 26.   [2] Vol. iii. p. 281.

the manual working class attend the pictures more frequently than clerks, shopkeepers and shop assistants.[1]

The evidence from the inquiry made by the British Institute of Public Opinion, however, does not support such a conclusion. Clerks went more regularly than any other occupational group; skilled workers and members of the profession went least of all. These findings are tentative since the total for each group was only small. For this reason the figures are not given in detail.

The last and most important question remains. What do Jack and Jill see when they go to the movies, and what effect does film-going exercise on them? The best point of approach is to describe the contents of films, and we are in the fortunate position of having Dr. Dale's detailed analysis of 1,500 films produced during the period 1920-30.[2] Five hundred films were taken from each of the three years, 1920, 1925 and 1930, being almost the whole number produced: their contents were carefully analysed on the basis of a comprehensive trade review of each film. In addition, 115 of the films were viewed and examined in greater detail, while for another 40 pictures the script was previously read, and on viewing, a full shorthand account was taken of every aspect and every incident in the films. The films examined in greater detail were chosen in a manner which ensured that they were sufficiently representative of the whole 1,500.

It may be said that since the films were American

---

[1] The results of the analysis of the questionnaires recently made by London Films Production Ltd. do not help since clearly there was very great selection in those who completed the form and, therefore, the sample is in no way representative.
[2] Dale, Edgar, *Contents of Movies*, New York, 1935.

and they are not necessarily representative of the fare offered to British audiences. But it is well to bear in mind that during 1929-35, a period covered completely by the operation of the Cinematograph Act, 1927, with its quota for British films, 10,839 films were registered under that Act. Of this total only 1,795 were produced in England and the "vast majority" of the remainder, 9,044, came from America.[1] It seems, therefore, that American films are representative enough so far as British cinemas are concerned. Perhaps also it should be remembered, as a check to undue complacency concerning our home products, that it is especially British films which have experienced difficulty in securing the Censor's full agreement.[2]

When the films are classified according to their main theme, what results are reached? The following Table speaks for itself:

Type of Picture.[3]	1920		1925		1930	
	Number.	Per Cent.	Number.	Per Cent.	Number.	Per Cent.
Crime	120	24·0	148	29·6	137	27·4
Sex	65	13·0	84	16·8	75	15·0
Love	223	44·6	164	32·8	148	29·6
Mystery	16	3·2	11	2·2	24	4·8
Comedy	59	11·8	63	12·6	80	16·0
War	10	2·0	11	2·2	19	3·8
Others	7	1·4	19	3·8	17	3·4
TOTAL	500	100·0	500	100·0	500	100·0

[1] *Kinematograph Year Book* (1936), p. 12.
[2] Rotha, Paul, *Celluloid* (London, 1931), pp. 8-10: "The average British picture of today is far more offensive than its American confrere."
The Australian Censor comments in his 1935 Report: "British films are going back to the unenviable position of 1931, when the percentage of such films finally rejected was about twice as great as those of American origin." Quoted, *Kinematograph Year Book* (1937), p. 29.
The same complaints come from Canada; see *Sight and Sound* (Summer, 1937), p. 58.
[3] Dale Edgar, *op. cit.*, p. 17. The various categories are briefly as

Thus Crime, Sex, Love, Mystery and War in each year accounts for more than 80 per cent. of the films produced. Comedies form an increasing proportion of the total, and all other types of films amount to no more than 3·8 per cent. at their highest.

Perhaps it would be as well, before turning to Dale's more detailed analysis of the contents to notice a survey made of the films actually shown in Liverpool. This will reveal what correspondence there is between the movies produced and the movies actually presented. The statistics were collected during 1929-30 and again in 1932. The classification employed is not the same but is sufficiently similar to Dale's to enable a comparison to be made.[1]

Type of Film.	1929-30 Per Cent.	1932 Per Cent.
Social dramas	45	37
Thrillers	22	30
Musical	11	5
Comedies	11	22
Western	7	1
War	2	1
Miscellaneous	2	4
Total	100	100
Number of Films examined	648	155

follows: Crime: blackmailing, feuds, corruption in politics, gangsters, outlaws. Sex: living together without marriage, adultery, " Women for sale " stuff, bedroom suspense, courtship, historical romance. Mystery: murder mystery, ghosts, emphasis on weirdness. War: spying, characters as soldiers, with or without actual scenes of warfare. Comedy: includes musical comedy. Others: history, exploration, children, animals as central characters, social propaganda. It is interesting to note that of the last type of film there were four in 1920, two in 1925, and none in 1930. Of course, it will be appreciated that often elements of several categories were found combined and that each film has been classified according to its main theme.   [1] *Survey of Merseyside*, vol. iii. p. 282.

Adding the first two categories together we get 67 per cent. for each year, which is comparable to the 75 to 80 per cent. of similar films actually produced. Musical and comedy films account for 22 per cent. and 27 per cent. respectively, in the two years: the corresponding figure in Dale's Table is 16 per cent. for 1930. Thus, on the basis of these Liverpool statistics it seems clear that the proportions in which the different types of films are produced form an adequate index to the proportions in which they are actually shown on the screen.

Turning to Dale's more detailed examination of the contents it is interesting to learn the main ends of conduct motivating the characters. Are they concerned merely with their own interests? Do they strive to benefit those immediately around them or are they in the main driven by a desire to assist the whole community in which they live? For the 883 leading characters involved in the 115 films[1] the results are as follows:

	Per Cent.
(a) Individual goals: conduct which would mainly accrue to the benefit of the individual himself	65
(b) Personal goals: "where he was trying to achieve something for a small group, all of whom he knew well," e.g., his family	26
(c) Social goals: the benefit from the course of action followed "would accrue not merely to himself or to a group with whom he is personally acquainted, but primarily to humanity in general," e.g., apprehension of criminal	9
Total	100

---

[1] Dale, op. cit., p. 187.

Less than 1 in 10 is concerned with achieving ends lying outside his own immediate circle!

In what settings do we find these egotistical people with their very restricted sympathies? Of the residences depicted in the 40 films, 69 per cent. were wealthy or ultra-wealthy, almost three times as many as the moderate group, while the remainder, a mere 5 per cent., were poor or indeterminate.[1] Could anything be more just and damning than the following comment from a well-known British producer? "If you try to reproduce the average sitting-room in Golders Green or Streatham it is apt to come out looking like nothing in particular, just nondescript. It is true that I have tried lately to get interiors giving a real lower middle-class atmosphere—but there is always a certain risk in giving your audience humdrum truth."[2]

On the basis of the 40 pictures the chances that during any films at least one of the leading characters will appear in formal dress is 3 in 4; 68 per cent. of the women appeared in evening dress, 33 per cent. of the men in full morning dress. Dale justly remarks that his enquiry reveals the motion pictures as "placing heavy emphasis upon standards of living far beyond the level of the group of persons who see such pictures."[3]

Against this preoccupation with luxury, perhaps there can be placed the fact that 10 per cent. of these pictures used a library as an interior set. Here seems stress upon matters of the intellect, until it is remarked that in none of the pictures was a character shown reading

---

[1] Dale, *op. cit.*, p. 39.
[2] Hitchcock, Alfred, *Sight and Sound* (Summer, 1937), pp. 61-62.
[3] *Op. cit.*, p. 78.

a book! The use of libraries is merely another aspect of the same emphasis, for it is only in wealthy homes that libraries are to be found.

Perhaps common everyday forms of labour and activity are depicted vividly, so that the cinema patrons, recognizing themselves, feel that their mode of existence has received the sanction of the screen? Again we are doomed to disappointment. Of the 583 men more than 20 per cent. have no occupation, are of independent means, or no indication is given of their employment. More than 50 per cent. of the women come under one of these three headings. Professional, commercial or academic, workers account for another 25 per cent. of the men. Illegal occupations, 11 per cent. of the characters, occur as frequently amongst the men as any other single category apart from those whose occupations are unknown. Military and naval male characters form 10·5 per cent., while for both sexes theatrical occupations account for nearly 9 per cent. of the total. "It is notable that ordinary labour is not once included. A few agricultural labourers exist only because there are Western ranges in the pictures. Were the population of the United States, the population of the globe itself, so arranged and distributed there would be no farming, no manufacturing, almost no industry, no vital statistics, almost no science, no economic problems and no economics. Such a world would speedily starve to death."[1]

It is striking that if and when ordinary people, such as soldiers, appear on the films they are almost invariably figures of fun. An excellent illustration of this attitude is to be found in one of the most finished

[1] Forman, H. J., *Our Movie-made Children* (New York, 1933), p. 44.

British films to date—Pommer's *Farewell Again*. The story is based on an actual incident when soldiers, returning to England after some years' service in India, found that they were redrafted to the Near East, and that as a result they would have only a few hours in England instead of the leave they had been anticipating for so long. Six of them—two officers, four men—have very definite reasons why they do or do not want to reach England and the story is based on their fates. One soldier had deserted his wife, whom we see obviously working night and day to earn a living. She finds him, causing him to collapse in consternation, amidst shrieks of laughter from the audience: in the treatment accorded to her by the film there is no suggestion of sympathy for her hard struggle. Another soldier is worried by the continual taunts that the child his wife has borne after his departure is "posthumous," to use his own expressions. This ends with a punch on the jaw of the man mainly responsible for the taunting. Again the audience is amused. If we remember the treatment accorded to such a theme by Strindberg, the contrast is sufficiently sharp to need no emphasis. Without recounting all the varied stories it can be said that the soldiers, although experiencing real troubles, are merely comedy figures, the only one to suffer and to face tragedy is the Colonel in command who must leave his wife at home with the full knowledge that she is mortally ill.

Film producers have remembered clearly the complaint made by Frederick the Great on seeing *Hamlet*, that it was unseemly for a common fellow like a grave-digger to utter such wise words.

As shedding further light on the conduct of the

characters we must note how far they uphold the socially accepted standards in regard to relations between the sexes and the criminal code. In the 115 films seen no less than 35 of the leading characters had "illicit love as a major goal," and 7 of these were the hero or heroine who are, of course, the characters presented to the audience as attractive. The percentage of the characters shown as married is very slight indeed compared with the proportion outside the cinema world, and in the 10 pictures (out of 40) in which some problem of married life was a major or minor theme only one baby had arrived. The coming of another was inferred at the end of a second picture.

When we turn to the question of crime on the films an astonishing condition is found. In the 115 films no less than 449 crimes were attempted or committed![1] In 84 per cent. of the 115 films there were one or more crimes. The chance of seeing a film which did not contain a crime was thus less than 1 in 6. Perhaps they were only minor delicts, mere venal offences? Almost 100 were murders, by far the largest of all the categories of the crimes. Perhaps these murders or attempts at murder were committed by the bad men of the films and these were duly punished? Nearly 1 in 5 were the handiwork of the hero or heroine and punishment was meted out (or inferred) to only 25 per cent. of the criminals: the remaining 75 per cent. was evenly balanced between those who received extra-legal punishment, in the main accidentally, and those who went scot-free.[2]

With all this evidence before us is it too much to say that the cinema is concerned to depict people who

---

[1] Dale, *op. cit.*, pp. 105, 119, 133. [2] Dale, *op. cit.*, p. 145.

are completely wrapt up in their own affairs or those of their immediate associates—of wider interests it is almost impossible to discover any signs—who do none of the manual labour without which our world could not exist, who have scant regard for standards of morality, or interest in the preservation of the race, and yet who move predominantly in luxurious surroundings and in the main escape retribution for their misdeeds at the hands of the machinery of justice? Truly they have "earned nothing and begotten nothing" and yet they live on the fruits of the land.

Is there any real evidence that this moving panorama, which the people of all countries and of all ages daily witness, plays any direct rôle in their lives? Is it not forgotten as soon as seen, dismissed for what it is, an insubstantial shadow? Emphatically this is not the case. Even the very youngest children remember 60 per cent. of the incidents in a film recalled by adults, and so far from forgetting them they sometimes actually recall more at the end of many months.[1] Such results confirm the facts brought to light more than twenty years ago when films were technically much inferior to the present productions and when their projection was exceedingly poor according to modern standards. In 1917, essays were secured from 6,701 children on the picture they liked best of all those they had seen at the cinema. "In one of the schools about thirty girls had promised their teacher in 1914 not to go to the cinemas during the War. In spite of this . . . they were able, with one exception, to give good accounts of films they had seen more than two

[1] Holaday and Stoddard, *Getting Ideas from the Movies* (New York, 1933), Chapter III.

years before."[1] If any lesson were carried in their memory for even a quarter as long a period their teacher would have been more than gratified. The dullest children become animated at the mention of the films, and often teachers are astonished at the wealth of detailed information on the lives, habits and rôles of innumerable film stars which will be poured out by children whom they have long ago abandoned as congenitally incapable of absorbing knowledge.[2] A *prima facie* case for believing that the films register an impact on all the audience is established by the evidence relating to children, for they are not different in kind from the adults, they merely show clearly at work an influence which, in the case of their elders, may or may not be obliterated by other forces. It is this question of whether the obliteration does in fact occur which has to be answered.

Particularly for the juvenile just starting work, it must be remembered that the cinema tends to be his only adventure in ideas. The world lying outside of his own daily, restricted confines is interpreted to him mainly by the films. As the following Table shows, there is a definite process, as soon as he leaves school, for his decreased interest in reading and outdoor sports to be replaced by a greatly enlarged attendance at the cinema.

A century ago, even if collier youths could not read, did not know who Jesus Christ was and had never heard of Queen Victoria, nevertheless they knew all

[1] *The Cinema*, National Council of Public Morals (London, 1917), p. 275.
[2] The value of the cinema as a method of imparting information to students of all ages is now being realized. Unfortunately, Great Britain is lagging behind in the provision of projectors in schools. Less than 1,000 schools are so equipped in this country, while in the United States more than 20,000 schools have their own apparatus for showing films.

the exploits of Dick Turpin and could detail the prison-breaking escapades of Jack Sheppard.[1] Similarly,

LEISURE ACTIVITIES OF JUVENILES [2]

	Per Cent. of each Sex with Interests as Recorded.					
	Boys.			Girls.		
	Before leaving School.	At 15+	+ or −	Before leaving School.	At 15+	+ or −
Some kind of outdoor sport or game, excluding cycling or walking	57·8	49·8	− 8·0	36·4	22·9	−13·5
Reading	53·0	51·9	− 1·1	57·0	44·7	−12·3
Cinema	28·9	45·6	+16·7	25·2	36·5	+11·3

to-day their environment offers no incentive to find exciting the everyday facts around them [3] or to seek knowledge by difficult and arduous paths. Whereas previously, in a search for something different, something outside of their own drab existence, yet something which could be easily assimilated, they delighted in the exploits of those who have been brave enough or strong enough to defy law and order, they now have recourse to the cinema, where all that is denied to them can be enjoyed vicariously. It is at once their nurse and comfort, their guide and entertainer. There is more

[1] " But it is to be especially remarked that, among all those who had never even heard such names as St. Paul, Moses, or Solomon, there was a general knowledge of the character and course of life of Dick Turpin, the highwayman, and more particularly of Jack Sheppard, the robber and prison breaker." *Second Report of the Commissioners on Child Labour*, vol. xiii. (1843), p. 170.
[2] *Survey of Merseyside*, vol. iii. p. 219.
[3] The one exception is the surprising knowledge of mechanical gadgets and machines which is often displayed by such youths.

than humour in the remark which the *New Yorker* recently put into the mouth of a young girl. "I never read any books now. If they're any good they make the grade for the movies."

As regards the impact made on the general mass of the people by the cinema it is sufficient to quote from the President's Research Committee:[1]

"Although the motion pictures is primarily an agency for amusement it is no less important as an influence in shaping attitudes and social values. The fact that it is enjoyed as entertainment may even enhance its importance in this respect. Any discussion of this topic must start with a realization that for the vast audience the pictures and 'filmland' have tremendous vitality. Pictures and actors are regarded with a seriousness that is likely to escape the casual observer who uses formal criteria of judgment. Editors of popular motion picture magazines are deluged with letters from motion picture patrons, unburdening themselves of an infinite variety of feelings and attitudes, deeply personal, which form around the lives and activities of those inhabiting the screen world. One editor receives over 80,000 such letters a year. These are filled with self-revelations which indicate, sometimes deliberately, more often unconsciously, the influence of the screen upon manners, dress, codes and matters of romance."

Discussion of the social implications of the cinema usually centres around the point whether it induces delinquency, a very narrow aspect of the problem. On this topic diametrically opposed views are advanced. Often it is argued that the cinema is good because if the children were not there they would be open to other and greater dangers, a pathetic failure to realize that this is no defence of the cinema, merely a condemnation of the conditions existing outside of it. Often it is said that the cinema has no tendency to

[1] *Op. cit.*, vol. i. p. 209.

induce crime. Most of the persons expressing such views have little direct evidence for their opinions—perhaps exception should be made of Dr. Emanuel Miller, the psychologist, who claims to have discovered no deep impact of the cinema on the young delinquents he has treated.[1] The relation between the cinema and delinquency is scarcely a topic which falls within the scope of the present work, but the opinion may be expressed that a very strong case emerges from the evidence carefully collected by Professor Blumer and Dr. Hauser, in *Movies, Delinquency and Crime*, or again by Blumer in *Movies and Conduct*, that incitement to crime comes from seeing some films and that crime technique is often learned whilst enjoying a film.[2]

A similar conclusion emerges from a recent German enquiry. The author stresses that most of the inmates of the Borstal institutions seem to have been very regular attenders at the cinema, and that very often their offences showed a conspicuous resemblance to incidents in films seen just previously by the delinquents.[3] The following quotation from a young offender is typical. "I believed that the career of criminals is the only profession to satisfy one's desires for adventure.... The art of the crime film is such that one can imagine them to be translated straight from life. I was led astray since in these films the attractive sides of criminal careers were in the foreground...."

[1] *Sight and Sound*, No. 20, p. 132: "The films no more produce criminals than the amorality of our dreams induces us to commit crimes."
[2] Burt, Cyril, in *The Young Delinquent* (London, 1925), pp. 143-150, argues that films have little direct responsibility in stimulating crime. At the same time he is careful to stress that undoubtedly they exercise a very potent influence in more diffuse but not less important aspects of social behaviour.
[3] Funk, A., *op. cit.*, *passim*.

In considering the larger question of the extent to which movie-going conditions interests and attitudes, a moment's reflection shows that the impact of the films, or of any force exerting an influence on the minds of people, will be dependent upon the strength and direction of other agencies at work. If these are non-existent, the cinema will have a clear field. If they operate in the same general direction, the cinema will reinforce their impact. If they operate against the trend of influence exerted by the cinema, then a conflict will be set up in the minds of those who go so regularly and frequently.

If, as is believed to be the case, the vast majority of the cinema audiences belong to the lower middle and the working class, and if further, as is being argued, they very largely lack contact with any social institution or organization which directly or indirectly integrates and rationalizes their situation for them, they are fully exposed to the blast of the cinema. Movies become "the real stuff." And the greater the lack of social integration, the greater the influence of the cinema. This fact is recognized by Blumer and Hauser;[1] nevertheless they are surprised by it.

"In recent years motion pictures seem to have become an important agency in transmitting patterns of thought and behaviour. Yet, *peculiarly*, the influence that they exert in this respect seems to be in *inverse* proportion to the strength of family and neighbourhood and school and church" (italics inserted).

But other investigators, who have examined what in the context may be claimed as a crucial instance, a high-rate delinquency area, explicitly adopt this con-

[1] *Op. cit.*, p 161.

clusion. The well-known American sociologist and specialist in juvenile gangs, Thrasher, writes,[1] with immediate reference to gangster films: "In a crowded section stimuli and patterns of this character would be more dangerous than in any other section of the population, particularly since there is great lack of restraint, inhibition and emotional stability in such a section." The conclusion seems eminently reasonable when it comes from a delinquent boy himself. "If I would have had work and parents and a home," writes a Borstal boy in the Germany enquiry already referred to, "then I would not have been so easily led astray by the films."[2]

The high-rate delinquency area merely exposes in cruder colours what can be discovered in the other poorer urban districts. Meeting with scarcely any other intrepretation of the world, the cinema audiences are conditioned into believing that the world of appearance which they know so intimately is the reality and all outside is mere illusion. "Movies is the real stuff. They ain't like it is at home. That ain't real life—home. It's just hollerin' and fightin' all the time, and kids. Pa's drunk. Ma yells and kids' crying. You see things in the movies that are different—it's another life. Fine clothes, cars . . ." said a seventeen-year-old Chicago boy,[3] and he expresses vividly the reactions of a vast number of his companions of all ages.

Whilst, as has been pointed out, discussion tends to centre on the results of depicting crime on the screen, it is chiefly the immense emphasis upon relations between the sexes which reacts most forcibly on the

[1] See Forman, *op. cit.*, p. 271.   [2] Funk, *op. cit.*, p. 131.
[3] Mitchell, *op. cit.*, p 133.

audience. With the adolescents this is expressed by a specific interest in love. "The influence of scenes of adventure, travel, gay life, fine clothes, wealth, luxury, success, heroism and so forth is quite pronounced, yet apparently the chief theme emerging in the day-dreaming of adolescents is that of love." "My interest in girls was sure awakened by the motion pictures. I remember one hearty fall I took for Clara Bow. Boy, did I fall hard: but, oh well, what is the use ... many times I came to my senses in the midst of a hero act, much to my sorrow, as my mother called me ... to perform some chore around the house." The effect on conduct—and incidentally the dangers attendant on trying to collect such evidence—are well shown by the following extract from a confession by another youth, of twenty years of age. "The other night I escorted a girl to a movie who is usually very strict about such matters as kissing.... Upon coming out of the movie and getting in the car I noticed that she moved over very close to me and cuddled up to me, laying her head on my shoulder. Remembering this paper I had to write I tried to kiss her!"[1] And whether the impact is specifically sexual or not,[2] they, their married sisters and brothers, their mothers and fathers, are all conditioned into believing that nothing exists beyond mere personal problems, questions of personal relationships. Belief in the efficacy of isolated, individual effort is continuously instilled, the hero, *ex hypothesi*, is invariably his own saviour, and such prospects as corporate

[1] Blumer, *op. cit.*, pp. 65, 67, 113.
[2] An array of evidence, surprising in its scope and unanimity, can be found in Blumer, *op. cit.*, and Blumer and Hauser, *op. cit.*, *passim*, and Forman, *op. cit.*, Chapters XIII and XV. See also Burt, *op. cit.*, p. 149.

activity, of uniting together to tackle the problems which invest the world is never once allowed to cross their cinema-bounded horizon.

"Or I would be stepping out of a luxuriously appointed machine with some society queen richly attired at my side. I would enter a fashionable night club, whereupon the manager would rush over . . . bringing to my table the choicest foods and the rarest wines. After an epicurean feast I would depart for my private box at the Opera." "The movies have made me dislike restraint of any kind. They have also made me dislike work."[1] "Fine clothes, cars. Poor people want these things too and they ain't got them. Then it's soon over and you come out on the street and it's the same old thing for you."[2] These quotations, from young people, bring out strikingly another aspect of the impact of the cinema—the dislike of work and the desire for luxury, the reaching after ease and comforts only to find them denied in the cold, hard world of everyday life. Gaining for a few pence admission to a mansion, the equal of which can scarcely be found even in Fifth Avenue or Park Lane, the patrons of the cinema experience for the space of two hours the joys of fine clothes, rich food, elegant rooms; they float serenely through all the intricacies of formal dining or highly organized social functions, and when they travel it is invariably reclining on the soft cushions of the smoothest limousine. Their two hours are up and they must scramble for a place on the 'bus or tram, eat a simple supper and hurry to bed in time to ensure that next morning they will hear

[1] Blumer, *op. cit.*, pp. 64 and 159.
[2] Mitchell, *op. cit.*, p. 133.

the alarm clock summoning them to another day of toil, exactly similar to the one that they are so glad has just ended. How can they feel other than discontented? How can they avoid being disturbed if, bound to a life of unremitting work, their faithful mentor, who embraces them so readily and so warmly, teaches them to despise all but riches and pomp? How can they avoid being at war with themselves when they witness the social ascent of the hero through his own efforts and realize at the same time how unsuccessful they themselves have been? Quite apart from the complete dissolution of all ethical standards which occurs in the presentation of the story in films, quite apart, that is to say, from the absence of a clear-cut standard in terms of which social problems are handled in the theme of the movies,[1] those who see them must experience conflict, must be confused and bewildered so long as what they see and absorb is so greatly at variance with their daily lot.[2] Emotionally disintegrated

[1] Blumer and Hauser, *op. cit.*, p. 149: " The same picture may frequently present a form of life as something attractive and alluring and yet imply that it is something that is dishonourable and to be condemned. For example, many pictures treating crime are likely to play up luxury, ease, power and popularity, suggesting incidentally that they may be attained easily by questionable methods, yet at the same time they may end by depicting the ultimate misfortune or ill fate of the criminal."

[2] There is even experimental evidence of the formation through the cinema of an ambivalent attitude in young children. Peterson and Thurstone recount in *Motion Pictures and the Social Attitudes of Children* (New York, 1933), pp. 40-44, that, in various cities in U.S.A., children who went frequently to the movies and those who did not, more than 400 in each group, were tested by questionnaires for their attitudes and interests. Far more of the movie children wanted to be a popular actor than of the non-movie children, far more of them preferred to know about a girl just appearing on Broadway rather than a girl just starting her medical training; yet there was no difference between them concerning " chorus girls are to be admired " or whether " chorus girls lead shady lives," and to the question whether " chorus girls are worth-while members of society," *less* movie children answered in the affirmative than non-movie children. " The tendency is consistent through all the populations and for both sexes and is one of the eleven most reliable differences which we have found." Thus we find, as the result of movie going, an increased interest in and desire

by the violent demands made on their mood and receptivity, demands, moreover, which are continuously and rapidly changing,[1] their abrupt transition from the padded and sheltered world of the screen to the rough and tumble of their ordinary life leaves them in a state of confusion. For a short while they may have escaped into the realm of the free. But they must pay the penalty of day-dreaming, of disillusionment, of being unfitted to tackle the problems which confront them.

In view of the tendency which is growing in the film industry for specialist cinemas to be erected, it is worth discussing the contents of the news-reels which form an important item in this development. Two enquiries are available to serve as a basis for examination of the items shown. One was conducted in America, the other in England.[2] The American investigation covered 118 reels released by X Company and 87 reels released by Y Company. The English survey was much smaller in scope and covered 296 items. When the subjects are arranged according to their frequency of appearance, the striking facts emerging from both surveys are the enormous predominance of sports over any other single category and the extremely high rank of military and naval items.

---

to enter personally the theatrical world coupled with an increased condemnation of its personnel. Can this be described in terms other than the growth of guilt feelings arising out of the conflicting forces which leave their imprint on the children?

[1] " The kaleidoscopic change that is involved in mood and receptivity of the spectator is so great that emotionally it may put demands upon him which make him callous or leave him indifferent to the ordinary requirements of emotional response arising in his workaday world." Blumer, *op. cit.*, p. 199.

[2] Dale, *Contents of Movies*, p. 201, and Ritchie, David, *Sight and Sound*, No. 11. The former covered 1931 and 1932, the latter those reels shown in London in February, 1933.

Sporting events appeared in 74 per cent. of the 118 X reels and 94 per cent. of the 76 Y reels: they appeared in 14 per cent. separate X items, and 30 per cent. separate Y items. Of the English items 30 per cent. depicted sporting events. In both the American and English reels this was easily the largest single category. We find once more that the emphasis is heavily on leisure activities—the frequency in the English items of sporting events equalled that of all the travel, political, social, commercial and industrial items put together. Thus in news-reels is found the same trend as in the entertainment films. Attention is diverted away from the common man and the everyday facts of life to the performances of those who permanently or temporarily have shed the obligation to earn their living.

When the news-reel does confront us with reality it is chiefly with references to war. For both enquiries the next largest category after sports was that containing naval-military-war items: they appeared in 54 per cent. of the X reels and 61 per cent. of the Y reels, whilst 13 of the English items came under this heading. Again the same tendency is well marked in the entertainment films; of the 40 films scrutinized by Dale, 13 contained characters who at some point appeared in a uniform of one or other of the services.[1] We might well claim the right to be free from such reminders so long as the treatment accorded to the items does nothing to stress the horror and brutality of war but rather shows, in sharp contrast, the brightness and lure of naval and military life.

If this be the state of the cinema to-day, must it

---
[1] Dale, *Contents of Movies*, p. 78.

necessarily be so? The answer is that the films, particularly in America, are an extremely sensitive reflection of the social atmosphere existing at the time. Since during the past five or six years that country has been experiencing an upheaval, the extent of which has been scarcely appreciated on this side of the Atlantic, certain new currents are visible in the cinema. Thus, when the clean-up of the big gangsters occurred, culminating in the imprisonment of Al Capone, the new heroes of the gangster films were the G-men, federal officials, appointed to eliminate gangsters from public life. When prison riots occurred and much adverse publicity was given to the conditions in prisons, films dealing with such themes were rapidly put on to the market. When a judgment was given, probably for the first time, against men who had taken part in a lynching, Fritz Lang, the well-known German producer now working in Hollywood, produced *Fury*, a film dealing with a lynching in the Southern States. Perhaps the most remarkable of these sociological films is the recently produced *Dead End*. A juvenile gang is shown as the products of the wretched East side tenements in which they have been brought up. The hero is a victim of the same environment, who, after struggling for years to qualify as an architect, is unable to make a living from his profession. He gains money only by shooting a much wanted gangster. The bitter contrasts between the rich and the poor who live cheek by jowl is underlined, and the film is in fact a striking analysis of the conditions which produce criminals.

The film differs so much from the usual American scenario that it is necessary to pause and ask how it could have been produced. Perhaps one is entitled to relate its appearance to the growing emphasis in the United States upon the need for building new houses. The hero speaks strongly of his lifelong dream of pulling down the tenements and building decent dwellings, and unless this point is meant to be brought out it is otherwise irrelevant to have made him an architect. Moreover, the film deals only with delinquency and gangsters, an aspect of our society which may be described as pathological, and which, the treatment suggests, may be eliminated.

The analysis of *Dead End* brings to light one feature which all these sociological films have in common. Under different guises each deals with the same aspect of social conditions—crime. This suggests that however concerned with contemporary movements film producers might desire to be, there exist certain definite limitations within which they must work. An analysis of these limitations might throw light upon the relation of the screen to its audiences and their reactions to it.

The main characteristic required of a film is its ability to attract a large audience, otherwise it brings no profit. The vast proportion of the audience under present conditions will be untutored and uncultured, unable, therefore, to appreciate subtle or complex situations. Hence, they will be unable to indulge in flights of fancy or to follow sympathetically films which make large calls on their imagination. The demand, therefore, is for realistic themes handled in a straightforward manner. What, for the vast majority of these people, is realism? Touching upon one or more of the problems with which they are surrounded every day of their lives. And when we ask in turn what are these problems, they are for the poorer the continual struggle to obtain money, with the conflict which this entails, and further, their treatment at the hands of officials and officialdom of all kinds. Those a little higher in the social scale are troubled by problems of how to run a small business, to compete successfully with larger rivals, to secure promotion in the commercial world. Moreover, consciously or unconsciously, a high percentage of cinema patrons have the feeling that they do not "belong" to society. They feel that it is not run for their benefit, and, whilst it would be absurd to talk of their being in a state of revolt, it remains that they are sufficiently tainted with dislike of their conditions and mistrust of those who seem responsible to witness appreciatively a person or group who acts in opposition to the accepted norms. In addition, there remains to them, as stressed in an earlier chapter, the interest in sex, the preoccupation with personal relationships, the craving for excitement, for relief from monotony.

Perhaps there will be some surprise at the stress placed upon the need for realism. Is not the normal diagnosis that the cinema serves essentially as a method of escape? Does it not allow its devotees to "forget themselves" for two or three hours? Does not everybody drop their cares as they enter the cinema even if they must shoulder them again as they leave? All this is true, and it is well known that films without the usual happy ending are seldom, if ever, good box-office propositions. Nevertheless, except perhaps in comedies and musical shows, it is essential that the audience shall recognize situations and themes with which they are familiar and which have some relation to their own lives. Without this quality the film will not appeal.[1] As an example, Wells' *Shape of Things to Come*, whilst it created some stir on its presentation and whilst the fact of the story being by Wells was some guarantee of its attracting attention, succeeded, in many working-class cinemas, in rapidly emptying the house. For them it had no merit because it failed to connect with any aspect of their own lives. When we come to a film which probably caused as great a furore as any before or since, Mae West's *I'm No Angel*, it seems clear that the reasons for its success were not merely that it portrayed a woman displaying her charms, but also that the film contained very pungent if indirect comments upon some aspects of our society. To take one example: did it not seem to show, what many people already believed, that justice so far from being blind, could be influenced by the compliments paid by the fair defendant to a juryman and to the judge? Maybe there was justice on her side, but does the judge pay a social visit to every one of his successful defendants? Thus the success of the film is not to be explained solely in terms of sex: it appealed to many strands in the mental make-up of the audience. It is noteworthy that the effect of the increased censorship which the film caused to be instituted has not been to eliminate the "sex stuff" from Mae West's later films but to delete any social realism. And it is further noteworthy that none of her films since *I'm No Angel* has repeated its success.

[1] It should be pointed out that this sense of realism in an untutored person is conscious only negatively. He can say what does *not* conform to it. It is much more difficult, if not impossible, for him to express what does conform to it. And this, after all, is in accordance with the accepted fact that in criticism of any intellectual or artistic work it is easy to condemn. The good—and rare—critic is the one who can also say what is right.

But whilst the demand by the audience is for realism, the producers of the movies have also their own problems to solve in trying to meet this demand. Even if we credit them with the desire to produce realistic films it is extremely difficult for them to do so. Their hands are not free. They must strive after realism but they must not be too realistic. Anything savouring of politics is not allowed to appear in the films. Speaking at the Cinema Exhibitors' Association Conference in June, 1936, Lord Tyrrell, President of the British Board of Film Censors, drew attention to "the creeping of politics into films." He continued, "From my past experience I consider this dangerous. Nothing would be more calculated to arouse the passions of the British public than the introduction on the screen of subjects dealing either with religious or political controversy. I believe you are all alive to this danger. . . . It is difficult to foresee to what lengths it may go . . . unless some check is kept on these early developments."

And this direct, immediate, censorship is merely the outstanding aspect of the framework within which the producer must work, providing him with both positive and negative limits. He must carry out the general orders which are periodically issued by the financiers of Wall Street who finally control the cinema industry.[1] He must portray society so that those who are its figureheads, the rich and the leisured, shall appear in a favourable light: he must show the beneficence of

---

[1] Rotha, Paul, *op. cit.*, p. 55 : " The tremendous impetus behind the whole American film is largely brought about by the wishes of Wall Street, the virtual controllers of policy in the Hollywood and other American studios." For an analysis of the financial structure of American film industry, see *World Film News*, November, 1936.

such forces as patriotism and religion: he must demonstrate to his audience that the world is not without brightness, not without hope, that everything is possible to those who have the necessary determination. If he must observe all these ordinances he must, in consequence, be careful to avoid infringing the codes and standards of the leading sections in society; it means that certain topics are forbidden to him and that a certain mode of treatment must be accorded to the others. Alternatively, he can try to avoid all the social quicksands which surround him by turning to comedies and musical shows, and Dale's figures reveal that only in the production of this category of films has consistent and substantial increase been made.[1] Moreover, extravagant, luxurious, musical shows offer a vicarious satisfaction to those who never experience riches in their own lives. Yet all the time the producer must try to cater for the need for realism.

The vast proportion of cinema audiences would, however, strongly resent having their attention *consciously* directed to their troubles and difficulties. This desire to escape—in opposition to their unconscious need for realism—arises from one of the predominant characteristics of modern society, the depersonalization which has taken place. The people are left with the feeling that they do not "belong" at their work, that as human beings they play no real rôle, that in the factory, office and shop their proper designation is a number. Hence, though rooted in grim reality, they believe that their real life is found in a brighter and more spectacular setting.

The producer meets this two-sided demand by the

[1] See p. 124.

production of "social dramas," in the theme of which the audience is able to recognize an aspect of their own lives. But the statement is always in terms of a luxurious setting which satisfies the demand for experiencing wealth and ease. The mode of treatment also enables the films to depict that the rich are not a closed group; with reference to the cinema a critic remarks that if the hero is needy "the national custom of marrying our employers' daughters may be relied upon to remedy this."[1] In reaching its happy conclusion the film often suggests that in his work the employee meets opportunities of making decisions or exercising initiative which, in actual fact, would never come his way. But in thus painting reality larger than life the movies fulfil the important function once more of giving assurance that the world does contain the opportunities and possibilities which the people so ardently desire. The technique of a film scenario may be summarized as choosing a situation with which the audience can identify themselves but treating it in terms of their dreams.

The device which the producer employs is to make all his characters, Minerva-like, spring into existence fully developed. The impecunious hero—more than two-thirds of the heroes in the forty pictures were classed as moderate or poor by Dale [2]—the rich *deus ex machina*, the sinister, wicked, gangster are all presented out of the void, and little, if any, attempt is made to help us to understand why some of the characters are poor, some rich, some wicked and depraved. There is scarcely a suggestion that they

---

[1] Russel, Ferguson, in *World Film News*, August, 1937.
[2] Dale, *Contents of Movies*, p. 47.

are creatures of their environment. The emphasis is very much the reverse, that every man's fate lies in his own hands; failures are due to personal defects. The whole world is painted in terms of individuals' characteristics, but an analysis is rarely attempted of the origin of those characteristics. Thus, whilst the theme of a film may, at some point or another, touch upon one of the crucial questions of to-day, or may even have it in the centre of its plot, the treatment accorded is unhelpful towards a real understanding of the processes at work: confusion is the price paid by the spectator.

When the producer strives to cater for his patron's demands for thrills, he finds an excellent method in crime films. They offer an opportunity of presenting mysteries, fighting, chasing, capturing, all the necessary ingredients for excitement, and they also show a person or persons in revolt against society, but a revolt which does not call into question the whole structure. Thus they are capable of providing an outlet for the anti-social impulses brought to the cinema. But, at the same time, the producer must not present the criminals in a completely unattractive light.[1] To do so would make the whole film unappealing and would, moreover, by withdrawing all sanction from those who rebel against society, alienate his audience. Hence, willy-nilly, a film often calls into question, explicitly or implicitly, many of the accepted codes of behaviour

[1] "It's my opinion that once the audience's sympathy is aroused, a character may enact any crime, however fundamentally repellent, without losing the audience's respect. The murder committed by Fonda (in *You Only Live Once*) was so horrible that I admit we were tempted to change the story. But . . . we justified his crime. To do it, we had to present him, in the early sequences, as a victim of circumstances, as a boy helpless and afraid, caught in the law's mesh, convicted for a murder of which he was innocent." Fritz Lang, in *World Film News*, July, 1937.

without offering a substitute which will stand the test of application to the affairs of the world outside. A process of erosion occurs, sapping the established fabric, but no work of rebuilding is undertaken.

But over and above all is the cult of the trivial, of the merely abnormal and sensational. Cinema audiences can find nothing exciting in their workaday world and the producer may scarcely approach an analysis of these conditions. He must perforce resort as often as possible to showing the world's champion tobacco-eating mule, the gentleman who squats on a pole longer than most people, or films whose stories are so trivial and improbable that they must be seen to be disbelieved. So long as the everyday events and the central problems of society must be avoided, the main alternatives are the peripheral trivilia.

As a last comment, the following foot-note may be reproduced from the *Kinematograph Year Book*, 1935: "The title of the film *Voltaire* has been altered to *The Affairs of Voltaire.*"[1]

[1] P. 124.

Part II

FOOTBALL

PERHAPS the main alternative to the cinema, if in any way it be an alternative, is football. Football is attracting wider and wider circles of adherents, players and spectators, particularly amongst women and girls.

Whilst there are comprehensive statistics for the cinema, little information is available concerning football, and the position is complicated by there being three codes, with no contact between them. Association Football—Soccer—is the most widely played: its adherents are to be found in all parts of Great Britain and amongst all social classes, although, as is noted below, this position is changing. Rugby Union, the handling code with fifteen players on each side, keeps itself severely aloof from the Rugby League, whose game is played with only thirteen players. The real difference is that the latter allows professionalism: it was on this question that the League was formed in 1895 as a breakaway from the Rugby Union, which, being based on the Public Schools and their Old Boys, would have nothing to do with people who earned their living by running with the ball. It would be a nice exercise in investigation to discover why in cricket it was considered sufficient to mark the distinction between amateur and professional by the mere provision of separate entrances on to the field at the headquarters of the game, and whilst, in Soccer, amateurs may play together with or against professionals, no such mingling may occur in Rugger. The probable answer is to be found in the history of the Amateur Football Association which, attempting to exist independently of its parent body in 1907, was forced seven years later to return to the Football Association through lack of worth-while opponents amongst its own ranks. The decline has gone so far that the famous Corinthians have this season made an arrangement to operate with the Casuals as one Club, an indication that the policy of the Public Schools of turning more and more to Rugby is having the inevitable effect of drying up the flow of recruits. In other words, whilst in cricket and Soccer it is impossible to play first-class matches for a whole season without including professionals, in Rugby there is no need to go beyond the ranks of the amateurs in order to arrange a full fixture list.

The Football Association is the most important in view of its wide ramifications and its large impact on huge numbers of people. The F.A. was founded in 1863, but the real developments did not come until twenty-five years later when professionalism was recognized. Shortly afterwards the beginnings of the present system of League matches, International fixtures and Cup ties, were organized, and "thus was ensured the spectacular phase of football which has proved so beneficial to Great Britain as an antidote to political, industrial and civil unrest."[1] To-day, in England and Wales, there are 88 teams in the three Divisions of the League. Scotland has 38 teams in its two Divisions, and Ireland 26 teams, a total of 152 first

[1] Catton, J. A. H., *Athletic News Football Annual*, 1936, p. 8.

teams (some clubs regularly place two teams in the field) in Great Britain and Ireland, playing each Saturday from April till August, apart from frequent matches in the mid-week. These are the teams whose fortunes are followed with such interest by so many millions and whose victories or losses occupy the space in the national dailies. But they form little more than one-third of the clubs employing professionals: it is estimated that they number 400 altogether and that at least 5,000 professionals are engaged.[1] To watch these professional and amateur players the public pay throughout the season for admission to some 20,000 matches.[2]

The attendance varies from 136,000, at an International match, to a few hundreds at one of the smaller amateur games. The total attendances are enormous: during 1936 in the struggle for the Football Association Cup, from the third round proper—a total of only sixty-three games—2,162,000 persons attended, paying £172,000 for admission.

Throughout the whole season 1936-37, H.M. Customs and Excise collected £422,200 [3] in respect of entertainment tax on admission fees to football matches. The total sum paid by the spectators is calculated with sufficient approximation if the tax is multiplied by slightly more than five, giving a figure of, say, £2,250,000. Deducting the portion paid by spectators at Rugby games [4] a sum of £1,950,000 is reached as

---

[1] For many of the details that follow I am indebted to Mr. S. F. Rous, Secretary of the Football Association, whose kindness I have much pleasure in acknowledging.

[2] For details of amateur games played, see Chapter IV, p. 229.

[3] This figure and other information was kindly placed at my disposal by H.M. Customs and Excise.

[4] The total is calculated at £450,000, of which only £300,000 is liable for entertainment tax: tickets at 6d. or less are not taxed.

the total amount collected for admission to Association games. On the basis that the average price of a ticket, exceeding 6d., is 1s. 3d., it follows that the total number of spectators during the season is approximately 32,500,000. This excludes all who pay 6d. or less, and no basis exists, unfortunately, for estimating their number. Probably they are more than one-quarter and less than one-half of the people already included, and so the total number of spectators who have paid during the season may be estimated to be between 40 and 48 millions.

Some further idea of the finances involved can be glimpsed from the sums which are paid by one club to another for the transfer of a player: the deal is done between the clubs, the player involved having little voice in the arrangement and receiving only an infinitesimal portion of the money. Arsenal, in 1934, paid £10,890 for the transfer of Jack from Bolton Wanderers. In six weeks during the 1935-36 season Aston Villa, in an effort to avoid relegation to the Second Division, spent £35,500 in purchasing seven players. Altogether during that season they spent nearly £45,000 on players' wages, bonuses, benefits and transfers, and it is one of the curiosities of football that they failed to stay in the First Division—the first occasion on which this famous club had been relegated. Transfers costing £5,000 "have become common" during the last fifteen years and do not now call for comment,[1] but at least it should be put on record that for one player alone, Hugh Gallacher, the Scottish international, fees amounting altogether to £20,000 were paid in less than ten years.

[1] *Athletic News Football Annual*, 1936, p. 36.

The Rugby League has its strongholds in Yorkshire and Lancashire, although in very recent years it has penetrated to the South; two professional clubs attempted to establish themselves in London, and the final for the Challenge Cup is played at Wembley Stadium. In its two home counties it is a serious rival to the older Soccer, there being 29 major teams in addition to their reserves and the 350 amateur clubs which exist. In 1935 the attendances at the Challenge Cup matches, a total of thirty-one games, amounted to 557,300, and the sum of £35,154 was paid for admittance. Apart from these, no exact details of spectators and the sums they pay are available, except that approximately 600 professional matches are arranged during a season. On the basis of the slight evidence which exists, an estimate of five million spectators paying a little more than £200,000 for admission may be ventured.[1]

The last of the three codes is the Rugby Union, confined solely to amateurs and gradually ousting Association football as the game for the Public Schools and their Old Boys. In the United Kingdom there are about 150 major teams, playing during a season not less than 2,500 matches, for the majority of which an entrance fee is charged to the spectators. The gates vary from a few hundreds to many thousands at International matches, and any estimate of their total size is perhaps little more than a guess: a fair average for the games where an admission fee is charged is probably 2,000, giving a total attendance of 5 millions. The average amount charged for entrance is not

---

[1] I have to acknowledge the kindness of Mr. John Wilson, Secretary to the Rugby Football League, in supplying me with the details quoted.

less than 1s., and on this basis £250,000 is paid each season.

The following Table gives a summary of the estimated attendances and amounts paid:

Code.	Spectators.		Amounts Paid.
	Class.	No. (millions).	
Association	Admission at more than 6d..	32	£1,950,000
	Admission at 6d. and less (Estimated average 4d. per head.)	10	167,000
Rugby Union	All	5	250,000
Rugby League	All	5	250,000
TOTAL	—	52	£2,617,000

Part III

RACING AND GAMBLING

The aspects of sport so far treated have been confined to the number of spectators and the amounts they pay. These sums are negligible, however, when compared with the money which goes into betting and gambling on sporting events. The latest comprehensive estimate of the annual turnover in Great Britain for betting and gambling [1] is £350 to £400 millions, with profits of £50 millions per annum.[2] The total is larger than the turnover in any single industry in this country with the possible exception of the building trade. An indication of the relative amount spent is that the nation's annual milk bill amounts to approximately £100 millions, equal to one-fourth of the total spent during the same period on backing chances of various descriptions. Details of the items composing the total are interesting:

	£ (millions)
Horse-racing	250
Greyhound betting	50
Football betting	30
Lotteries, newspaper competitions, automatic gambling machines	20
Total	£350

All the items have been estimated conservatively, and probably, therefore, the total shown is an under-assessment. It is significant that on their figure of

---

[1] It is not necessary for our purpose to distinguish between these two and the terms will be used synonymously.
[2] *The Economist*, 29th February and 7th March 1936.

£230 millions, which excludes all street bookmaking, the Control Board comments that "even this is considered by some experts to fall short of the actual sum which changes hands in the course of a year in betting transactions."[1]

In the face of these figures it is clear that the practice of betting is more widespread than at any previous time, and that more money than ever is spent in this direction. And striking as the figures are, more striking is the fact that popular betting seems to be almost completely a growth of the last hundred years. It is true that in the eighteenth century there were a large number of gaming clubs in London at which much money passed in card-playing and dicing. But their patrons were confined to the aristocrats and the wealthy, no one else could gain admittance, and outside of such clubs there exists but slight evidence of gambling. If we search the writings of Wesley, who during his long life of eighty-eight years (1703-91) delivered advice and admonitions now filling fifteen volumes, it is possible to find only two slight references, and these are directed against "the gamester" rather than against general gambling. The extent of his works and their detailed character, ranging from exhortations against tea-drinking to advocating "The Duty and Advantage of Early Rising," make it certain that if, during his time, betting had been prevalent amongst the poorer people he would have tackled the evil.[2]

[1] Racecourse Betting Control Board, First Annual Report (1929), p. 56.
[2] At the same time it may be noted that in 1739 the Society of Friends found it necessary to exhort " especially the youth, to avoid all balls, gaming places, horse races, those nurseries of debauchery and wickedness. . . ." *Printed Epistle of the Yearly Meeting of the Society of Friends*, 1739. Probably the greater concern of the Quakers with gambling arose from the higher social standing of the members of their sect compared with the people to whom Wesley addressed himself.

By the beginning of the nineteenth century gambling even amongst the wealthy people had tended to decrease; it was no longer the open institution it had been in the West End Clubs. In 1844 a House of Commons Report, whilst stating that "A wager was proverbially known to be an English way of settling a controversy," goes on to add, "In the last century (*i.e.* the eighteenth) the practice of betting was much more common in this country than it is now." In support of the conclusion that gambling had declined and was not at that time a widespread occurrence, the following extracts from the evidence given before the Committee may be quoted.

The Chief Magistrate of Marylebone Court, replying to the question: "Do you believe that there is much gambling prevalent among the poorer class of society?" said: "I should think only in that little way of which I have spoken, boys tossing up for halfpence in the streets. I do not know that this is any very great extent of it so far as my observation goes." A police inspector called to testify before the Committee [1] and in whose mind "there is no doubt" that gambling is very prevalent amongst the lower classes, produced no more evidence in support of his belief than a recent case he had conducted against a coffee-house keeper who allowed gambling for 2d. on his premises. Mr. Thomas J. Hall, Chief Magistrate, Bow Street, did "not think that amongst the labouring classes much gambling does go on in London." This evidence must be accepted as conclusive since these witnesses were eminently in a position to form a well-founded

---

[1] Select Committee of the House of Commons on the Gambling Acts vol. vi, 1844.

opinion. Yet twenty years later (1867) we find a writer who is very well disposed towards the poorer people commenting regretfully upon the rapid spread of betting habits among the working class—"a fact now greatly deplored by its most thoughtful members."[1] The same story of the increase in gambling was told by B. S. Rowntree who, making his social survey in York at the beginning of this century, was much struck by the prevalence of betting.[2] A year later a Select Committee of the House of Lords confirmed that his findings were valid for the whole country. They were convinced that "betting is generally prevalent in the United Kingdom, and that the practice of betting has increased considerably of late years especially amongst the working classes."[3] A few years later, after the War, another Select Committee expressed amazement at "the extent to which betting exists at the present time." "Indeed it is stated that there is scarcely a works in the country employing more than 20 workmen where one is not a bookmaker's agent, and this Your Committee believe to be near the truth."[4] In 1933 a Royal Commission was constrained to observe that "It is in densely populated centres, particularly in poorer working-class neighbourhoods, that gambling has become a social factor which the State cannot disregard."[5]

[1] Ludlow and Jones, *The Progress of the Working Class* (London, 1867), p. 189.
[2] Rowntree, B. S., *Poverty* (London, 1901), p. 143. Towards the end of last century the well-known novel, *Esther Waters*, written by George Moore, has, as one of its main themes, the spread of betting on horse racing both in the county and in the town.
[3] Select Committee of the House of Lords on Betting, 1902, para. 1.
[4] Select Committee of the House of Commons on Betting, 1923, paras. 30 and 14.
[5] Royal Commission on Lotteries and Betting, 1932-33, Cmd. 4341, para. 208.

Even since these words were written there has been an enormous expansion in a very important and large field of betting, *i.e.*, football pools. Thus the quotations given seem to show that widespread indulgence in gambling has developed very recently. The present indications are that it will continue to grow.

To understand how the existing condition has been reached it is necessary to trace three strands which are all very closely inter-related: the developments in the field of sports and gambling itself, the changing social background against which these developments have occurred, and the altered attitude of successive Governments to betting.

As early as 1388 there appears on the Statute Book, "It is accorded and assented That (all) Servant of Husbandry or Labourer, nor Servant, Artificer, nor of Victualler . . . shall . . . leave, all playing at Tennis or Football, and other Games called Coits, Dice, Casting of the Stone, and other such importune Games."[1] The purpose of this Act seems to have been twofold, to prevent games interfering with more serious pursuits and to ensure that Archery was not neglected. This policy was followed by future Governments. Perhaps the most determined attempt was made by Henry VIII, who passed three Acts on the subject, the last, 1543, entitled "An Act for the Maintenance of Artillery (Archery) and debarring of unlawful Games." The Act laid down what must be done in leisure time and what was forbidden. "Every man being the King's subject, not lame, decrepit nor maimed . . . except spiritual men Justice of one Bench and of the other . . . shall use and exercise shooting

---

[1] 12 Ric. II, c. vi.

in long bows, and also have a bow and arrow continually ready in his house." It further enjoined "that no manner of Artificer or Craft man of any handicraft or occupation, husband man apprentice labourer ... or any servingman ... shall play at Tables Tennis, Dice, Cards, Bowls ... at times apart from Christmas."[1] The Act provided that quarterly proclamation of its contents should be made—an indication of the importance attached to it. Nevertheless, the attempt to control the games which might be played was a failure, and future legislation confined itself exclusively to the question of controlling or eliminating gambling. Charles II's Parliament brought wagering and betting within the criminal law by enacting against "deceitful, disorderly and excessive Gameing," and providing very heavy penalties if the amount at stake exceeded £100.[2] These provisions were repeated during Queen Anne's reign, with the further restriction that if the amount lost at one sitting were £10 or more, then the loser was at liberty within three months to recover the money by Action of Debt. It is interesting that the Statute specifically exempted the Royal Palace during occupation by Her Majesty from any such limits.[3] In the meantime the Government had established State Lotteries during William III's reign, imposing a fine of £500 on any person attempting to promote a competing lottery. This was the position of the law in relation to betting and wagering till 1741 when charges were made in the amount of money which

[1] 33 Henry VIII, c. 9.   [2] 16 Car. II, c. 7.
[3] 9 Anne, c. 19. Its provisions were constantly tightened by new Statutes, but it is clear that the law remained a dead letter, no action taken under it succeeded. See Select Committee of the House of Lords on Gaming Laws, 1844, Minutes of Evidence, 1165.

could be laid on a horse race. It was declared illegal to enter a horse when the stake offered was less than £50. Parliament had been moved to legislate because "the great number of horse races for small plates, prizes or sums of money, have contributed very much to the encouragement of idleness."[1] Thus the State's ground for interfering with wagering had now shifted from the need to promote a continual supply of archers to the desire to ensure that the lower classes worked: the remainder of the population were allowed to gamble, always subject to the provisions of the loser being able to sue for his money if it were £10 or more and to the sum at stake not exceeding £100. It is a striking commentary that this remained the legal position whilst the Bucks and the Corinthians gambled wildly during the second half of the eighteenth century.

Changes were occurring in other directions which were destined to affect very considerably the attitude to gambling. As the original trading adventure had gradually developed into the common law company, in reality a huge partnership, so there arose at the same time a traffic in the transferable shares which each partner held. Often large profits could be earned by such trading ventures, but perhaps as often the perils of overseas trade resulted in a loss. Hence, investment in such enterprises was extremely speculative, but the high profits which could be earned gave a keen edge to the growing taste for these gambles. During the same period there grew up the practice of time bargains, the settlement of a transaction in Government stock by the loser merely paying over any difference arising from changes in the price of

[1] 13 Geo. II, c. 19.

the stock during the days between contracting and settling the bargain. The increased banking facilities and the easy flotation of limited liability companies eventually led to one of the most astounding episodes in British finance when innumerable companies were promoted for any and every object: the public were actually prepared to subscribe to a company "whose objects will be promulgated hereafter." The South Sea bubble inevitably collapsed, some made fortunes, many were ruined, but these disappeared and were soon forgotten. It was the fortunate who remained on view and whetted people's appetite for share gambling with its lure of large profits. Henceforward a powerful and increasing section of the public consistently strove to exploit the new fields of finance. Nevertheless the authorities, secular and ecclesiastical, were opposed, and exercised their influence against the spreading of practices which they believed to threaten both the morals and the structure of their society.

The Government, in 1719, had condemned public companies as tending to "the common grievance, prejudice and inconvenience of His Majesty's subjects," and the Act [1] proceeded to indict them as common nuisances. This Act remained on the Statute Book till 1825, a period of more than a century, and it was not till 1855 that the right of incorporation without a special Act of Parliament was permitted. Still more striking in our eyes are the provisions of an Act, passed in 1734 [2] and remaining in force till 1860,[3] which fixed a penalty of £500 against those who indulged in "the

---

[1] 6 Geo. I, c. 18.   [2] 7 Geo. II, c. 8.
[3] 23-4 Vic. c. 28 repealed the Stock-jobbing Act.

wicked, pernicious and destructive practice of stock-jobbing, whereby many of His Majesty's good subjects have been and are diverted from pursuing and exercising their lawful trades . . . to the utter ruin of themselves and their families."

In their stand against time bargains the Government was supported by at least one of the religious sects. From 1788 till 1849 the Society of Friends felt so strongly against stock-jobbing, "which is a species of gaming and altogether inconsistent with our religious principles," that to prevent "such disgraceful practices" on the part of any member, whether as principal, agent or broker, the monthly meetings should "not fail tenderly to advise and deal with such; and if they cannot . . . induce him to relinquish the practice, to testify against and disown him."[1] In the editions of the *Rules of Discipline* published after 1849, however, all mention of strictures against gambling disappear. Not till 1911 is the question once again discussed, but this time in a much more general form. "In the first place it is essential that we should dissociate ourselves from all participation in or encouragement of gambling and the gambling spirit. . . . We encourage our members to inform themselves and others as to the extent of the evil . . . and to promote legislation for its suppression."[2] The date of 1849 is significant, since a few years previously the laws had been considerably amended by the repeal [3] of the Statute making illegal stakes of less than £50 in a horse race, and this alteration was quickly followed, in 1844, by a complete overhaul of the existing

---

[1] *Rules of Discipline*, the Religious Society of Friends Supplement, 1849, p. 142.
[2] *Christian Practice*, Religious Society of Friends, 1925, p. 127.
[3] 3-4 Vic. c. 5.

legislation concerning gambling, by Select Committees of the two Houses.

The situation facing them was difficult. For several centuries there had been on the Statute Book enactments in restraint of gambling. In practice these were ignored and betting for large sums daily occurred. So long as the bets were between men of standing who knew each other—bookmakers were still a comparative rarity—they could agree upon disregarding the law and could trust each other to pay in the event of losing. With the increasing wealth and growing social mobility resulting from industrialization, the betting and gambling field was invaded by upstarts with no morals but much knowledge of the law. Hence, they were prepared to decline to pay heavy losses, knowing that any action for recovery laid the plaintiff open to proceedings under the criminal law for excessive gambling. They were, moreover, prepared to start actions, tantamount to blackmail, for penalties in respect of large-scale betting by any well-known sportsman who tried to draw up new regulations controlling those allowed to use the betting rings on the racecourses.

Most of the witnesses before the Committees considered that all betting should be made legal and subject to all the ordinary processes of law. The Committees themselves thought otherwise. The House of Lords considered that "the law should henceforth take no cognizance whatever of wagers," and "that debts so contracted should be recovered by such means only as the Usages and Customs of Society can enforce for its own protection." Their Report continued, "The Committee have reason to hope that in thus imposing upon honest Men a Necessity of greater Caution and Reserve, the System of excessive Betting will be restrained by ... Considerations of Prudence...."

The House of Commons were more historical but no less optimistic. "In earlier periods of European civilization it was thought to be the duty of Governments to exercise a minute superintendence and control over ... private actions of the members of the community ... and to protect them against the consequences of their own improvidence.

This notion was not confined to despotic Governments....

Such regulations are out of date and nobody now disputes the opinion of Adam Smith that Governments ... if they look well after their own expenses ... may safely trust private people with theirs." Thus the Committees of the two Houses were completely in accord: the House of Commons' said *laisser-faire*, the House of Lords' *caveat emptor*. The result of their joint recommendations was the Gaming Act, 1845, which is the basis of the present legislation concerning betting and the effect of which is to allow betting for any sums on any issue, but to prevent any dispute which may arise being taken to law. The law was tightened against gaming houses, but the wording of the relevant sections and of future Acts made it possible for judgment to be given that they did not apply to betting rings on racecourses. In other words, the position was established which obtains to this day, that ready-cash bookmaking was permissible only in the betting ring: elsewhere it was illegal. Credit betting could be done anywhere.

The impact of this new Act with its interpretations

was soon felt, particularly in horse racing. One or two meetings, Doncaster and Epsom, for instance, had had traditionally a popular character, attracting large crowds from all over the country. At Newmarket, the headquarters of the Turf, however, the meetings were still a preserve for a "few gentlemen on horseback." By 1850 the financial possibilities had been realized of charging a comparatively low admission fee and allowing ready-cash bookmakers, who had rapidly sprung into prominence with the removal of all the former legal restraint. The result was an immediate increase in the numbers attending: the "sport of kings" now became the pastime of the people. Its popularity has continued to grow, till in recent years it was officially estimated that "445,039 . . . represents about one-tenth of the total number who visit racecourses in a full year." [1] To this figure of four and a half millions must be added all those watching without paying entrance fees, who number at some meetings fifty times those actually paying.[2]

Horse racing is now a large and important business employing many thousands of people and absorbing millions of capital. Whilst owners are still prepared to lose a surprising amount of money for the sake of the social prestige which arises from having one's colours on the Turf, horse racing is increasingly becoming a rationalized industry in which large profits can be made. In a single year one owner has secured in Great Britain £65,000 from stake monies alone and shared two million francs in France. The stud fees to be charged for a Classic winner make the stakes

---

[1] Racecourse Betting Control Board, First Annual Report, 1929, p. 9.
[2] *Ibid.*

of £10,000 or £12,000 comparatively negligible, even apart from the sum for which the horse could be sold. An offer of £100,000 has actually been refused for a Derby winner. When it is remembered that the admission relating to greyhound racing, that it could not continue to exist without betting, applies also to horse racing,[1] it will be realized how closely betting is woven into the whole social and economic structure. Not only is it a large industry in itself, it sustains more than one large industry.

But a proper appreciation of the present position cannot be obtained without taking into account developments in other fields. The growth of speculative finance in its early stages has already been mentioned, but the story must be brought up to date so that its full impact may be realized. The quotations given from the *Rules* make it clear that the Quakers drew no distinction between gambling on a racecourse and gambling on the Stock Exchange. Less than a century ago it was still possible to find this view held in official quarters. Thus the Commissioner of the City of London Police was being cross-examined before the Select Committee of the House of Commons on Betting. Being asked concerning the amount of gambling in the City, he pointed out that not much gaming occurred, "He (the gambler) would be more likely to be detected in the City, except at the Stock Exchange where gentlemen of all pursuits are known to speculate extensively."[2] To-day it would be

---

[1] The experiment has never been tried in this country of organizing races without betting. In America the experiment has been attempted more than once. Each time it has failed and betting has had to be introduced in order to maintain the racing.

[2] Select Committee of the House of Commons on Gaming, 1844, Minutes of Evidence, 783.

difficult to imagine such a coupling together of Stock Exchange transactions and ordinary gambling, but it remains that, apart from one small provision, the law knows no distinction between Stock Exchange speculation and other wagering contracts. More than this, time bargains, which are intended to be settled by the payment of differences only and do not involve taking up the stock in question, form the majority of the transactions on the Stock Exchange. Yet they are in direct contravention of its Rules and all such contracts are void under the Gaming Act, 1845.[1] In other words, the distinction which current morality would draw between speculation through a stockbroker and speculation with a bookmaker has arisen only recently. It is not to be found in the law of the land and it is expressly repudiated by the Rules of the Stock Exchange itself. And that this line is now drawn does not alter the objective characteristics of either class of transactions. They are both gambling.[2]

Similar considerations arise when we turn to examine the insurance world. The proportion of policies in which the proposer has an insurable interest at stake, *i.e.*, he would be materially affected if the contingency against which he is insuring actually arose, is very high,

---

[1] Halsbury, vol. 27, p. 259.
[2] The economic impact of business speculation, from which its defence is usually derived, is adequately summarized by the following footnote from Webb's *The Decay of Capitalist Civilization* (London, 1923), p. 24 : " Some part of this speculation may be defended as an indirect, but we think cumbersome, way of equalizing prices. But legitimate speculation has in recent years been submerged beneath an elaborate superstructure of commercial gambling not only in securities but in essential foodstuffs and raw materials ; the dealings in ' options ' and ' futures,' in wheat, cotton, etc., the practices of ' short-selling,' ' rigging,' ' bolstering,' ' hammering,' ' unloading,' ' switching ' in gambling on ' specified margins,' are all ways of getting rich—often fabulously rich—without producing anything else but the maximum amount of uncertainty in the earnings of all classes of producers and in the prices paid by all classes of consumers."

but nevertheless it is possible to effect "honour policies" on any event, sporting or otherwise. In the commodity market the same element of speculation is present, and it is understandable that after a full examination of gambling and business B. S. Rowntree was forced to write, almost apologetically, "The writer is aware that in urging the avoidance of gambling in commercial transactions he exposes himself to the objection that gambling and commerce are apparently inextricably associated. He does not, however, seek to maintain that any hard and fast line can be drawn. . . ."[1] The simple fact is that no line at all can be drawn, yet the kind of speculation which is conducted in business forms such a large part of the lives of many middle- and upper-class persons that for them the really interesting portion of the newspaper is the City column or the latest market prices.

Since these people occupy the most prominent positions in society, and since their norms set the general standard of conduct, it is not surprising that gambling is regarded by most as having become socially sanctioned.

So far only a portion of the legal framework and some of the conditions which made possible the spread of gambling have been described. What was the stimulus to the actual process whereby the position has been reached in which four out of every five of the poorer families in London bet from time to time.[2] The Royal Commission, which conducted the most thorough investigation yet made into the whole

---

[1] Rowntree, B. S., *ibid.*, p. 173. See also Select Committee on Betting, 1923, p. xlii. para. 1.   [2] *New Survey of London*, vol. ix. p. 281.

problem, should be allowed to speak for themselves: "One of the main causes, perhaps the most potent, in the growth of gambling has been the increased facilities for organizing gambling."[1] It is worth spending a few minutes describing the development of these facilities in order to show how absolutely ubiquitous they are. The spread of horse racing has already been mentioned. It was increasingly accompanied by newspaper publicity, which multiplied from the 1890's onwards when the impact of compulsory education was beginning to be felt. A growing number of people were just able to read, but were without intellectual interests and largely without suitable reading material. These formed an admirable market for the popular Press which quickly found that, next to war, the best selling news was sport. Hence the emphasis on horse racing, with forecasts of results, on football and athletic meetings which, together with cycle races, formed at one time an important and extensive field for betting.

This emphasis has tended to grow rather than to decline, so that to-day the sales of one popular national daily fluctuate widely at one time of the year compared with another as the result of its excellent service for flat racing being necessarily suspended during the winter months. The early editions of the evening newspapers are little except guides to racing form: if racing were stopped they would have no reason for their appearance. All this means that the fortunes

[1] Royal Commission on Lotteries and Betting, Final Report, 1931-33, Cmd. 4341, para. 208. See also Select Committee of House of Lords on Betting, 1902, para. 5: "the increased prevalence of betting throughout the country is largely due to the facilities afforded by the Press and to the inducements to bet offered by means of bookmakers' circulars and tipsters' advertisements."

of newspapers are closely bound up with racing of all kinds and so with betting.

In addition to devoting large space to sport with its concomitant of betting, the papers directly promoted gambling by their own competitions. Thirty years ago Masterman described forcibly the process as he had seen it developing under his eyes.

"We have been nourished . . . in this unreal world of sport and gambling, we began with our boys' papers and guessing competitions. We were insensibly led on to efforts after a pound a week for life by estimating the money in the Bank of England on a certain day or amassing gain in hundreds of pounds for guessing words or the last line of 'Limericks.' On the Sabbath, committed by our parents to some such literature as the Sunday Syndicated Press, we found there the same cheery game, smeared with grease of piety, rewards and prizes here for guessing anagrams on Bible cities. . . . We were led on to talk and read and chatter about 'sport' in biography of various football heroes, in descriptive reports of football matches. . . . Our thoughts and growing interest were sedulously directed away from consideration of any rational or serious universe. . . . The work of corruption—the word is not too violent—in the matter of frivolous gambling competitions is a systematic whole beginning with the papers designed for boys and children. . . ."[1]

So far from declining, newspaper competitions after the War increased to such an extent that it was possible to win £20,000 by correctly forecasting the results of football matches. This particular branch of their activities was closed by the Betting and Lotteries Act,

---

[1] Masterman, C. F. G., *The Condition of England* (1909), pp. 92-93.

RACING AND GAMBLING

1934, which prevents newspapers from offering prizes for the forecasting of results of any events. It was undoubtedly a serious blow to them, but such competitions as their ingenuity can discover are still open to them for exploitation.

But newspapers were having fresh material to feed to their public.[1] New sports with their additional opportunities for betting were continually appearing. Moreover, the new sports were continually giving opportunities for fresh periodicals, till to-day nearly 210 sports annuals and periodicals are published in Great Britain. Only if all the religious publications are added together can a greater number of journals be found dealing with a single topic.

For our purpose the most important of the new sporting attractions is greyhound racing: not only can it be staged right in the centre of urban areas, but its very existence is bound up with betting, without which it could not survive for a single day.[2] And the importance of greyhound betting cannot be gauged by comparing its total of £50 millions per annum with the £250 millions for horse racing. The sums spent are comparatively so small that it represents probably a greater total number of bets. This is supported by the frequency of greyhound meetings compared with horse racing. At "7 horse racecourses within a radius of 15 miles from Charing Cross there were 187 days' racing a year, whereas in the same area there were 23 greyhound tracks with over 4,000 days' racing. In

---

[1] For an analysis of the contents of newspapers see Appendix to this Chapter.
[2] *Question.* " I take it you would admit frankly that except for the betting, these greyhound tracks could not exist ? " *Answer.* " Yes." G. Picken, Chairman, National Bookmakers' Protection Association, Ltd., before the *Royal Commission on Lotteries*, Minutes of Evidence, 7991.

the city of Glasgow there are no horse racecourses, but there are 5 greyhound tracks with about 1,400 days' racing."[1] At some tracks no entrance fee is charged. The owners are content with the profits they secure from the operation of the totalisator. In a recent municipal election a new party intervened in the shape of a greyhound track company which was willing to provide swimming baths free of charge to the ratepayers, and to finance the building of a railway station in exchange for nothing more than permission to erect a track in the district.

That greyhound tracks can be reached with little difficulty, that any admission fee charged is low, that the meetings are held in the evening, that the considerations involved in determining the likely winner are few and simple compared with the factors involved in horse racing, that totalisators are available to give the punters confidence they are securing reasonable odds, all these factors have tended to draw in a large public which previously had done no betting.

Another recent development with very important cumulative effects is the opening of innumerable shops with pin-tables and the installation of such machines in restaurants, public-houses, cafés, anywhere the public is likely to congregate with a moment to spare. The sum involved with an automatic playing machine, of which pin-tables are the most popular form, is only 1d. a time, but the total earnings must be so high that there is considerable incentive for their proprietors to extend their use. Pin-tables embody so perfectly the characteristics demanded of a modern amusement

---

[1] *Ibid.*, para. 252. The number of days' racing on organized tracks is now limited to 104 per annum.

that they call for special comment. The game is played by projecting a ball and allowing it to follow a course where it must negotiate several hazards, ending, if the player is lucky, in a hole worth a high score. No physical effort is required, no skill is demanded, the game is short and hence sustained attention is unnecessary. Above all at the end there is the possibility of winning money. A child of two can play as well as an adult. Alekhine, Borotra or Bobby Jones would have no advantage over the inmate of an asylum. The necessary qualifications are simply the possession of one penny and the ability to pull a small handle five or six times. Is it surprising that one London shop, even though it has only pin-tables, can pay a rent of nearly £8,500 per annum?[1]

Moreover, the bookmakers have been incessantly extending their facilities, assisted all the time by the host of tipsters who try to make a living from selling alleged winners. Their anxiety to expand the business is easily understandable in the light of confessions such as that of "The Deluded Sportsman," who seems scarcely to merit at least the first term, when he says that he has made in one day a profit of £5,000 from cash bookmaking.[2] In addition to ceaseless circulars by post, offering a high limit of credit and very convenient methods of placing bets, some bookmakers even employ street canvassers who go from house to house, as though they were trying to sell groceries. All this is over and above the widespread organization which has been set up, including street runners, milkmen and other door-to-door tradesmen, to carry on the illegal

[1] *Gambling Machines*, National Anti-Gambling League (pamphlet).
[2] "The Deluded Sportsman," in Rowntree, B. S., *Betting and Gambling*.

practice of street betting, so that now no one need have the slightest difficulty in putting money on any race. But not only have the bookmakers spread their net further, the Government itself has taken a hand in the game, both directly and indirectly.

Since 1845 the legal status of betting had remained unchanged, but in 1926 the Chancellor of the Exchequer proposed a tax of $3\frac{1}{2}$ per cent. on credit betting and 2 per cent. on ringside bets. The Government, who already received indirectly from racing and betting a considerable revenue through the use of telegraph and telephone facilities by the Press and by bookmakers, now tried to raise money directly on the betting turnover. The attempt was relinquished three years later owing to the difficulties experienced in collecting the tax, but inevitably the conclusion was drawn that by its action the Government of the day had given betting a new status. This conclusion was enforced by the introduction and passing of a Bill which empowered the setting up of a statutory body to operate totalisators on horse racecourses. The Racecourse Betting Control Board started work in 1929 and has now established an organization which enables it to provide pari-mutuel betting on practically every racecourse or point-to-point meeting in Great Britain. The Government does not derive benefit from any surplus they may have. It is devoted to improving the breed of racehorses, and latterly also to the promotion of training in, and research into, veterinary surgery.

The concessions did not end there. In 1934, against the recommendation of the Royal Commission on Lotteries which had reported in the previous year, the establishment of totalisators was allowed on greyhound tracks. In the course of the debate on the same Bill, the Government withdrew the proposed ban on credit totalisator betting on football results, making possible its remarkable expansion of the past three or four years. Thus, during the last century the attitude of successive Governments towards betting has undergone a very deep change. Starting in 1845 with a refusal to recognize the existence of any wagering contracts except negatively, *i.e.*, they were and are prepared to suppress all gaming houses, they have ended by specifically permitting betting on most racecourses and by refusing to attempt the suppression of credit football betting through "Pools." The one stand in which they have been consistent is the refusal to recognize ready-cash bookmaking off the course. If they were successful in attempts to abolish this practice it would mean that only those with sufficient cash to visit a racecourse or sufficient standing to be granted credit could bet. It is notorious, however, that street bookmaking continues to flourish, only mildly irritated by the efforts of the authorities to deal with it.

Very little has been said so far on one of the most important developments in betting, the promotion of "Football Pools." They are a happy example of those all too rare cases where the interests of each party concerned coincide. The bookmaker much prefers them to the older form of straight betting with fixed odds, and his clients are also with him in this preference. The reason for the bookmaker's choice is that whilst the contingency was very remote, it was possible in the past for him to lose. Now he must win, he cannot lose, for under the rules drawn up by himself he is entitled to retain a certain proportion of the total amount subscribed. The proportion is sometimes specified, sometimes not, but it is always sufficient to cover his expenses and to afford him a handsome profit. It is perhaps the one business so far discovered which is absolutely certain of declaring a dividend.

The backer also prefers Pools for two reasons. Under the old system all his money was lost if his forecasts were not absolutely correct. In a Pool, however, the prize has to be won: each week it has to be shared amongst those with the best forecasts. It can and does happen, therefore, that a man's coupon is not completely correct but, nevertheless, because no other is more accurate, he participates in the prize money distributed. Secondly, the prize he wins may be infinitely larger than his winnings could be by betting. Hence the backer feels that he has a better chance with a Pool than with a straight bet. As the result, Football Pools have grown rapidly. They were threatened with suppression when the Bill, which finally became the Betting and Lotteries Act, 1934, was first introduced. It contained a clause prohibiting any Pool betting other than through racecourse totalisators. Presumably as the result of strong opposition from the Football Pool Promoters Association, Lord Londonderry beat a graceful retreat on behalf of the Government. Since "there are considerable disadvantages in isolating and singling out for special restrictions only one method of the course betting," the Government "propose . . . allowing the continuance of office pari-mutuel betting . . . in connection with such sports as horse racing and football matches."[1] In other words, the Pools could

[1] 91 H.L. Deb., 5 s., 779.

continue and, armed with this official refusal to suppress them, they have gone from strength to strength. The Football Association's attempt to eliminate the Pools in 1935, by withholding permission to use their fixture list, was completely unsuccessful. And from the total of £8 millions mentioned in 1933, it is probable that they now handle not less than £50 millions per annum.

The Postmaster-General announced that, during the three months September-November, 1935, his department had collected in the seven towns where Pool promoters are mainly situated an average of 5,371,000 postal packets per week. Assuming that 20 per cent. of the coupons despatched by the Pools are not returned by the recipients—probably this estimate errs on the high side—there still remains nearly $4\frac{1}{2}$ millions completed coupons. One coupon almost invariably represents the investment of at least two persons, often three or four participate in its completion. It follows, therefore, that at least 10 million persons are interested in Pool betting each week throughout the season. This figure represents 35 to 40 per cent. of the adult population of this island!

Football Pool betting is, therefore, the most popular pastime ever known, excluding cinema-going. On what is its enormous appeal based? Primarily the attraction is the possibility of winning money. Most people are poor and most are concerned with methods of securing greater wealth: the Pools seem to offer opportunities which do not exist elsewhere. For many the sum expended in Pool betting is an investment to be charged to the weekly budget as regularly as the cost of life assurance or National Health contributions.

Thus in a small workshop in the East End of London only one of the workers out of the ten employed professes to have any knowledge of football form. But all of them regularly subscribe 6d. a week which is handed over to their *cognoscente*. He alone knows how the coupon is completed. When the match results are announced the rest cannot share the excitement of discovering how their bets have fared, for they have no idea of the games that have been backed. Their sole concern is to learn on Monday morning whether any winnings are due to them.

It is to be expected that people who from their youth up have been forced to learn that "wealth is virtue," in Balzac's phrase, should seize the only opportunities which seem to offer the hope of great reward. What a temptation it must be to a labourer, who earns less than 40s. a week and who knows that however industrious and efficient he may be his earnings will never increase to any extent, that for a mere 6d. there is actually the chance of his winning many thousands of pounds. What else offers such tempting baits? When one reads an accountant's certificate that during a single season a Pool promoter paid more than four million prizes, and when in the same attractive leaflet one sees the picture of those who have been the fortunate winners of any sum up to £30,000, who can resist the thought that it could as easily be their face and not that of someone else which shines above the reproduction of a large cheque? The social function of betting as holding out to poor people an escape is well understood by J. M. Keynes. "It is depressing," he said, "for an individual to look forward to a life of poverty without the slightest possibility of any amelioration in it. If everybody for quite a small deduction from their wages, (for lottery tickets), always had just the possibility of something turning up, I see no evil in it."[1]

It is no wonder that when John Hilton[2] invited letters explaining why the writers spent money on the Pools, so many were received which stressed "the hope that you will secure more of this world's goods than you can possibly obtain otherwise." One writes of "one day winning a sum which would remove the sense of insecurity that is always hanging over our home." Another explains that they invest "a modest 6d. or 1s., because one day we may have the luck to win a decent sum and so put an end to this strangling existence which we lead." A third, a widow, tells him that "this week I have had a letter from the Council saying that if I do not pay the remainder of my rates, I have already paid half, they will take proceedings against me. I am telling all this to explain . . . think what it would mean to be able to pay my rates at once, instead of wondering every time there is a knock at the door if it is a policeman with a summons. . . . I can still see the funny side of life and I enjoy a good laugh."

It is little use quoting the laws of probability to illustrate to such people the foolishness of thus trying to reach security. They have had experience of the workings of chance, often their whole life is at the mercy of the god, and many fully realize the futility of their conduct. But what else can they do? Faced

---

[1] Royal Commission on Lotteries and Betting, Minutes of Evidence, 7865.
[2] Hilton, John, *Why I go in for the Pools* (Allen & Unwin Ltd.). All the following quotations are from the booklet unless otherwise indicated.

with the certainty of not having enough and the possibility, however slight, of one day reaching affluence, is it not natural that they clutch at the straw? How many have sufficient adjustment or resignation to adopt the attitude of the woman shopkeeper in Lancashire who writes, "I'm not innocent of this form of gambling . . . the futility of the thing forced itself upon me . . . if I had the money I would go to a naturopath. That's why I gambled . . . and why I'm now without much hope of ever having enough, putting the money by." She expresses classically the Scylla and Charybdis of the vast proportion who gamble, "the futility of the thing," "putting the money by, without much hope of ever having enough."

The lack of an assured living and the desire to attain security is not a sufficient explanation of the habit of gambling. If it were, it would be difficult to understand why some soldiers, whose security of livelihood is equalled only by that of prisoners, are amongst the wildest gamblers.

The urge for excitement and even the mere desire to have some kind of break in the monotony of everyday life is a very potent force making for gambling. "Filling in the family coupon makes a bit of excitement. That may be a good thing, for work and bed day in and day out gets monotonous," is the verdict of a boilerman. Even a professional worker, whose life is likely to be a little varied, confesses to "the thrill on Saturday of hearing the results from the B.B.C.," while another explains the attraction of the Pools in terms of ". . . just *excitement*. A pleasant spice to daily life, a condiment to enliven the weeks of winter." In many cases the desire for excitement or change mingles with the economic motive, which has been stressed, through the hope of winning sufficient money for a holiday otherwise unobtainable. "One day I may win and get a holiday on the Continent. . . ." "I had a lucky line a few months ago and it meant a whole load of anxiety lifted from me and a week spent with my young daughter in Scotland."

A third important strand in the motives leading to gambling, especially Pool betting, is that it acts as a link between people who participate. It gives them something in common, a never-failing topic of conversation in lives which otherwise tend to be empty. Filling in a Pool coupon is mostly a family affair: everybody can discuss the respective merits of Arsenal or West Bromwich Albion. There are comparatively few complications involved: the study of football form seems simple against trying to follow horse racing form, and all the family are able to arrive at their own opinions, to listen in collectively to the results being announced on Saturday evening over the wireless, to chaff each other during the week, and especially afterwards when the respective hopes have or have not materialized. Even the simple fact that Pool gambling means a postal packet arriving regularly, always with something fresh in it, is an added attraction to the many persons who are otherwise without links to the outside world. This aspect of Pool betting as fellowship is fully realized by one of the most efficient promoters. They have established their own "Circle," asking patrons to introduce their friends as members; it issues a Log containing bright and chatty snippets; every week the "Chief" addresses a letter to his "friends" and often he refers to his "family," all of which gives those who spend their money the feeling of "belonging": it almost seems something more than a mere betting transaction.

Thus the history of gambling is one of a rapid and extensive development due to new sports arising which could form a basis of wagering, to the systematic and ceaseless pushing of betting and to the provision of new facilities, such as the totalisator on the racecourses and the Pool in relation to football, all bringing in an ever greater public. The way for this spread of betting has been eased by the disappearance of almost every vestige of Government opposition [1] and by the fertile ground in which the bookmakers could sow their seed.

For the rich, betting is merely an extension of their normal habits and is bound up with many facets of their lives.

"There is something more than the mere eventuality of a chance which prompts us to the enjeu. . . . There is mixed up with our eagerness for the stakes the most varied elements of business and pleasure: cash-books, ledgers, dividend warrants, indignation meetings of Venezuelan bond-holders, coupons, cases of champagne, satin-skinned horses with plaited manes, grandstands, pretty faces, bright flags, lobster salads, cold lamb, fortune-telling gypsies, barouches and four and 'Our Aunt Sally.'" [2]

For the poor, it is the one thread which binds them

---

[1] The Government reserved the right to take further action if the social consequences of betting were shown to be harmful. See Lord Londonderry's speech, 91 H.L. Deb., 5 s., 779. A powerful campaign has recently developed for action against Pools, but the Home Secretary was " not satisfied that it is necessary in the national interests to establish special machinery for the regulation of these Pools."

[2] Sala, G. A., quoted Steinmetz, A., *The Gaming Table*, 1870, vol. i. p. 135.

to their vision of Paradise: "Our future life seems pretty hopeless, with me just a labourer. Now you can picture our home and how we sit and think and puzzle of some way of getting out of the rut, but so far only the Pools have presented a hope, very slight I admit." [1]

[1] Hilton, John, *op. cit.*, p. 21.

[APPENDIX

APPENDIX TO CHAPTER III

TWELVE DAILY NEWSPAPERS AND ELEVEN SUNDAY NEWSPAPERS, PUBLISHED IN LONDON. ANALYSED ACCORDING TO THEIR CONTENTS.

Type of Display.	The Times, Daily Telegraph.		Other Daily Newspapers.		Total.		Sunday Times, Observer.		Other Sunday Newspapers.		Total.		Grand Total.	
	Inches.	Per Cent.	Inches.	Per Cent.	Inches.	Per Cent.	Inches.	Per Cent.	Inches.	Per Cent.	Inches.	Per Cent.	Inches.	Per Cent.
Sport	508	6·6	2,480	13·6	2,988	11·4	1,039	13·0	4,406	19·4	5,445	17·7	8,433	14·8
Stage, Cinema, Wireless	417	5·5	927	5·0	1,344	5·1	413	5·2	1,715	7·5	2,128	6·9	3,472	6·1
Social Gossip	367	4·8	1,225	6·7	1,592	6·0	399	5·0	1,797	8·0	2,196	7·1	3,788	6·7
News of political, financial and economic interest	2,363	30·7	3,624	19·7	5,987	23·0	1,534	19·3	1,995	8·8	3,529	11·5	9,516	16·7
Book reviews	109	1·4	—	—	109	·4	611	7·7	130	·6	741	2·4	850	1·5
Stories, serial and short	—	—	768	4·2	768	2·9	—	—	775	3·4	775	2·5	1,543	2·7
Accidents, mishaps	47	·6	330	1·8	377	1·5	46	·6	367	1·6	413	1·3	790	1·4
News of criminal or passionate interest	207	2·7	1,399	7·6	1,606	6·2	19	·2	1,246	5·5	1,265	4·3	2,871	5·2
Advertisements	3,137	40·8	5,668	30·7	8,805	33·9	2,965	37·3	6,509	28·6	9,474	30·8	18,279	32·2
Miscellaneous	529	6·9	1,965	10·7	2,494	9·6	934	11·7	3,780	16·6	4,714	15·5	7,208	12·7
	7,684	100·0	18,386	100·0	26,070	100·0	7,960	100·0	22,720	100·0	30,680	100·0	56,750	100·0

NOTES.—The weekday was a Tuesday which was chosen to avoid the week-end bias towards sport. The midday editions of the evening papers were excluded. If these had been added they would have greatly increased the percentage devoted to sport, since they are little but guides to form and summary of forecasts for horse and greyhound racing.

The papers analysed were: *The Times, Daily Telegraph, Daily Express, Daily Herald, Daily Mail, Daily Mirror, Daily Sketch, Daily Worker, News-Chronicle, Evening Standard, Evening News, The Star: The Observer, Sunday Times, Sunday Express, Sunday Graphic, Sunday Pictorial, Sunday Referee, Reynolds News, Sunday Dispatch, The People, Sunday Chronicle, The News of the World.*

CHAPTER IV

ORGANIZATIONS FOR LEISURE

PART I

YOUTH

UNTIL almost the middle of the last century the only organizations in the United Kingdom which catered for the leisure of the working class were the Sunday School and the beer houses. The working men, women and children followed the rule laid down for them by Sir James Graham in the House of Commons, that the life of the poor must necessarily be limited to eating, drinking, sleeping and working.

The bleakness and drabness of English urban life was notorious amongst continental observers. The Public Commission, which during the 1830's examined the health of towns, reported that in Lancashire only Preston possessed a public park, and only Liverpool had public baths.[1] "If the people of Manchester want to go out on a Sunday, where can they go?" asked a Frenchman, who during that period studied English conditions.[2] "There are no public promenades, no avenues, no public gardens and no public common ... everything in the suburbs is closed against them, everything is private property; in the midst of the beautiful scenes of England the operatives are like the Israelites of old, with the promised land before them, but for-

---

[1] See Hammond, J. L., *The Growth of Common Enjoyment* (Oxford, 1933), p. 4.
[2] Faucher, *Études sur l'Angleterre*, quoted by Hammond, *op. cit.*, p. 5.

bidden to enter into it." Why was, as Hammond asks, "the richest country in Europe judged by its wealth, the poorest country in Europe judged by its social amenities?"

As we have said in an earlier chapter, the poverty of social life in the towns was in fact closely related to England's wealth. The aristocracy ignored city life, the clergy avoided it if at all possible. The manufacturers feared that amusements might divert the attention and so lessen the efficiency of labour. Thus all amenities but Sunday School and the public-house were absent on the Sabbath: it was impossible to think of establishing new institutions for "common enjoyment." All efforts of progressive people were primarily concentrated on breaking through the strict sabbatarian rules. Everyone who studied and supported this issue came to the conclusion that "leisure was the privilege of a class," and that "leisure therefore came to assume class significance." [1]

Thus the National Sunday League [2] addressed the people in these words [3]: "While on Sunday the wealthier classes have their libraries, pictures, pleasure-grounds, clubs and subscription botanical or zoological gardens, and are waited on by their domestic servants —not only without reproach, but with the approval of all excepting perhaps a very few ultra-sabbatarians—

[1] Hammond, *op. cit.*, p. 10.
[2] The League described its character and aims in the following terms: " The National Sunday League recognizes neither sect nor party : it simply concerns itself with the social, moral and intellectual progress of the people; and beyond claiming for them a freedom from ascetic restraint in regard to the observance of Sunday, has no desire to interfere in spiritual matters. . . ."
[3] National Sunday League: Address to the public on the Sunday opening of the Crystal Palace, Great Meeting held in St. Martin's Hall, 7th December 1858.

is it too much to ask that the industrious classes, confined six days to their daily labour, should have the public institutions opened to them on that day? Is the miserable plea that a few attendants must be on duty sufficient to deprive *thousands* of working men of their chance of visiting the public galleries, libraries and places of instruction, for the maintenance of which they actually contribute by their taxes?"

The case was stated in similar terms fourteen years later by Councillor Jesse Collings in the Birmingham Town Council.[1]

"If you can buy a share in the Crystal Palace, or if you can subscribe a guinea to the Edgbaston Botanical Gardens, you can enjoy art and nature righteously; but if you are so poor that you can possess books, and pictures, and gardens in the only way in which the poor can hope to possess them, namely in their corporate capacity, then such enjoyments become oppressive to the consciences of certain other men, many of whom by their own confessions derive the utmost delight in doing in their own homes that which they so strongly object to be done in the Public Libraries and Galleries of the town."[2]

---

[1] Speech "On the Resolution to Open the Public Art Gallery and Free Reference Library on Sundays." March, 1872, published by the National Sunday League, p. 12. Finally, "the resolution was put and carried amid great cheering by a majority of 27 against 15."

[2] Even the Select Committee of the House of Commons on Public Houses, 1854, came to the same conclusion: "The system that suffers the singing saloons of Manchester and Liverpool, and Cremarne and the Eaglé Tavern Gardens, to be open on the Sunday, and shuts in the face of all but the proprietors and those who may have free admission to the gardens of the Zoological Society and the vast and varied schools of 'ocular instruction,' provided within the grounds and building of the Crystal Palace, is scarcely consistent. The National Gallery and other places of public instruction are paid for by the Nation; and it does not seem to your committee reasonable that these places should be closed upon the only day that it is possible for the majority of the population to visit them without serious loss."

The change of attitude towards workers' recreation which became at last noticeable from the middle of the last century onwards, may be traced to three different yet closely related trends in the history of the time. Improvements in technique made it possible to consider freeing labour of some of its burden by shortening the working day; the growing self-consciousness of the workers, as represented by the Chartist movement, led them to demand free hours and amenities, especially since leisure was so marked a political issue, and leisure facilities had become an important political weapon.

Thus, as Hammond quotes in *The Bleak Age*,[1] with reference to Manchester, "on one occasion, and one only, such institutional gardens as existed were opened to this melancholy population: 'On the holiday given at Manchester in celebration of Her Majesty's marriage, extensive arrangements were made for holding a Chartist meeting, and for getting up what was called a demonstration of the working classes, which greatly alarmed the municipal magistrates. Sir Charles Shaw, the Chief Commissioner of Police, induced the mayor to get the Botanical gardens, Zoological gardens and Museum of the town, and other institutions thrown open to the working classes at the hour they were urgently invited to attend the Chartist meeting. The Mayor undertook to be personally answerable for any damage that occurred for throwing open the gardens and institutions to the classes who had never before entered them. The effect was not more than two or three hundred people attended the political meeting, which entirely failed, and scarcely five shillings worth

[1] P. 53.

of damage was done in the gardens or in the public institutions by the work people, who were highly pleased. A further effect produced was that the charges before the police for drunkenness and riot were on that day less than the average of cases on ordinary days."

And finally, the ill effects of time and money spent in the public-house, drunkenness and delinquency, aroused the concern of industrialists and humanitarians. Provisions for spare-time activities were started gradually as it was recognized that if the workers "pass their leisure in habits which are weighing them down into pauperism,"[1] their industrial efficiency was seriously threatened. There were, indeed, grave signs that such a state of affairs was approaching. Jesse Collings reported[2] that at a recent meeting in Manchester, presided over by the Bishop of that city, a paper was read which stated that there were 3,302 drink shops in Manchester and Salford; and into ten of those one Sunday " there enter 5,928 men, 3,002 women and 890 children, giving an average of 982 persons to each house, or over 100 per hour."

The paper further stated, that in Manchester 151 spirit vaults, 229 public-houses, 1,027 beer shops had been watched and the visits to them on one Sunday were, 120,122 by men, 71,111 by women, 23,285 by children.

The streets of the industrial towns were "filled by night with bands of young savages."[3] But "it was not till the later decades of the nineteenth century when the ruffianism of youths had reached such a

---

[1] Collings, Jesse, *op. cit.*, p. 20. [2] *Ibid.*, p. 15.
[3] Russell, C. E. B., *Lads' Clubs* (London, 1932), p. 6.

pitch as to become an absolute danger to the community that attention was thoroughly roused." [1] Such gangs as the "Bengal Tiger" and the "Forty Row" in Manchester stimulated efforts which were destined to result, in our day, in the "Nation Wide Movement" for "Fitness" and "Fellowship" of the "Working Lad."

There were everywhere signs of the "new social spirit." In 1847 the Ten Hours Act was passed and the industrial towns started to provide public parks and libraries. After 1850 "rich men began again to use their money to improve their cities," [2] but, on the other hand, the playing of games in London parks on Sundays was prohibited until 1922, and the playing of matches even until 1934. Such restrictions and the continued existence of long hours for men and of drudgery for women [3] frustrated attempts by the workers themselves to form spontaneous and independent institutions for recreation, the more so since the squire, the vicar and the manufacturer took the task of improving the poor energetically into their own hands. It is their partnership which characterizes the history of leisure institutions in this country and which makes it a record of philanthropy and patronization.

Facilities were provided with the aim of rescuing the downtrodden and preventing rowdyism. Interest centred around young people, who were especially conspicuous for their wild escapades, rather than around adults. Religion supplied the pattern of behaviour which these boys', and later the girls'

[1] Russell, C. E. B., *Lads' Clubs* (London, 1932), p. 6.
[2] Hammond, *op. cit.*, p. 11.   [3] See preceding Chapter, Part III.

organizations, tried to inculcate into their members. "It was to men who already had some connection with rough boys as teachers in ragged schools and Bible classes that the idea first came of keeping their pupils out of mischief by providing harmless amusement, at the same time humanizing them by the influence of closer personal intimacy than a mere weekly meeting in class allowed." [1]

The Church by participating energetically in the rescue work felt that they were also rescuing themselves. The necessity of justifying the existence of organized religion by doing good works, not by faith alone, was the principle which helped to shape the Evangelicals and the Christian Socialists, the Young Men's Christian Association in 1844, the Young Women's Christian Association in 1855, later still Toc H in 1919. Thus these organizations found in social problems a field for their activities, in the educational needs of the fourteen to eighteen group, slums and unemployment.[2] Moreover, by taking part in and supplying the moral principles of such social work, organized religion secured new adherents. This motive was strongest with Nonconformist and Church of England youth organizations. The first, the Boys' Brigade, was founded in Glasgow in 1883 by Sir William Smith, who wished to promote the "advancement of Christ's Kingdom among boys." The Church of England Lads' Brigades followed much later in 1891; the corresponding girls' organizations, the Girls' Friendly Society in 1876, Girls' Guildry in 1900, and

---

[1] Russell, *op. cit.*, p. 8.
[2] Viz., the title of a pamphlet by the Archbishop of York: *The Wageless: A Social Asset*, or that of V. S. Hoyland, *Digging with the Unemployed*, S.C.M. Press.

the Girls' Life Brigade in 1902. "Each Brigade company was and is attached to some place of worship, and attendance at a Bible class was and is compulsory."[1]

Religious policy is less dominant and less strict in the Boys' Clubs, in which, on the whole, the recreation of their members was always more in the foreground than the measures for their moral education. However, if not religious instruction, the religious "spirit" is one of the corner stones of the Club Movement. A club leader stated: ". . . the proper relationship between manager and member is that of brotherhood. . . . This can only be achieved through the recognition and worshipping together the same Father."[2]

Another one deplores the fact that: "Very few boys have the opportunity of praying in their crowded homes. Club prayers provide that opportunity. Through short talks, not only on religion but policy, the club policy can be instilled into the boys!"[3]

The warden of the Brighton Boys' Clubs holds that sport is the best avenue to religion. ". . . it must surely impress the smaller lads in the Club when they see the Club's finest boxer taking the litany at the Club service, and the captain of the football team reading the lesson, and the winner of the billiard championship announcing the hymns."[4]

Thus "religious spirit" and "club spirit" are regarded as mutually supporting each other, and the essence of the first has been very clearly defined by Russell, who was one of the pioneers of the movement and who has, in conjunction with his wife, written its

---

[1] *New Survey of London*, vol. ix. p. 141.
[2] Reported by Russell, *op. cit.*, p. 167.
[3] *Ibid.*, p. 164. [4] *Ibid.*, p. 158.

standard handbook. "Tell the boys the truth that the Christian life is hard and difficult, not enjoyment in this sense, but sacrifice, sometimes humiliation in the eyes of the world, a voluntary daily seeking and bearing of the Cross."

To make such ideas acceptable, and the attempt has by no means been neglected in recent years, a more complex system of values, of symbols, and of organization had to be developed than was set up by the founders of these institutions. The aim of rescuing poor boys from the evil of the street, the "penny-gaffs" and the public-house with the help of religious influence, was superseded by more positive objectives.

The youth organizations more and more turned to inculcating special behaviour-patterns amongst their members. It had at the outset been stressed by the founders of clubs that boys who worked all day long were badly in need of opportunities for playing indoor and outdoor games. Indeed, Russell puts "Recreation" as the first object of the club, "the direct benefit of the boy rather than that conferred on the community by the removal of turbulent elements."[1] It was held that recreation was best calculated to protect boys from evil influences, and at the same time recreation should be the chief means of educating them.[2] "To brighten young lives and to make good citizens"[3] is, for

---

[1] *Ibid.*, p. 14.
[2] "The movement, if it is to be a movement, must express an ideal which will become progressively clear to boys, to club leaders and to the public alike. A club is not an institution to keep boys off the streets by providing them with indoor amusements and outdoor athletics. It has a very positive end in view, and its amusements and athletics are only the means by which that end can be achieved. Its aims are twofold, to raise the standard of fitness for life and to create good citizenship." The National Association of Boys' Clubs, *Principles and Aims of the Boys' Club Movement*, p. 19.
[3] Salford Lads' Club.

instance, the object of one club, and that of another,[1] "to provide a bright and pleasant place in which working lads and young men may spend their spare time with profit and pleasure; and to exert every possible influence for their moral elevation." It became necessary to elaborate the notion of citizenship and the code of morals which should form the basis of club life.

That working boys were utterly unprovided for in their spare time was first realized by clergymen and influential citizens in industrial towns. In the work they undertook to remedy this state of affairs they were financially supported by and dependent on rich landowners, manufacturers and, in general, people with money.[2] In the attempts they made to attract and to educate the boys they had, therefore, to reckon with two different attitudes, those of the patrons and those of the patronized.

Boys from factories and workshops resent everything which recalls school; they do not wish to be educated. They are realistic, they wish to have freedom, independence and an outlet for their energies. On the other hand, patrons do not want to provide these boys merely with amusement, they want to educate them according to the standards of their own education, that is to say, according to the ideals of the Public School. The Boys' Clubs have become a "truly British institution,"[3] by reconciling these two apparently conflicting aims.

---

[1] The Proctor Gymnasium and Hulme Lads' Club, Manchester.
[2] Their relationship with Public Authorities is only recent. See p. 208.
[3] *E.g.*, "The real rules of a club lie in an unwritten tradition formed by the club and preserved by its members." *Aims and Principles, op. cit.*, p. 14.

One idea soon helped in combining them; the idea of the club as a community, or of team spirit, fellowship, brotherhood as it was and is called in subsequent youth organizations. To inculcate group loyalty amongst members was the chief administrative necessity. By this means alone could some sort of discipline be achieved which, especially in the very early clubs, *e.g.*, in the Working Lads' Institute and Home, founded 1870 in Whitechapel, and in the Hulme Boys' Club, founded 1886 in Manchester, was seriously lacking.[1] The club could benefit only boys who were not too irregular in their attendance or too disorderly. Through group loyalty only could a system of internal government be carried out which was neither totalitarian nor democratic, in which the "leader" gives the orders and makes the decisions, whilst the boys, nevertheless, feel that they have some say in the matter.

"There should be just enough emphasis on the word 'boys' to make it clear that self-government in a Boys' Club is self-government under control and always with inspiration."[2] There should be no difficulty, since "any adolescent boy is quick at recognizing the natural leader, and will follow his leadership so long as it is given in a spirit of co-operation and not of condescension."[3]

Moreover, the idea of group loyalty is inherent both in street gangs and in Public Schools, the Boys' Club has the task of transforming the objectives of the one into the objectives of the other. "The gang . . . is a natural social unit; what has to be done is to direct the spirit of the gang towards a constructive and

---

[1] See Russell, p. 9.   [2] *Principles and Aims, op. cit.*, p. 16.
[3] *Ibid.*, p. 18.

socially useful end. The gang spirit repressed is often a nuisance and a danger. Expressed, it may become a social force of the first importance."[1] It is found that "boys as they grow up want to form societies of their own for the expression of like tastes or the pursuit of some agreed end—a team, gang or 'click,' such a society evokes loyalty. A member of it accepts leadership and will obey rules agreed upon for safety or success. . . . The strength of the appeal to comradeship lies in its being absolutely natural and almost universal, it brings vast numbers of boys into the clubs, unselfconscious and ready to be their natural selves. Its weakness lies in the danger that it may end where it begins, leading nowhere and getting nothing done."[2]

That this weakness be overcome "the club movement must then adopt a definitely patriotic national aim,"[3] which is expressed in terms and fostered with methods almost identical with those of the Public School. Thus we are told that "the club itself will create an influence and a collective personality of its own. This club personality has first to be created. It has afterwards to be perpetuated. It becomes in time the club spirit and tradition which, more than any individual personality, must be the real influence for good in the club. The club leader himself embodies it."[4] And just as in the school so in the club, "games must be used . . . to foster the growth of the team spirit that will shape not only his (the

---

[1] *Principles and Aims, op. cit.*, pp. 6 and 19 : " The club as an organization appeals quite simply and directly to two natural instincts which are peculiarly strong in the adolescent. These are the instinct for play and the instinct for comradeship. The combination of these two instincts calls forth a corporate activity for the common weal ; and the boy is taught to use them in the club so that in manhood he can put them to the service of the nation."
[2] *Ibid.*, p. 13.   [3] *Ibid.*, p. 14.   [4] *Ibid.*, p. 9.

boy's) play, but his whole life. Through the team spirit, new moral and social values may be given to every 'recreational' activity in a club ... games themselves must be so organized that they will teach boys to 'play the game'—at home, and in the workshop, as well as in the club, a boy who has learnt to play the game for the game's sake, to play for his side rather than for himself, to be a good loser and a good winner —generous in defeat and modest in victory—to accept a decision in the right spirit, to be chivalrous and unselfish, and ready to serve others—such a boy has indeed a good start on the road of life. To help boys to learn how to play the game in this sense is the club's task, and club sport must be organized to this end."[1] The great promise for success is that "keenness, sportsmanship, fair play, friendship—all these are inherent in British boys; reliability, unselfishness, persistence, and many other qualities which come of nurture rather than nature, have to be inculcated by practice when the club has given the natural qualities of boyhood freedom of expression and encouragement."[2]

The club leaders, therefore, set themselves consciously the object of building up an institution which "must do for the working boy what the public school has done for the privileged boy."[3] This side of the work is stressed whenever the movement appeals to the public, that is to say, to its actual and potential patrons. *The Times* said in a leading article [4]: "The purpose of the boys' club is the same as that of the private and the public school—to make the boys want

---

[1] *Ibid.*, p. 10.
[2] *Ibid.*, p. 10.
[3] Henriques, Basil, *Club Leadership.*
[4] 4th May 1937.

to exercise and develop body and mind by doing things for themselves and doing them the best way. That desire—in the schools very largely the result of tradition and environment—must depend for the poor boys on the personal influence of the men who take charge of their leisure. And that influence can best be exerted —perhaps, can only be exerted—within a voluntary association like a boys' club."

Similarly, Annual Reports of clubs and their federations stress this note. "Your sons," says such a report,[1] addressing its subscribers, "sheltered by the traditions and privileges of some great school, pass those malleable years building bodies, broadening and deepening minds, laying foundations of character for the demands of the future. The sons of Bermondsey spend them in long working hours on tricycle or van, in factory or workshop...." But "... the gulf which place and circumstance make is accidental and the spirit may easily and victoriously bridge it. Here, in Bermondsey, was something very like a part of Oxford—achieved not by a welter of lavish apparatus or noble buildings, but by a vigorous and assured positivity of spirit. There are plenty of clubs better equipped, with more ground, more houses and more money to play with; but here was the right stuff out of which is made, in youth, the background for satisfactory living. The only analogy for any grown man is with his own youth. If you think of your own school or university, of the best times you had there, of the best friends you made, of the best —because the most intangible and elusive—experiences you knew, and good times and friends and experience

[1] Annual Report of the *Oxford and Bermondsey Club*, 1936.

are what these clubs, over many years, have been giving to these Bermondsey boys.

The connection with Oxford is strong and the likeness is strong."[1]

This 'likeness' is fostered by bringing as often as possible the club members in direct contact with Public School life and its pupils. Almost every big school runs a club,[2] and "at both Oxford and Cambridge Universities there are organizations which are concerned in advancing the Club movement."[3] Outings for club boys to the great schools and to the old universities are arranged, various camps provide opportunities "that may otherwise not occur, for boys from public and secondary schools to meet and make friends with boys from clubs,"[4] and the Jubilee Trust has even enabled six club boys to join the Public Schools Exploring Expedition. "It is satisfactory to know that the leaders of the Expedition were well pleased with their conduct."[5] We are told that through these methods "Class feeling becomes absurd in boys' clubs where Public School and University men come not merely to 'run' or manage them, but to enter fully into their life, regardless of class, wealth or education. Clubs are not places where the rich and highly educated satisfy their conscience by good works. They are

[1] *Ibid.*; this quotation comes from an article reprinted in the report, which originally appeared in *The Evening News* on 19th June 1936.

[2] Another example of this co-operation is, for instance, the fact that at the Annual Conference for Club Leaders, 1937, the principal address was given by Mr. Spencer Leeson, Headmaster of Winchester College, on "English Education and the Boys' Club Movement."

[3] Annual Report, National Association of Boys' Clubs, 1932-33.

[4] Annual Report, Lancashire and Cheshire Association of Boys' Clubs, 1936-37.

[5] Annual Report, N.A.B.C., 1937. It is there also reported that "Seven club boys were present at the Olympic Games as the guests of the German Government, their travelling expenses being paid by the Jubilee Trust, which was responsible for the whole organization of the party."

places where fullness of life can be found by sharing interests and occupations."[1] On the other hand, Russell,[2] the pioneer of the movement, came to the conclusion that "the Public School boy is almost trained at the Public School to look upon a boys' club as a charity or mission, and therefore the healthy-minded boy is very often anything but attracted to the club which is run by his school. He has to pay a subscription to it every term or every year, and that is the end of it. But even that is better than that he should patronize his school's club. . . . The very idea of 'helping' in a club is wrong."

"The patriotic, national aim" which the Club Movement wishes to foster has been given a special name, "the Gospel of Fitness."[3] "To the club it must always mean the fitness of the whole boy for complete manhood. Boys themselves will interpret it according to their needs and opportunities. Club leaders will develop it along the lines most natural to themselves. It can be applied simply to any of the objectives which any club with a purpose has in view. With equal simplicity it lends itself to interpretation in its physical, mental and moral aspects. . . . If it is possible to crystallize the practice and ideals of the clubs into a single word, that word is Fitness. But it must be fully interpreted. So interpreted and so understood it might be gloriously inscribed on the banner under which every club boy would fight the battles of adolescence and win his way to manhood." And finally, it is stated that "the fitness which is inculcated and provided for is presenting itself . . .

[1] *Principles and Aims, op. cit.*, p. 18.   [2] Russell, *op. cit.*, p. 52.
[3] *Principles and Aims, op. cit.*, p. 14.

to the public as an incentive to provide more and better clubs in order to build up a fitter race. A nation of fitness, fit to play its part, in the empire and the world." [1]

The aims of the Boys' Clubs, Fellowship and Fitness, are shared by all other youth movements, although each gives them a different expression. The Boys' Clubs are more free from religious symbolism, "make-believe," discipline, militarism and leader-worship than any other. They are based on play and group loyalty in its simplest and most natural forms. They cater predominantly for one age group, the fourteen to eighteen years old, and for one social group, boys in factories and workshops. Whatever may be the language of the Annual Reports, life in the clubs themselves is largely ruled by common sense. Adolescent boys go there because they wish to have company, to play games, to indulge in hobbies and perhaps even because they are, subconsciously, searching for some stable interest. Boys of that age do not much frequent

---

[1] The scheme for " Fitness " may also be quoted from the same source : " The following is a simple scheme showing how the term ' Fitness ' in its physical, mental and moral significance can be applied to some of the objects of club life :

A. *Fitness for Citizenship:*
    1. Physical—Healthy habits and interest in questions of public health.
    2. Mental—Fairmindedness, tolerance, independence of mind.
    3. Moral—Team spirit, brotherliness and patriotism.

B. *Fitness for Manhood:*
    1. Physical—Self-control.
    2. Mental—Sympathy and fairness.
    3. Moral—Understanding of true love and false.

C. *Fitness for Work:*
    1. Physical—Energy.
    2. Mental—Skill and enterprise.
    3. Moral—Conscientiousness.

In a similar way the term ' Fitness ' can be applied to other phases of life, *e.g.*, Fitness for home, for play, for service, for leadership, etc., etc." *Ibid.*, pp. 10, 11, 20.

public-houses. They are convinced that they are grown up and no more in need of education, so much so that they hesitate for a while after they have left school before they join any organization which is designed for young people. "The club age group of fourteen to fifteen is small and indicates a lapse of time between leaving school and joining a club." [1]

But not all of them are completely absorbed by their interest in girls, although for many there are only two things in the world which count—girls and bicycles.[2] There is no doubt, therefore, that an institution such as the Boys' Clubs has a most important and most valuable function to fulfil.

On the other hand, there seems no inherent reason why it can exist only as a voluntary organization, maintained by the grants of private individuals. "We may observe," says Russell,[3] "that there is nothing that a boy resents more than the imputation, however delicately hinted, that in becoming a member of a lads' club he is in any way becoming a recipient of 'charity.' Those responsible for the management of clubs should do all in their power to justify and to foster this feeling. In general the members do pay a very fair proportion of the cost of their clubs, and sometimes considerably more than half the cost of their annual encampment."

It is true, of course, that boys of that age, who receive their first wages in factories and workshops, are unable either to provide or to maintain solely by their own contributions the equipment they need for

---

[1] *New Survey of London*, vol. ix. p. 167.
[2] This direction of interests was clearly shown in the accounts of their free time given by the twenty lads, see Chapter II, p. 84.
[3] Russell, *op. cit.*, p. 52.

their sports and for their hobbies. The principle of financial support from outside is, therefore, recognized by any club at the outset. "There are hardly any federated clubs that make even a pretence of being self-supporting." [1]

Russell [2] says on this point: "It is with deep regret that we must state that the discrepancy between boys' payments and total expenditure is, as a rule, most marked in clubs which make the spiritual welfare of their members the most conspicuous goal of their efforts. The thought inevitably suggests itself that either boys cannot be induced to pay much for the privilege of belonging to what is called a religious club, or that the managers in the zeal for the winning of souls overlook the importance of preserving a spirit of independence among their members."

At present each federated club is autonomous, "headquarters both for London and the United Kingdom can only act in an advisory capacity," [3] and it relies very much on the financial support of local influential people. Similarly, it is dependent on the supply of local voluntary leaders, leisured men, the clergy, rotarians, members of Toc H, of Public Schools and sometimes even of Rover packs. Yet leaders are very scarce and local financial support insufficient. It is more and more realized that club managers need to have a special training for their task, but under the present system the clubs cannot afford this. Of 1,500 club leaders there are only 120 "professionals," *i.e.*, they are paid for full-time work,[4] and some of

---
[1] *The New Survey of London*, vol. ix. p. 159.
[2] Russell, *op. cit.*, p. 54.   [3] *The New London Survey*, vol. ix. p. 158.
[4] I am indebted to the N.A.B.C. for this and other information in the following pages.

them do not run one club only but have to look after a small group of clubs. So far, only short training courses are provided by the National Association of Boys' Clubs, week-end courses and an annual ten days' training course; more intensive instruction is arranged individually by referring the person concerned for a certain time to a club. "Nearly every club we have seen is more or less under-staffed, and is glad to accept the help of almost anyone who is willing to give it, without preliminary inquisition into any special capacity for the task." [1]

Such a situation makes it more and more necessary for clubs and their federations to appeal to and co-operate with public authorities.[2] The trained personnel of the Evening Institutes take charge, under some schemes of special activities in clubs. The N.A.B.C. has during the last year received substantial grants from the Commissioner for the Special Areas in order to establish new clubs, and it is hoped that more help will be forthcoming from the Physical Fitness Campaign.[3] However, whilst from this money capital grants have been made to clubs, considerable portions of it have been used to extend the existing administrative staff, to appoint new organizing secretaries at county and national headquarters, so that attempts to gain the financial support of private people can

---

[1] Russell, *op. cit.*, p. 55.

[2] Local Authorities had, under the Education Act, 1921, Section 86, power to assist clubs in various ways. For further details see Appendix, Chapter V.

[3] Well-known charitable Trusts have equally supported the Boys' Club Movement, *e.g.*, £25,000 have been given by the Jubilee Trust during 1936-37, and the Carnegie United Kingdom Trust, who continually assists, has made a special library grant to clubs, of which 480 groups, including also some Scout Troops and Brigade Companies, have so far availed themselves.

be intensified.¹ And such efforts have, in fact, been successful.² However, the student of social administration is puzzled by the position which has thus arisen. Government departments and local authorities assist a voluntary organization. Yet by doing so they do not gain control. Some of their money is even spent in securing new private supporters who, through being in direct contact with the federations, are in a position, if they wish, to exercise influence. In other words, public money is used to make the organization more "voluntary" than ever. Moreover, this state of affairs is by no means confined to the Boys' Clubs, it exists, at present, in the whole sphere of voluntary social service in this country. At least so far as the Boys' Clubs are concerned the position might as well be reversed. Existing voluntary help might be pooled by Government departments and by local authorities and employed to the fullest measure under their control.

Local authorities have already given examples of what they are able to do. Institutes of Leisure, Youth Community Centres on New Housing Estates and the Men's Junior Institutes, represent a compromise between

---

[1] See also *The British Social Services*, PEP (London, 1937), p. 174. 'It is of considerable interest to observe that while the public services tend more openly to borrow from voluntary experience and personnel, an opposite tendency is visible in the growth of a salaried bureaucracy of the voluntary services. According to the 1931 Census, persons employed by social welfare societies in England and Wales had almost reached 10,000, and the category in which they were included showed an increase of no less than 84 per cent. since 1921. These voluntary societies by 1931 could offer paid employment to as many persons as the blast furnaces, or as the manufacture of linoleum, of butter and cheese and condensed milk or of explosives. Evidently the salaried staff of the voluntary social services is still growing, and its influence is increasing in spite of the expansion in the personnel of the public social services which is also taking place. We must therefore anticipate some convergence in points of view.'

[2] See Annual Report, 1937, N.A.B.C., p. 3.

evening instruction and recreation. The principle that the "adolescent needs different fare," that he must be educated by means different from those employed at the Elementary Schools has been established.[1] With him recreation and instruction have to be combined.

This achievement may be ascribed to the Club Movement. Its present extension is due mainly to the "new social spirit" of the late nineteenth century, the War-time concern with increasing juvenile delinquency and the present interest in National Fitness. The oldest club whose history has been recorded was established in 1876;[2] eleven years later there already existed in London a number of unrelated clubs which linked themselves together in the London Federation of Boys' Clubs. New clubs were founded all over the country. When the increase of juvenile delinquency during the War caused public alarm it was Russell "who . . . suggested to the Home Secretary that the solution of the problem lay, not in the opening of further reformatory and industrial schools but in stimulating the organizations working amongst boys and girls. . . . The boy, his imagination fired and anxious to do deeds of daring, must be given legitimate opportunity for his adventurous spirit. So the Home Secretary called together representatives of the Clubs, Scouts, Guides, Brigades and similar bodies to form

---

[1] The strong dislike against schooling expressed by so many adolescents as soon as they start work is one extremely disquieting aspect of their whole condition. It arises from several sources. They have gained a spurious freedom (Chapter II, p. 86) and so resent restrictions which are imposed. They can perceive little utility, now that they are away from school, in the knowledge which was there given to them. Therefore, why be bothered further with such a place? Thirdly, it may be, although this is probably the least operative factor, the method of education was inefficient.

[2] But clubs were certainly in existence in London and Manchester from 1850 onwards.

the Home Office Juvenile Organizations Committee,[1] with Russell as chairman, to assist him in dealing with the problem. An investigation made by this committee into the history of the acts of delinquency of 7,000 youngsters in five large industrial centres clearly proved that in the lack of opportunity for self-expression in the dark winter evenings and the leisure time of the week-end lay the root cause of this increase in delinquency. So this committee called for further activity from the organization."[2]

At present there are 77 Juvenile Organization Committees in England and Wales, and Youth Organizations, with the exception of the Brigades, have all gained ground. The number of clubs in the United Kingdom has grown markedly in recent years.

Year.	No. of Clubs.	No. of Members.
1926-27	679	79,284
1937-38	1,500	150,000

REGIONAL DISTRIBUTION OF BOYS' CLUBS AND SCOUTS

Districts.	Clubs.				Scouts.	
	Clubs.		Members.			
	No.	Per Cent.	No.	Per Cent.	No.	Per Cent.
London and Home Counties	540	47	29,619	33	160,182	45
Eastern Counties	14	1	4,235	5	13,021	3
Lancashire and Cheshire	198	18	25,188	28	52,424	15
Eastern Midland	24	2	2,030	2	18,483	5
Western Midland	228	19	15,949	18	39,774	11
South-Western Counties	48	4	2,973	3	20,507	6
Northern Rural and Yorkshire	47	4	5,628	6	35,669	10
Northumberland and Durham	56	5	4,490	5	18,228	5
Total, England	1,155	100	90,112	100	358,288	100
Wales	64	—	5,713	—	16,841	—
Ireland	1	—	42	—	9,229	—
Scotland	86	—	7,749	—	55,134	—
GRAND TOTAL	1,306	—	103,616	—	439,442	—

[1] The Central Juvenile Organizations Committee was actually formed by the Home Office in 1918; it was later transferred as an advisory committee to the Board of Education. [2] Russell, *op. cit.*, p. 13.

London accounts for one-third of all members in England, and Lancashire for more than one-quarter, whilst the Table, for 1936-37, shows that the Scouts are also strongest in the same two districts.

Moreover, there are scores of non-federated clubs in the United Kingdom,[1] people know of their existence, but nobody can estimate their number. They are church clubs, gamble clubs, street clubs, some might equally well be described as gangs, and all, except the church clubs, have arisen spontaneously. Thus their existence testifies that young people need social organizations and wish them to be as independent and informal as possible.

Neither the Brigades nor the Scouts respond to this particular need, and, moreover, neither of them caters largely for this particular group. The "essential method" of the Brigades is, in the words of the *New Survey of London*,[2] "the combination of religious training with military drill and discipline." Bible classes, weekly parades and drills are the main activities undertaken. "The Movement sets little store by recreation as such."[3] The founder, Sir William Smith,

---

[1] The National Association of Boys' Clubs, which was formed in 1923, has laid down the following conditions of affiliation. Any club can affiliate which:
  (i) Has headquarters.
  (ii) Charges a membership subscription.
  (iii) Has a membership which comprises at least fifteen boys between the ages of fourteen and eighteen.
  (iv) Has a responsible head and committee of management.
  (v) Meets at least twice a week.
  (vi) To open at all reasonable times to be visited by an accredited officer of the Association.

Old Boys' Clubs can also be affiliated if they are "directly related to a boys' club, and wholly or mainly recruited therefrom."

Thus the smallest federated clubs have fifteen members; the largest club in England, with a membership of 3,542, is in Norwich.

[2] Vol. ix. p. 145.   [3] *Ibid.*, p. 145.

had insisted that "Christ wants the whole boy as a boy." The "promotion of habits of Obedience, Reverence, Discipline, Self-respect and all that tends towards a true Christian manliness," was his goal. He stated, in an address to the Scottish National Sabbath School Convention, 1887, that "Boys are inherently fond of soldiering and drill, and we decided to take hold of this fact and use it for Christ."[1]

The Church of England followed his example in 1891 and founded the Church Lads' Brigade, which perhaps emphasized military symbolism more than the Nonconformist organization. They wish to foster the development in boys of the "principle of patriotism and good citizenship during peace," and to train them "in the event of a national war to take their places in defence of their homes and country." And, indeed, from 1911 to 1930 the Church Lads' Brigade was recognized by the War Office as a cadet unit; it had a heavy death-roll during the War. After the Armistice, however, there followed "a reaction against anything of a military appearance and against organized religion. From these reactions the Brigade movements . . . naturally suffered,"[2] and they have not since recovered the ground lost.

In the meantime another youth movement which had evolved its own symbolism had grown. The Scouts and their activities are too well known to need detailed description. Founded in 1908 by Baden Powell, "it differs in method rather than in object from the movements that had preceded it."[3] It also aims at educating "the whole boy" by appealing primarily to his spirit

---

[1] Quoted in *New Survey of London*, vol. ix. p. 141.
[2] *Ibid.*, p. 144. [3] *Ibid.*, p. 165.

of adventure. "It is expected that every Scout shall belong to some religious denomination and attend its services."

"Every boy on being enrolled as a Scout, makes the following promise: [1]

"On my Honour I promise that I will do my best to do my duty to God and the King. To help other people at all times. To obey the Scout Law."

The organization of Scouts, with its combination of local autonomy and central supervision, is more elaborate and more unified than that of any other youth movement. However, the total number of Scouts has been steadily declining in recent years. It is mainly "the very poor percentage of First Class Scouts in this country" [2] which has worried the headquarters commissioners. "From evidence that has reached me during this year from widely separate sources it would appear that we are not making sufficient effort to discover the wishes of the boy, and having dicovered them, shape our programmes accordingly." [3]

Numbers had been increasing from 1918 to 1933, but since then there has been a steady falling off in all ranks. This may be due to the fewer births during the War years, it may be due to deeper causes. The present position is indicated by the following summary: [4]

---

[1] Wolf Cubs make this promise :
>   I promise to do my best ;
>   To do my duty to God and the King ;
>   To keep the Law of the Wolf Cub Pack ;
>   And to do a good turn to somebody every day.

The Cub Law
The cub gives in to the Old Wolf ; the Cub does not give in to himself.

[2] *The Boy Scouts' Year Book*, and 28th Annual Report, 1935-36.
[3] *Ibid.*, p. 18. [4] See Scout Census, 1937, for the complete statistics.

	Cubs and Scouts.	Commissioners and Officers.
England	312,016	20,492
Scotland	48,298	2,083
Wales	11,845	1,501
Ireland	8,020	421
Total	380,179	24,497

In addition to the above there are 38,779 Scouters, giving a Grand Total of 443,455, all ranks, in 10,771 groups.

More than half of all groups are "controlled," *i.e.*, in direct touch with a religious organization.

The Scout movement is more concerned with boys of school age than with adolescents.[1]

Section.	Age Group.	Number in 1937.
Cubs	8–11	147,882
Scouts	11–18	201,103
Rover Scouts	18 and more	31,194

It has this feature in common with the Brigades.[2] Similarly, the social complexion of both Scout troops and Brigade companies is predominantly that of non-manual workers, whilst the Clubs are recruited mostly from poorer boys. The make-believe and symbolism of these organizations certainly appeal to young people whose childhood lasts longer than their actual physical growing up.[3] Moreover, this symbolism, with its uniforms and its rule that local groups should be self-

---

[1] However, all youth movements were at first concerned with elder boys. Junior organizations were started by the Church Lads' Brigade in 1912, by the Scouts in 1916, and by the Boys' Brigade in 1920.

[2] "Scouts and Brigades in fact cater for younger boys than clubs." *New Survey of London*, vol. ix. p. 165.

[3] "Scouting is really based on an exceedingly acute appreciation of pre-adolescent boyhood." *New Survey of London*, vol. ix. p. 63. At the same time it should be stressed that an enormous amount depends upon the local scoutmaster and officers. "Dens" have been visited where the attitude has been admirable, completely rational and humanistic, in fact strongly pacifist.

supporting, is expensive. Poor boys can neither afford the romantic emotions, nor the discipline nor the shillings which it requires. Whilst, therefore, 124 out of 187 Public Schools had Scouts in 1936,[1] there are comparatively few groups in the poorer London districts. The *New Survey of London* has established that this is also true for the Brigades. "It appears that in the inner ring of boroughs a greater number of boys over school age are in clubs than in brigades or scout troops and probably about as many as in the two together."[2] Their sample enquiry into the occupations and the educational record of members of youth organizations which is, unfortunately, the only one of its kind, brings out the same point.[3]

Whilst the Clubs have the smallest number of boys engaged in clerical work or still at school, they have a surprisingly high number of members who are doing skilled manual work. Of all Club members 62·7 per cent. are either still at school, are black-coated or skilled workers. Hence, it seems that even the population of the Clubs is not really as representative of working-class adolescents as is commonly assumed. On the contrary, this and other evidence point rather to the conclusion that a select group of boys from their respective districts join the Clubs. At the same time, however, the membership of the Scouts and the Brigades is certainly even more selected.[4]

---

[1] *The Boy Scouts' Year Book, op. cit.*, p. 31, where it is also stated that ". . . in the case of the Public Schools the necessity for propaganda decreases as there are comparatively few Public Schools without Scouts left, and in many of these cases we have only to wait for a change of Headmaster."

[2] *New Survey of London*, vol. ix. p. 162.

[3] *Ibid.*, p. 194, see also on the same page the Table of the proportions in the different movements of members who continued their education after fourteen years of age.

[4] *Ibid.*, p. 194.

We may conclude that none of the three major youth movements in this country have so far attracted the bulk of young people who come from artisan homes. Only the Clubs touch considerable numbers of the working youths and are primarily concerned with the fourteen to eighteen group. None of these organizations really deserves the name "Youth Movement," in the sense that the German Youth Movement prior to the War deserved it, since none has been started and developed entirely by youth itself. The Clubs have a philanthropic, the Brigades a religious and militaristic basis, and the Scouts one which, in a peculiarly modern way, is a mixture of all three ingredients, adding deliberate educational purpose. Each one of them wants "the whole boy," their philosophy centering around Fitness and Fellowship. The local autonomy of their groups is combined by the Brigades and Clubs with attachment to a national organization, whilst loyalty to the leaders and the leader is the principle which unites all Scouts. Since all these movements are voluntary and depend financially on private benefactors, very little sound information is available about their work. The occupations and the educational records of their members are never referred to in their Annual Reports, nor the fluctuation of membership and the frequency of attendances.[1] The patrons and the officials take their aims for granted, hence it does not occur to them to undertake an inquiry

---

[1] This acceptance of the aims of youth organizations is so well established amongst their personnel that even the otherwise very comprehensive survey of *Youth and Leisure*, see p. 221, does not deal with either of the two points referred to above, which are so vital to the subject. The question of fluctuation of membership is not mentioned, whilst that of the occupations of club members is occasionally hinted at, but no attempt is made to summarize the position.

into the actual impact of their activities. No questions can be asked in Parliament about their use of the public money they have received, nor can Ratepayers' Associations write their customary polite letters requesting information. This absence of an opportunity to scrutinize from time to time the work of these organizations and their lack of spirit of self-criticism are the most conspicuous deficiencies at present.

The other organizations for youth and leisure hold to the same principles and display the same features. The Y.M.C.A. steadily developed from 1844, when it was founded, and has flourished since 1882, the year its National Council was established. Religion has been the basis of its varied and comprehensive programme. "It is the Association's ultimate task to represent the Lord of all Life to every boy and man within its reach as their Lord and Master, and to prepare for and look for the coming of His Kingdom." [1] To-day the Y.M.C.A. runs hostels, amongst them are five hostels for transferred juveniles, housing 220 boys, Scout Troops, "the British Boys for British Farms" scheme, Military Centres, Clubs for Boys and the unemployed, and Holiday Camps. In 1935,[2] "40,000 boys have come under the direct influence of the Association." [3] In 1937 sixty-one of the Y.M.C.A.'s Boys' Clubs, the Red Triangle Clubs, which had a

---

[1] *Fitness for What?* The Annual Report of the National Council of Y.M.C.A., 1937, p. 43. In 1885 the first international conference of Y.M.C.A., which took place in Paris, adopted this " Charter that binds together the National Unions in the World's Alliance of Young Men's Christian Associations :—' Young Men's Christian Associations seek to unite those young men who, regarding Jesus Christ as their God and Saviour according to the Holy Scriptures, desire to be His disciples in their doctrine and in their life, and to associate their efforts for the extension of His Kingdom amongst other young men.' "

[2] This is, unfortunately, the last year for which such figures are available.

[3] Annual Report, 1937, p. 43.

membership of 8,173, were affiliated to the N.A.B.C. "The club method is time honoured in Association practice. Keep-fit classes have been held for fifty years in the Y.M.C.A. and are attended now by more than 30,000 boys and men." [1] It seems, however, according to reports from social workers that, apart from such special schemes as those for unemployed and transferred boys, the Y.M.C.A. deals mainly with elder youths of the black-coated type. Russell holds that "the two castes, for such they really are, do not readily mix, and as a rule few young men will transfer their allegiance to a typical branch of the Y.M.C.A. when they become too old for a boys' club in a poor district." [2] Thus the impact of the Y.M.C.A. lies certainly, at present, much more in its tackling of special social work, such as care of the unemployed, provision of hostels and holiday camps, than in its guidance of industrial youths in their leisure time. Perhaps more than with other youth movements there appears to be in the Y.M.C.A. and the Y.W.C.A. a spirit of open-mindedness and enquiry.

Toc H, a recent religious movement of War origin, which was re-established in 1919, is primarily concerned with young men above adolescent age. It is an organization, with a rich store of symbolism, attracting primarily black-coated workers. "The headings of the Four Points of the Toc H Compass—a simple summary of its purposes and plans"—are:

1. Fellowship: "To Love Widely."
2. Service: "To Build Bravely."
3. Fairmindedness: "To Think Fairly."
4. The Kingdom of God: "To Witness Humbly." [3]

---

[1] Annual Report, 1937, p. 39.   [2] Russell, *op. cit.*, p. 234.
[3] This and the following quotations come from the Annual Report, 1937, or from a pamphlet headed "Facts for New Friends of Toc H."

"Toc H believes that the sickness of the world is due to the fact that men do not understand the minds, lives and needs of their fellows; this ignorance Toc H seeks to destroy by active thinking and active doing." Hence, Toc H acts "as an auxiliary force of manpower for the recognized social services," undertaking among other tasks "leadership and comradeship of boys and younger men in clubs, camps, classes and Scout groups."

Toc H, therefore, assists voluntary societies; it runs hostels and clubs for boys, it provides, in short, the "cadets" for these youth organizations. Toc H itself "is no mass movement. It is essentially a personal affair, and it grows slowly because it depends on individual example and conviction." Young men from sixteen upwards are eligible for membership, which totals, at present, approximately 30,000.[1] One leader, "Tubby," presides over the movement, which is thus linked together, although its Marks and branches have a good deal of independence.[2] "While Toc H, where it has become firmly established, is steadily learning to bear an increased part of the cost of the necessary Staff, it has been and still is true that much pioneering work is only made possible by the discerning support of men and women who cannot themselves take active part, but help Toc H because they believe in it. These friends become Toc H builders and make monthly or yearly payments."

Not only the "whole boy" but also "the whole girl" is developed by youth organizations in this country.

---

[1] There exists also a sister organization, the Toc H League of Women Helpers.

[2] In 1937 there were 633 Toc H groups in the home counties and 278 overseas.

The girl groups are so similar in aims and methods to those of the boys that they do not deserve a special analysis.[1] With the exception of the Y.W.C.A., which was founded as early as 1855, and the Girls' Friendly Society, which began its activities in 1875, they were all established at the beginning of the twentieth century, most of them following the example of some "brother" movement. The girls were thought of later than the boys, for industrial employment was less frequent amongst them and they included far fewer "turbulent elements"; their organizations, however, were centralized at an earlier date. The National Council of Girls' Clubs was formed in 1909, whilst the National Association of Boys' Clubs came into existence only in 1923. The former is mainly the Federative Agency of existing National Societies, whilst the latter maintains its own extensive organization.

Centralization and unification of Girls' Societies was undertaken so early because the major aim and guiding principle was the same for all of them. Religion plays an even greater rôle with them than with the boys' organizations, and it was this community of outlook which provided a basis for co-operation.

Not only has each National Society dealing with girls adopted a religious motto, but also "in all the club unions affiliated to the N.C.G.C. Church clubs form a large proportion of the membership."[2] Religion, therefore, is an indispensable subject in the training scheme for club leadership which the National Council

---

[1] The more so since a very comprehensive survey of Girls' Organizations has recently been undertaken. See *Youth and Leisure*, Madeline Rooff, 1935.
[2] Rooff, *op. cit.*, p. 29.

of Girls' Clubs has developed. "In view of the importance of the religious basis of club work, a candidate, in order to qualify for a complete Diploma or Certificate, must have followed a course of study and practice arranged in co-operation with the Training Committee by the religious body to which she belongs, to which she will be referred immediately on registration. This body will endorse the Diploma or Certificate to the effect that the candidate has shown herself to be suitable, from the religious point of view, for club leadership. An incomplete Certificate may be granted to a candidate who omits this part of the training. Where a candidate has received training for inter-denominational work her Certificate may be endorsed by the Training Committee to that effect." [1]

Moreover, the churches themselves claim the allegiance of large numbers of young people.[2] "In many areas the week-night activities connected with the Sunday School provide the bulk of the opportunities for the leisure hours. The Sunday School Union works to develop the whole personality." [3]

Although the spiritual welfare of the girls is thus well cared for, not all age groups profit equally. Indeed the second major feature which distinguishes the "Sister" movement is the comparative neglect of the fourteen to eighteen group. In 1934 the total membership of the five national societies affiliated to the N.C.G.C.[4] was 229,576, divided as follows:

---

[1] Rooff, *op. cit.*, p. 104.
[2] No mention has so far been made, *e.g.*, of the Fellowships for young people which most of the local churches organize:
[3] Rooff, *op. cit.*, p. 33.
[4] These figures are extracted from *Youth and Leisure*, *op. cit.*, p. 237. The total membership of the N.C.G.C. at that date, including affiliated club-unions, was 271,387.

Under fourteen years old . .	86,611	girls.
Fourteen to eighteen . . .	45,707	,,
Eighteen and over . . .	97,258	,,

Whilst the Boys' Club movement is a deliberate attempt to attract working boys between fourteen and eighteen, no parallel can be found amongst the organizations catering for girls. Their primary concern, so far, has been with school children or young women past adolescence. Thus 75 per cent. of the members of the Girls' Friendly Society are over eighteen and most of those are domestic servants, whilst the Girls' Guildry, the Girls' Brigades, the Home Fire Girls and the Camp Fire Girls, and finally the Girl Guides, are primarily composed of juniors. Moreover, the clubs seem to do little to bridge over occupational differences.[1]

The Y.W.C.A., the organization which started Girls' Clubs in this country, the first being opened in Bristol in 1861,[2] also mainly provides for girls over sixteen. The social origin of its members is very varied.[3]

---

[1] " Some open clubs, where girls of all types make up the total membership, have, in practice, certain groups composed of one type of worker." Rooff, *op. cit.*, p. 80.

[2] The object of this club was " to provide the advantages, pleasures and safeguards of a Christian House for young women away from home influence and unprovided for in their houses of business." Quoted in *Our Eighty Years*, published 1935 by the Y.W.C.A. of Great Britain.

[3] The following percentage figures, published in the Y.W.C.A. Review, 1937, display the occupation represented in some Y.W.C.A. Centres :

ABERDEEN.—100 per cent. industrial.

BRIDGETON.—90 per cent. industrial, 10 per cent. domestic and business.

DAGENHAM.—90 per cent. industrial, 10 per cent. business.

DONCASTER.—10 per cent. business, 1 per cent. professional, 10 per cent. domestic, 25 per cent. industrial, 34 per cent. shops, 3 per cent. school, 5 per cent. home, 5 per cent. unemployed, 7 per cent. various.

GATESHEAD.—60 per cent. business.

LONDON CENTRAL.—31 per cent. business, 20 per cent. professional,

In 1934 the total number of girls of all ages enrolled in national organizations was 780,572, and the Girl Guides had by far the largest membership, the next in order of size were the Girls' Friendly Society, the Girls' Brigades and the Y.W.C.A.[1]

Attempts are being made at present to break down the separation of Boys' and Girls' organizations. Thus, "it is significant that while the falling off in club membership occurs when the girls began to be interested in boys," the report on *Youth and Leisure* states, "many groups which are springing up spontaneously all over the country are 'mixed.'"[2] The youth groups of political organizations, of the Co-operatives and of the League of Nations Union are mixed; none of them, however, has a considerable membership. The "Fellowships" directly organized by the churches are also in most cases concerned with both boys and girls. The Y.W.C.A. and the Y.M.C.A. are seriously considering the question of closer co-operation. We read in the *Y.W.C.A. Review*, 1937, that "the girl who didn't 'take to do with boys' used to be regarded as

19 per cent. domestic, 28 per cent. women and girls of leisure, 2 per cent. students.

SWANSEA.—10 per cent. professional, 40 per cent. business, 15 per cent. domestic, 15 per cent. leisured, 20 per cent. students.

In 1937 the total membership of the Y.W.C.A. was 40,000.

[1] For complete details see Rooff, *op. cit.*, p. 235. For the same year the figures for the Girl Guides were in England and Wales:

Section.	Age Group.	Number.
Guides	11–16	252,463
Brownies	7–11	162,790
Rangers	16 and over	51,595
Leaders	—	42,829

Since the Guides do not register their members according to the same age groups as the other national societies it is, unfortunately, impossible to arrive at an estimate of the proportion of the total fourteen to eighteen age group in Great Britain in touch with such organizations. The total of the fourteen to eighteen group, Girls, was in 1934, 1,415,000.

[2] P. 84.

the ideal club member. It is now seen to be natural and necessary that boys and girls together should find in the club not only enjoyment, but help in facing some of the terrific problems, both personal and world-wide, with which they are confronted."

Three noteworthy youth organizations do not separate their male and female members. The "Wayfarers' Sunday Association," which was founded in 1928, seeks to provide special Sunday Clubs for girls and boys. The girls form a committee called the "Bodyguard" which runs the Club, boys who have been introduced and proved to be good "Wayfarers" are registered as the "Service Corps." In 1934 this organization had nine centres, most of which were in London, and approximately 2,000 members.

The Young People's Adult Schools, an auxiliary to the Adult Schools, provide a type of club life different from any previously discussed. Members meet informally, exchange their views, listen to talks, everything is very informal and spontaneous. This movement has a religious basis; it is distinguished by its democracy, and its absence of symbolism and officialdom. In 1934 there were, however, less than 2,000 members of young people's groups.

The Young Farmers' Clubs, which after the War were introduced from the U.S.A.[1] by Lord Northcliffe, are an interesting educational and agricultural experiment. The Clubs are open to boys and girls between ten and twenty-one. "The central feature of the Clubs' work is the running, by each member, of some small agricultural enterprise," which "is regarded throughout

[1] The 4 H Clubs in America, the corresponding organization, has a membership of one million boys and girls.

as a miniature business and not as a hobby, and every effort is made to maintain a business outlook with regard to it. In some cases the necessary initial loan has been raised by local subscription or has been made by a local benefactor; finally, funds have often been raised by means of a bank overdraft under the guarantee of the members of the Advisory Committee." [1] Thus this movement, like the other voluntary organizations, is dependent on patronage and it has succeeded in finding generous patrons.

The central administration of the Clubs was taken over in 1928 by the National Council of Social Service, with the financial support of the Ministry of Agriculture. They formed an Advisory Committee of interested persons and appointed an organizer. The Committee called together in 1929 the leaders of all existing Clubs, and this meeting decided upon the formation of a National Association, to which the individual Clubs might affiliate. In 1931 a further generous grant from the Carnegie United Kingdom Trust made possible a considerable increase in the headquarters staff, and somewhat later still the constitution was modified and the present National Federation came into being as an independent body." [2]

During the last year the Ministry of Agriculture has, in addition, given an indirect grant. King George's Jubilee Trust and the National Farmers' Union have also helped financially.

At present the National Federation includes 310 Clubs, with 800 members in England and Wales. Since "it is, however, difficult to overcome social

---

[1] "Young Farmers' Clubs," Watson, Professor J. A. S., *The Scottish Journal of Agriculture*, vol. xvi. No. 2, April 1933.   [2] *Ibid.*

barriers in rural areas, it often happens that the sons and daughters of farmers, and not the children of farm labourers, are to be found in the Young Farmers' Clubs in the villages." [1]

The question should be asked, before leaving the youth organizations, of the proportion they cover of the total youth population. The position in one part of the country seems to vary from another, and whilst general estimates have been made concerning boys' organizations, no similar estimate is available regarding the girls. At Becontree and Dagenham, not more than 1 in 8 of the age groups five to seventeen years, boys and girls, belong to any society or association. Such a figure is low, especially since, as a rule, more children than youths are members. Therefore, if the ages were restricted to fourteen to seventeen years, the proportion would decrease still further. In Liverpool, of the girls fourteen to eighteen years, 38 per cent. belonged to the main juvenile organizations, whilst the corresponding societies for the boys claimed only 33 per cent. of this age group. These percentages are high, and it is also very unusual to find proportionately more girls than boys organized in their leisure hours. Probably the explanation of the high percentage organized lies partly in the helpful attitude of the local Education Committee, who readily assists juvenile organizations by such means as grants. In the case of the girls it is also partly to be explained by the large numbers employed locally in personal service. Domestic servants are foremost in their willingness to join social clubs, and in Liverpool a Union of Girls' Clubs has existed for as long as fifty years.

[1] Rooff, op. cit., p 22.

Sheffield shows a position nearer to the average over the whole country. One in seven of the boys and 1 in 9 of the girls were attached to one or other of the chief juvenile societies.

In 1928 it was estimated, for the country as a whole, that about 1 in 5 boys were to be found in an association such as is affiliated to the Juvenile Organization Committees. After a very complete survey in 1936, the British Medical Association confirmed this estimate.[1]

---

[1] Young, Terence, *op. cit.*, p. 224 ; *Survey of Merseyside*, vol. iii. p. 132 ; Owen, A. D. K., *Juvenile Employment and Welfare in Sheffield*, 1933 (pamphlet) ; Russell, *op. cit.*, p. 23 ; British Medical Association, Report of Physical Education Committee, 1936.

Part II

OPEN AIR RECREATION

ACCUSTOMED to our reputation as sportsmen, a foreigner might be interested to read "that over four million children had nowhere to play: that whilst Secondary schools were well equipped with playing fields, it was the exception rather than the rule to find similar provision made for children in Elementary schools." "Of rural areas it would be a generous estimate to say that not one parish in ten possesses a public recreation ground or open space, and in some counties the proportion falls as low as 1 in 44." [1] He would be startled to find that the description refers not to the distant past but to only a few years ago, and that although since its inception, in 1925, the National Playing Fields Association has been instrumental in securing open spaces for more than two million persons on a basis of 5 acres per 1,000 inhabitants, "the fringe of the question of providing adequate spaces measured by these standards has been hardly touched." "In Middlesborough there are only 5 acres for 5,000 persons," similarly in Derby. In London, the County Council must reject two-thirds of the applications for sports pitches from lack of accommodation. Thus, although each week during the Season approximately 40,000 amateur Association Football matches and 4,000 to

---

[1] The quotations and statistics concerning open spaces are all from literature kindly supplied by the National Playing Fields Association.

5,000 Rugby Union and Rugby League matches are played, it is clear that many would-be players are excluded through a deplorable shortage of pitches. The figures in respect of cricket are, unfortunately, unobtainable, but it is certain that the same lack of grounds exists. Moreover, sports grounds in big towns are tending to be swallowed in the builders' maw, in London at the rate of 1,700 acres per annum. In spite of the devoted efforts of the National Playing Fields Association, therefore, at least twice the area which they have secured all over the country for recreation and games has, in the capital alone, been transformed from open spaces into building land. In other words, so far from improving, the position has rapidly deteriorated. Town-planning authorities are now setting a minimum of 7 acres per 1,000 of the population. Provided they have powers to enforce such a standard in all places the newly developed areas will not repeat the bareness of both the towns and villages at the present time.

A brighter picture is presented when we turn to less organized open-air activities such as rambling, cycling and camping. More and more people of all ages are walking in the countryside, either in private parties or organized as members of clubs. The Youth Hostels Association provides accommodation for ramblers at 1s. per night and its membership is rapidly increasing. During the last five years it has trebled and is now approximately 80,000. A very high proportion, about 70 per cent., are under twenty-five years of age, probably men outnumber the women by 2 to 1, whilst "A rough estimate of occupational membership puts one-third as manual workers, one-half of the 'black-coat' group, and the remaining fraction as of the student university type."[1] The Camping Club of Great Britain and Ireland has sections covering canoeing and caravaning of all kinds, in addition to owning many permanent camp sites. Its membership is not large, approximately 8,000, the great majority being people who have time and money to spend in camping frequently at weekends and for touring or camping holidays abroad. Other organizations such as the Woodcraft Folk cater for juveniles, but their membership is even smaller, being only 3,000 or 4,000. The figures for such clubs do not give any real indication of the total numbers who are actively engaged in camping and touring, since mostly the participants are unorganized. Similarly, in rambling and cycling, the Ramblers' Association and the Cyclists' Touring Club have both increased greatly during the past twenty years, from 8,500 to approximately 38,000 in the case of the C.T.C. The increase in those joining is probably commensurate with the increase in the total of the persons rambling and cycling. It is certain that far more are engaged in these pastimes than at any time previously, and this seems a permanent change in habits affecting a large proportion of the youth of the country.

The participation in all such activities has undoubtedly been increased by the extension of holidays with pay for all types of employees. It was recently calculated by the Trades Union Congress that of those persons earning per annum £400 or under, not less than five millions now have annual holidays of one or two weeks with pay from their employers. The Government wish to increase the total by another

[1] *New Survey of London*, vol. ix. p. 21.

800,000, on the ground that this number of domestic servants should be included in any such calculation. Whichever figure be accepted, it means that a substantial advance has been made towards the desirable state where every person receives an annual holiday with pay.

One other open-air activity should be mentioned since it occupies probably a considerable portion of the free time of 600,000 to 1,000,000 persons. In the urban areas of England and Wales there were at the end of 1936, according to the Returns of the Ministry of Agriculture and Fisheries, 605,026 allotments. Each year the total number and the total area shows a slight decrease, compared with the preceding period, of between 1 per cent. and 2 per cent., mainly owing to the encroachments of the builders. The National Allotments Society Ltd. has affiliations of approximately 100 local societies, representing roughly 100,000 members. This figure is about one-half of those belonging to the corresponding French Association, and is probably the measure of the difference which allotment holding plays in the leisure habits of the workers in the two countries. In fact, it is stated that gardening forms the main occupation of the French labourer and artisans outside their working hours.[1]

[1] Beaudemoulin, Jean, *Enquête sur les loisirs de l'ouvrier français* (doctor's thesis).

Part III

BROADCASTING

NOTHING so far has been said about radio and its influence on leisure. The omission is deliberate. The detailed knowledge concerning the impact of wireless is slight, while practically nothing can be said *a priori* of the changes which it may have brought into leisure habits. Radio is not merely one unit: its import differs when it is broadcasting a message from the King at Christmas, a fireside chat by the President, or when the programme is dance music at 11.30 p.m.

Accordingly, the many detailed investigations which have been made into leisure habits regarding the radio tell us little. Did people stay at home deliberately to listen-in? Were they merely tired or lazy and so would have stayed at home in any case? Did they, in fact, listen or was the wireless merely switched on, forming a background which had to be overcome when conversation occurred? Even when we are told that radio listening is a regular habit, we still require to know what selection is exercised in the programmes heard.

In other words, it is difficult to say how radio has altered the manner of spending free time, and it is impossible to say whether it has brought about any general change in people's outlook. The one certain result is, perhaps, that interest in music, as shown by the sale of gramophone records and attendances at concerts, has in this country grown considerably since the introduction of broadcasting. That 8,500,000 wireless licences have been issued in Great Britain is clear evidence of the very large number who at some time or the other actually tune in, and it is evidence for not much more than that. Where, as in Australia, the broadcast descriptions of horse racing are excellent and attendances at the track itself often involve a journey of hundreds of miles, the effect has been to cause a very large drop in the numbers of spectators. The influence of wireless is clear in such a case. Where, as in the United States, commercial firms pay hard cash for purchasing time, and, moreover, as much as $7,000 to $8,000 per half-hour to the artiste, then it is a matter of importance to discover the impact of the programme. This is done by means of frequent door-to-door surveys, and presumably they are satisfied that people listen since they continue to sponsor the artistes. Accordingly, it is possible to say, when Eddie Cantor, Jack Benny or whoever it may be is broadcasting, that a certain and large number of people will have tuned in.

The influence of wireless, in short, depends in some cases upon the nature of the programme, and in others upon its relation to the general social and political atmosphere of the time. If attention is being directed to a particular topic by the events in Parliament or as the result of incidents in the international sphere, then an authoritative broadcast will be listened to by millions. The importance of radio in such a context is shown by the effects of the broadcast by Mr. Runciman just prior to the General Election of 1931. Perhaps a still clearer instance is that when the Austrian Nazis attempted a putsch in 1934, their first act was to seize the broadcasting station. On the other hand, some programmes can stand on their own legs. Thus a popular film or music hall figure is assured of a universal audience. The impact of radio also depends upon the strength of counter-attractions, and at the moment there is no known method of assessing these, particularly since they vary from day to day.

The uncertainty of the extent of the audience can, of course, be overcome by linking radio with an organization, either of its own as Group Listening— there are approximately 640 Groups in Great Britain —or with an already established one as broadcasting to schools. Clearly wide possibilities exist in such work. A further technical advance in joining wireless and television will perhaps result in an important and permanent change in the habits of people such as the films have caused. It may be doubted, however, whether such a change will occur until the two services combined cost as little as the cinema and until they become as realistic as the movie screen.

Part IV

ORGANIZATIONS FOR ADULTS

SINCE concern with the "right use of leisure" has only just begun in this country, there are at present few recreational organizations for adults, and those which exist have comparatively low membership. The rich are well provided with their traditional social institutions, their entertainment, their travel, their sports, their clubs, their committees and their honorary social work. Amongst the middle classes there exist a multitude of small and large societies, established for some definite purpose, some kind of sport, some branch of the arts, drama and choral singing.[1] Of all organized artistic activities, the latter two are the most flourishing. The British Drama League had, in November 1937, 3,983 members and 2,756 societies were affiliated. The League is in touch with about 5,000 other play-reading groups and societies. There are also 341 village societies affiliated, 34 county rural committees, and 25 other federations working in the villages.[2]

Another reason for forming and joining an organization is the desire for the interchange of professional and social experience or, related to the first, the urge

---

[1] " Choral and Orchestral Societies are active in many parts of the country and . . . on the whole by reason of high fees membership is drawn from the salaried workers or the leisured members of the community...." Rooff, *op. cit.*, p. 37.

[2] See *Drama*, published by the British Drama League, November 1937.

to undertake social work. The first motive stimulated in 1905 the foundation of Rotary in America, and in 1911 the formation of the first Rotary Clubs in England.

Whilst originally "vocation" was the Rotarian's main concern,[1] it has later become "service in vocation." Thus Rotary is now "a world fellowship of business and professional men united in the ideal of service." Only men in executive positions can join, and only one representative from each type of commercial enterprise in the locality. Lunch meetings "which the members are pledged to attend with a prescribed degree of regularity"[2] are a universal feature of Rotary and so is the undertaking of much social work, the choice of which is governed by local needs. Rotarians assist statutory and voluntary organizations and, since they are particularly concerned with youth, clubs for young people are in many places sponsored or maintained by them.[3] In England and Ireland, in 1937, there were 429 Rotary Clubs which had 19,719 members.

The second type of organization is represented primarily by the Settlements. Their "Mother," Toynbee Hall, was founded in 1884 by Samuel Barnett, the "pale clergyman of Whitechapel." He was assisted mainly by Oxford men, to whom he had "outlined his

---

[1] "In the early days . . . the 'Fifth object' of the movement was: 'To advance the business interests of the individual members of the affiliating Rotary clubs.'" See *Synopsis for Rotary*, published by the Rotary International Association for Great Britain and Ireland, p. 25. Nowadays (*ibid.*, p. 11) "Rotarians are not in Rotary to do business with each other."

[2] *Ibid.*, p. 7. A Rotarian is pledged to make 60 per cent. of the possible number of weekly attendances in the course of each year.

[3] The Soroptimists, a sister movement of the Rotarians, support and sometimes take charge of the Girls' Club.

plan of colonies of University men in industrial areas, where they would be brought into friendly contact with the people, where they would themselves learn as they helped, and where, as the natural leaders of the community, they would teach and join in local government." [1]

Toynbee Hall subsequently mothered many schemes of social reform and social research, and became a "home experiment in working-class education." [2] But perhaps the greatest importance of such places lies in their function as a neighbourhood centre. They establish a tradition for the youth of adjacent districts to join the settlement: men, women and societies know that there is a place where they can meet. Through such hospitality, interests and a variety of social contacts are brought into people's lives.

The need for such stimulation is recognized by two recently established women's organizations, one is operating in rural and the other in urban areas. The first, the Women's Institutes, was started in Canada in 1897 amongst country women. During the War they were introduced into England, the first Institute was founded in 1915 with the purpose of assisting food production, preservation and preparation. The sponsors were the Agricultural Organization Society and the Board of Agriculture, which in 1917 took over completely the propaganda for the Institutes, whilst policy was directed by a newly formed National Federation. The Institutes are still concerned with "better feeding" and thus they have gained the

---

[1] *The Times*, 21st December 1935.
[2] *Toynbee Hall*, 1844-5 to 1934-5, pamphlet.

support of the husbands, of whom one is reported to have said, "I'm all for the Institutes: they make a man's home comfortable." Competitions and exhibitions of cooking, dressmaking, millinery and upholstery are organized. The social side of the meetings is now more emphasized than at the beginning. Tea and some entertainment is provided at the afternoon meetings which are usually held once a month. Interest in local government is promoted, and special talks and lectures are arranged. The Institutes co-operate with Rural Community Councils and often assist Young Farmers' Clubs. They had approximately 350,000 members in 1937, almost all of whom were housewives. Such Institutes can only be formed in villages and small towns with a population of less than 4,000 people. Hence a somewhat corresponding urban organization has recently arisen.

The Townswomen's Guilds are really the offshoots of the suffragette movement. They were launched in 1929, a year after women had received the vote on the same terms as men, on the suggestion of the National Union of Societies for England Citizenship.[1] The objects of the Townswomen's Guilds are:

"1. To encourage the education of women to enable them as citizens to make their best contribution towards the common good.

2. To serve as a common meeting-ground for women irrespective of creed and party, for their wider education, including social intercourse."

Their actual programmes parallel those of the Rural

[1] This Union was originally the National Union of Women's Suffrage Societies, founded in 1897.

Women's Institutes, but instead of "feeding," "civics" is primarily emphasized. In 1937 there were 323 such guilds in England, 66 in Scotland and 26 in Wales. It is believed that amongst their membership business women are in a majority.

Similar Guilds and Women's Fellowships are organized in some places by the political parties, and by the Co-operative societies, and almost everywhere by the Churches.

The Community Centres on New Housing Estates also organize Women's Neighbourhood Guilds. On the whole, more attempts are made to organize social life amongst working- and middle-class women than amongst their husbands.

The majority of the men spend most of their free time either at home, in the garden or allotment, in the public-house or in the club. The number of such clubs, particularly working men's clubs, still seems to be growing.

With longer hours for drinking and at a lower charge, with better opportunities for rest and talk than in the public-houses, these clubs form a welcome alternative. A few have attempted to introduce some form of education amongst the facilities they offer, but their example has not been followed widely although the Union does its best to stimulate such interests. The leisure hours of the working man are still dominated by his tiredness and by his wish for complete informality.

In the circumstances, it is hardly surprising that "Industrial Welfare" has not been successful. The Industrial Welfare Society was founded in 1918 in order "to encourage firms to develop such voluntary activities as affect the safety, health, security and social well-being of their work people." At present, the Society is in touch with, and is supported by, approximately 1,000 firms, mainly the large ones. A special enquiry on physical education in industry undertaken by the Society in 1936,[1] revealed that more facilities were provided by the heavy industries than by the light industries, but that in the case of the former an even smaller proportion of employees made use of them than in the case of the latter. Most of the 88 firms which replied to the questionnaire issued by the Society, had more than 1,000 employees, the total number being 367,306. However, only 92,015, 25 per cent., were registered as members of the works' recreation schemes.[2] In the light industries 36 per cent. of the staff were members and 23 per cent. of that of heavy industries. "As regards the numbers who engage in systematic exercises figures are wholly incomplete. In no case did it appear to include any but a very small percentage of the employees. There is evidence of many classes which for years have struggled with small attendances and finally been abandoned." Thus the enquiry led to the conclusion that "a great many difficulties" hamper the successful running of works sports clubs, one of them being "a desire amongst workers to spend their leisure time away from the works and their fellow employees." And "finally it appears that, though much is being

[1] The Society supplied this evidence for the British Medical Association's enquiry into Physical Education. See the B.M.A. Report on Physical Education, 1936 (pamphlet). The results of the Society's enquiry which are referred to here were published in detail in *Industrial Welfare*, July 1936.

[2] "The figures on the numbers of participants in works physical recreation schemes can only be considered as very approximate to the real position. Most sports clubs have a register of membership, but keep no records of active participation." *Industrial Welfare, op. cit.*

done by employers, there is frequently some opposition from workpeople to the attempts which savour of paternalism. Leisure is felt to belong to the worker, and although welcoming help in the provision of facilities, in the organization of games there is desire for democratic control." [1]

"Where girls are active," says another recent survey,[2] "it is often found that the majority of the members work in the office staff and few are manual workers." In view of this failure some firms have adopted the alternative of providing clubs away from the factory in the centre of the town. Others "support local clubs which are open to girls of any occupation. Many of the large open clubs in the country with full-time paid leaders receive generous donations from firms or from those connected with large works. Many labour managers are also to be found as voluntary helpers in clubs and some play an active part in the local Union (Federation of Clubs) outside the factory." [3]

The oldest voluntary society in England providing recreation and education is free from patronization of any kind and its administration is democratic. The Adult Schools, started by a Wesleyan layman, William Smith, in 1798, were designed to teach reading and writing to industrial labourers on Sundays. The movement spread and in the middle of the nineteenth century it was the Society of Friends which sponsored this new form of popular education. The Friends'

---

[1] *Industrial Welfare, op. cit.*, similar views were expressed by the B.M.A. Physical Education Committee itself, for which this enquiry had been undertaken. "Recreational schemes for industrial workers will be most successful where employers while encouraging and providing facilities for physical activities leave the organization and maintenance to the employees."
[2] *Youth and Leisure, op. cit.*, p. 66.   [3] *Ibid.*, p. 68.

ORGANIZATIONS FOR ADULTS 243

First Day School Association fostered schools until, in 1899, their number had grown sufficiently to warrant the foundation of an independent National Adult School Council.

The forms and the objects of study changed with the changing times, soon other books, in addition to the Bible, were read, and the weekly meeting was transferred from the evening to the morning of Sundays. In its essentials, the free association of men and women devoting themselves to some common subject of interest, the movement has not altered, although it has been remarkably flexible in responding to new needs which have arisen. Nowadays, there are 1,160 Adult Schools in England, "with a total membership of 34,390 and an average attendance of 22,593, which is upwards of 65 per cent. of the whole." [1] Each year a lesson Handbook is prepared for the use of the schools.[2]

Literature, science, history and economics are discussed. "Extension work figures in 100 schools, Handicrafts in 137, Drama in 146, Lecture Schools or Courses in 90, Prison work in 35, and in 470 others there is Social Service work of alternative specified kinds. In the great Peace Ballot 602 schools took part; 231 had members attending Summer Schools, and 256 supported outside classes such as those of the Workers' Educational Association." [3] Week-end schools, holidays and correspondence study have been arranged as well. These schools have certainly led

---

[1] National Adult School Union, Annual Report, 1936.
[2] The last three Handbooks have the titles, *Personality in the Making*, *Achievement and Challenge*, and *Towards Community* ; each of them has a circulation of approximately 20,000 copies.
[3] National Adult School Union, Annual Report, 1936.

the way and are now co-operating with the more recent organizations for Adult Education.

Adult education cannot be described in the detail its importance warrants. Moreover, the task has elsewhere been recently done.[1] Three main branches may be distinguished. The Technical Colleges and Evening Institutes maintained by the local Education Authorities, providing tuition in vocational, particularly commercial, and non-vocational subjects: the Extramural work of the Universities, combined with that of the Workers' Educational Association in providing University Extension Courses, Three Year Tutorial Classes, Sessional and One-Term Lecture Courses, all in non-vocational subjects. These are supplemented in an important fashion by many of the Settlements throughout the country arranging their own lecture courses. Then come a large and heterogeneous collection of organizations and societies which arrange educational meetings either as their primary or subsidiary purpose. Their number is large and their membership varies.[2]

Technical Colleges and Evening Institutes are attracting more and more students. An analysis of the nearly two and a half million enrolments on the part of 956,224 students in 1936 shows that vocational subjects account for half, and that if English and Mathematics be included, since they are very largely of a commercial, strictly utilitarian, nature, the proportion is increased

---

[1] See Peers, Robert, *Adult Education in Practice*, London, 1934; Rowse, R. C., *An Introduction to the History of Adult Education*, 1933 (pamphlet); Cole, G. D. H., *The Condition of Britain*, London, 1937, chapter, "The Educational System." All these contain bibliographies. For an account of the worth of Evening Institutes, see *Adult Education and the Local Education Authorities* (H.M. Stationery Office, 1933).

[2] For a short account of their work and a list of their names, see *The Auxiliaries of Adult Education*, Williams, W. E., 1934 (pamphlet).

to three-quarters. Physical training is the only other subject to attract large numbers. A high proportion of these students attend to increase their knowledge of the process in which they are employed, as is shown by 331,000 enrolments for industrial subjects. An even greater group, the same students largely accounting for the numbers who have enrolled in Mathematics, Languages and English, are studying professional and commercial subjects. They number 476,000 [1] and almost all of them come with the object of passing some educational test necessary for advancement in their employment. It may be, for instance, to try to reach a higher speed in Shorthand, to get through a Civil Service examination, or to secure a minor professional qualification. Their total is growing, since it becomes ever more necessary to secure some mark of distinction if any hopes are to be entertained of progressing in commercial or industrial employment.

Very different is the Workers' Educational Association. There is no reward or certificate at the end of the course, attendance is completely voluntary and the subjects taught are non-vocational. Three out of every five classes arranged in the United Kingdom during the Session 1935-36 related to the social sciences; Literature and Dramatic Art accounted for another fifth. The number of students enrolled is nearly 60,000. It has grown slowly and almost without set-backs since the foundation of the Association in 1903. The official description of the work is "non-party-political and non-sectarian," but, as stressed by Professor Tawney in his Presidential Address,

[1] For the statistics given, see *Board of Education Report*, 1936, Cmd. 5564. The figures refer to England and Wales.

1936, there is an emphasis upon the first word of the title. The occupations of the students support this emphasis although the position varies from district to district. London, with 8 per cent. of the students, has only 5 per cent. of the manual workers; South Wales, with only 10 per cent. of the students, has nearly 25 per cent. of all the manual workers. Over the whole country nearly 30 per cent. are manual workers, whilst many of a further 20 per cent., who are women engaged in "Domestic and Home Duties," would belong to the same social category.[1]

One feature should be commented upon—the high average age of the students. A recent sample enquiry in London, confined to Three Year Tutorial Class students, gave it as 33·1 years,[2] and another, made in 1933, showed that those under 30 represented only 30 per cent. of the total.[3] Various explanations can be offered. Clearly the competition of the Evening Institutes is serious and considerably more than half of their students are under twenty-one years of age. Secondly, more boys and girls than previously have the opportunity to secure higher education, and hence only when they are older do they have recourse, if at all, to the W.E.A. Thirdly, modern work combined with modern amusements does not inculcate an attitude likely to breed a thirst for knowledge. There is no need to comprehend the world, in fact it seems there is nothing to comprehend; any realization of the need to replenish one's knowledge and understanding tends,

---

[1] For statistics of the Workers' Educational Association, see Annual Report, 1937.
[2] *Leisure of the Adult Student. A Sample Investigation in London*, Adult Education, March 1937.
[3] Peers, Robert, *op. cit.*, p. 61.

therefore, to come only with maturity. Probably considerable weight must be given to this explanation. Yet when the work is absorbing it can stimulate an interest in following all its ramifications sufficient to satisfy the most ardent educator. Thus, in 1934, a group of scientific instrument workers approached the authorities of Toynbee Hall requesting guidance. They were continually being asked to make surgical instruments the purpose of which they did not understand, and accordingly they were working "blindly," which was very disturbing. Could they get assistance? Lectures were arranged for them, the tutors to be mainly surgeons. Although started four years ago, the class is still continuing with large numbers regularly attending.

CHAPTER V

THE OUTLOOK FOR LEISURE

ARE there men and women for whom the problem of leisure does not arise? Do some seem to escape the difficulties experienced by the majority from the division between their working life and the rest of their day? There seem to be such fortunate people. They are found mainly amongst professional workers and artists, as members of the intelligentsia, perhaps, and this applies especially to members of the older generation, as independent merchants and manufacturers in a sufficiently large way of business to belong to the upper middle-class and, last but not least, as skilled workers. The characteristics which unite these very different types, enabling them to be put in a common category, may be listed. They all obtain satisfaction from their work. All of them have some sphere of independent action, or they are presented with problems and difficulties with which they must grapple and solve, as in the case of the skilled workers. They must employ and develop their faculties; none of them are automata. The satisfaction of turning out a completed piece of work, carrying through a completed operation or at least clearly understanding the part in the whole which their exertions play, is given to them all. Their work also makes continual demands on them in the sense that it is always presenting fresh problems to solve or giving rise to the need of acquiring new knowledge.

Because of this, and because, finding satisfaction in work, they do not desire to flee from it as soon as the immediate job is completed, the impact of their profession or work is clearly discernible in all their activities. There is for them no sharp break. They read books which have relevance to their job; similarly they attend lectures and follow courses of study; they move predominantly amongst people who have the same interests and so discuss the problems of their daily task while they are not actually dealing with them; they have tended to build up leisure time associations on a vocational basis; they see the world through the eyes of a man who is a painter, an architect or an engineer, as the case may be. It is notorious how a skilled artisan is reluctant to discuss or to follow activities which are not in some way related to his occupation. In short, the method of earning their livelihood determines for them their mode of living. And it does this in such a way that they obtain satisfaction. Hence they need not search for compensations in other directions; they do not require soporifics from the world of amusement. When they have recourse to it, it is not because they experience an uncontrollable urge. Moreover, and this point is of supreme importance, they will tend to bring to such aspects of their lives the same attitude and qualities of mind as are required and developed by their work.

Thus the one dominating common characteristic is that they work and that they find pleasure in it. Such a state, therefore, seems to be the precondition for solving the problem of leisure. But at the present time are there no steps towards a solution which might be taken in the field of leisure itself?

In this country the distinguishing feature of a vast amount of recreational facilities, outside the "machinery of amusement," is their philanthropic origin. Thus the activities in a club are stopped, and it is more than an apocryphal story, for the leader to announce, "You must all welcome Mrs. X, who so kindly provides us with our money." The effect on all concerned is unfortunate.

An attitude of mind is inculcated in the rich which is illustrated by the following quotation from *The Daily Telegraph*. "The social butterfly is doomed . . . débutantes will go, after the gaieties of their coming-out season, and learn the art of being citizens. . . . Mothers want to give ex-débutantes some alternative to the festivities. . . . The 'serious' round which ex-débutantes will do after the social round will consist of . . . learning about unemployment. . . . Débutantes are usually at a loose end when their season is over. They get bored if they stay at home. . . ."[1]

The club members tend, according to their temperaments, to be resentful or indifferent, to be uneasy and uncertain how to behave, to become mere parasites anxious to obtain anything that is possible, or to develop an attitude which is "more royalist than the King," doing their best to ape the manners and outlook of their benefactors.[2] And since the philanthropy

---

[1] 27th May 1936.
[2] That the rich have not always been anxious to act as models to the remainder is evident from the following extract of a letter written in 1850 by the Duchess of Sutherland who "fears that he (the local schoolmaster) may be led into temptation by his attendance at the cricket club on Wednesday evenings." "Could anything be said to him," she writes, "about the importance of his wife *not* being smart—the example will be important and she had very playful ringlets. *The Life and Work of Sir James Kay-Shuttleworth*, Smith, Frank (London, 1923), pp. 208-9.

is exercised through movements with vague aims such as Fitness and Fellowship, few who are its objects can remain unscathed. When there is a definite end in association, and particularly when this is an artistic or intellectual one, the harm is a little to seek, the good is obvious. Thus the Bermondsey Bookshop ran successfully for ten years arranging lectures and encouraging an interest in culture.

Most of the clubs and organizations have a leader, and it is not clear that due care is taken to stimulate amongst the members initiative and energy in the managing of their own leisure and recreation. One of the main spheres left for developing these faculties accordingly tends to be closed and the stultifying effects of their work are thereby reinforced. As we have seen, the Welsh miners, the North Country textile workers and engineers, have all shown that the working people are, in fact, able to organize their own forms of recreation.

The philanthropic and patronized forms of social institutions and organizations for leisure ought, therefore, to make way for others with a different basis. Can a legitimate sphere be found in this field for voluntary workers? The answer seems to lie along two lines. The relationship should be the reverse of that which tends to exist to-day, where public money is given to be spent by voluntary bodies beyond the reach of public criticism. Perhaps voluntary workers can be incorporated into schemes which owe their origin to the decisions of Local Authorities, as is the case in the basic social services at the present time. That is to say, their place would be assigned for them within the framework of official plans. Moreover, they could then act as an instructed conscience stirring the public and the authorities.

On what basis should the fresh institutions rest? The answer has been partly anticipated above. Local Authorities, and more recently Government Departments themselves under the Physical Training and Recreational Act of 1937, have powers to develop recreational and cultural amenities. As the Appendix to this chapter shows, the powers are extensive and varied. They range from the opening of libraries to the laying out of parks and sports pitches; from the arranging of concerts and lectures to the provision of summer camps for children. Grants can be made towards setting up Community Centres and maintaining Institutes of Leisure. Such provision should be greatly extended. Certain Local Authorities have adopted many of the powers permitted to them. Bermondsey has two excellent municipal lecture halls. Birmingham municipality arranges very fine concerts throughout the winter. Wigan has an Institute of Leisure. The London County Council provides Men's Junior Institutes which are in fact very much like clubs.

Not only should the existing powers of Local Authorities in the cultural sphere be used as extensively as possible, but they should be widened. No valid argument can be found against the elected representatives of a local area providing its residents with their recreational facilities. It is an arbitrary distinction which allows a municipality to include in its health services a convalescent home for getting people back to health and yet will not allow them to provide for adults a holiday home which would go far in keeping them in health. Local Authorities may teach people to swim or to play the violin; they may provide them with books and, since the libraries are interconnected the service is an excellent one, with exhibitions of pictures and with museums. They should also be able to maintain a repertory company, in 1929 a Bill granting general powers to adopt such a service was dropped "through congestion in the House of Commons," and to show films, thus giving an enormous impetus to the production of the better type of film which now is not made for lack of a market. At the moment only those dealing with health topics may be exhibited. The poorest people should not be excluded from sports merely because participation is costly. It should be easier for them to play football, tennis or cricket than at the present time when, owing to the lack of pitches in the first, the cost of equipment in the second, and from both causes in the last, many would-be players are excluded.

Of great importance would be the provision in each area of an Institute providing free or very cheap facilities for indoor sports, lectures, committee and rehearsal rooms and a theatre; in short, all those premises and accessories which constitute the framework necessary for encouraging initiative and enterprise in organizing spontaneous leisure. A beginning in this direction has been made by the Community Centres on the municipal housing estates and by the Institute of Leisure at Wigan. Glasgow Corporation plans to build a Centre costing £80,000: it is on this scale that provision should be made, at the same time ensuring, as the Board of Education and the Ministry of

Health recommend,[1] that the people themselves have control.

Seaside towns and inland spas have, under local Acts, extensively developed municipal services of the kind which have been discussed. The object has been, of course, to make staying in these resorts pleasant to the visitors. Is it not reasonable to suggest that the same efforts should everywhere be directed towards making a place attractive to its inhabitants?

The other chief avenue open for the provision of independent, non-commercial leisure is that Trades Unions should seriously cater for the recreational activities of their members. In Great Britain alone, of the Western European Powers, do the Trades Unions fail to provide clubs, lecture halls, sports grounds, holiday homes; in general, the facilities which are necessary for spending a varied leisure.[2] Trades Union meetings in this country tend to be merely a business discussion, often held in a room of a public-house. It is eminently desirable that they should be made more attractive by being linked with social and cultural activities. Moreover, Trades Unions would, by being associated with the recreation of their members, thereby assist in bridging the gulf which now separates, for the majority, work from leisure.

These steps, the provision of recreation facilities both by Local Authorities and by Trades Unions, seem to be the chief methods available not only for

---

[1] " Ideally, we consider that in order to develop corporate activity and a sense of responsibility . . . the management of the building should be vested in those who will use it." *Report on the Need for Youth Community Centres on New Housing Estates*, 1935.

[2] " It may seem curious that in British countries there are no institutions of this kind." Mequet, G., in " International Action for Workers' Spare Time," *International Labour Review*, November 1934.

raising the standard of recreation, but for drawing more people into leisure organizations than are members at the present.

A task which perhaps lies ahead is to evolve new forms of recreation. They seem to be necessitated by the numerous and important inventions which have resulted in fresh facilities for spending leisure. That is to say, we are only at the beginning of the impact of the cinema, the radio, the gramophone and the motor-car. It is difficult, therefore, to judge what their full effects will be. One result, however, can be stated. The old forms of unsophisticated amusements were good in that they often resulted from efforts by the people themselves, they were not merely passive entertainments. They are, however, now tending to be outmoded. Thus it is a symptom of more than local and particular difficulties that a discussion should appear in the organ of the Workers' Education Association on the unsatisfactory nature of the entertainment often provided at their social events.[1] It is precisely among these and similar bodies of alive and intelligent people that such new needs are first evinced. The problem to be solved is, on the one hand, to secure active participation by the audience. On the other, it must result in an entertainment whose standard does not compare too unfavourably with that obtainable from the radio, the cinema or the gramophone.

Each age and people have evolved distinctive forms of art and of enjoyment. The present will be no exception, but the conditions for solving the problems are becoming increasingly difficult. Most of the innovations for recreation induce passivity. Conscious

[1] *The Highway*, January, 1938.

attempts are now necessary to arouse activity among the audience in the same spheres as they can enjoy the world's leading experts. But the one need not exclude the other. Appreciation is heightened by participation in sport, in art and in all forms of culture. When a man has tried to make films himself he watches the screen with new eyes. When he has attempted to become proficient in any sport, to paint, to write, to play a musical instrument, he is given a fresh insight into the difficulties involved. He can savour with greater relish the work of those who have mastered the art.

At the same time, we often secure greater enjoyment from our own attempts although their imperfections are realized, than from witnessing the performances of the virtuosos. We experience the joy of physical energy in sports. We love to display ourselves in dramatics. We achieve large satisfactions from our own painting, our own playing, our own carving or needlework. These feelings and impulses are latent in everyone. They merely need to be aroused, and, moreover, only optimists can imagine that all the potential geniuses now born actually develop their capacities. Increased participation by the people, therefore, will produce more and more great figures in the world of sport and the arts since all will have the opportunity to discover the abilities they possess.

We have said that the necessary precondition for reaching a solution to the problems of leisure is that man should work and should find pleasure in it. This means first and foremost that in a satisfactory society the scourge of unemployment will be removed. The free time which is forced upon those out of work must be spread over the whole population. The unemployed will then be rehabilitated by once more taking their place as citizens, and the anomaly will be abolished of some persons being kept in enforced idleness whilst others are overworked.

Equally important is that each man should feel he is a useful and valued member of society, and, further, that work should be intrinsically pleasant. The first will be achieved when each knows that his daily labour is serving the common good. A rise in the social status of the performance of work must accompany such a change. All will be required to justify themselves in terms of the addition they make to the common fund of wealth. The fact, moreover, of having made this contribution, whatever its shape, will constitute a claim to social recognition, and the more efficiently the duties are performed the greater will be the claim. Very different is the position to-day where a man may be a first-class handicraftsman and yet obtain therefrom no standing or mark of social approbation. The great change that is necessary, in other words, is that our standards of value should be based upon recognition of work as the primary good. It will be no more than the acceptance of the actual position: this globe cannot continue to be inhabited unless a vast amount of labour is expended every moment. Work is the basic necessity and a well-ordered society must be grounded upon its recognition. The centre of a man's life will then be his daily labour. Accordingly, during his non-working hours he will not be engaged in a restless search for a justification of his existence.

When such a transformation of values has occurred great progress will have been made towards the second goal, of making work itself intrinsically pleasant. But the final realization will be a long and difficult process. The world is now only in the infancy of mechanization. The main forms of work are characterized by monotonous, repetitive operations, wearying to the body and stultifying to the mind. Machinery dominates the industrial field and the worker is a finely adjusted automaton to serve its needs. So long as this relationship exists, so long will man find it impossible to realize himself as an individual. So long, that is to say, as he is required to spend many hours a day possessed by the machine and carrying out puerile operations, he will be unable to exercise fully in any sphere the powers with which he is endowed.

Many forms of repetitive work which are necessary to-day will, perhaps in the distant future, be eliminated. The guess may be hazarded, for instance, that typing will eventually be superseded. Already there is the dictaphone which records our speech, and the steno-typewriter which enables shorthand to be written by a machine. The two may be combined: speaking into a machine will result in our words either being printed in full or in signs as are now used on the steno-typewriter. These will be sufficient, for it will then be part of education to read such signs as we now learn to read the alphabet. The possibilities of applied science in the domestic and the industrial field are limitless,[1] so that whilst the first onset of mechanization has taken all the savour from work without relieving man from the necessity of arduous

[1] For a sober yet brain-stretching account of the possibilities which exist in the application to industry of our present knowledge of physics and chemistry, see the essay entitled " Science and Industry," in *The Frustration of Science*, London, 1935.

labour, it can be envisaged that its final result will be to return to his activities a freedom so lamentably absent to-day: man will then possess the machines.

Paradoxical as it may seem, when necessities are being supplied by machinery, a large number of men might experience the joys of creative work by turning to handicrafts for their living. And this will be possible because the abundance of wealth will allow employment in ways which, whilst eminently satisfying, are not the most productive. All, moreover, will have the opportunity, by working only short hours under pleasant conditions, to cultivate their abilities and develop a richly endowed culture.

Such a picture lies in the far future, but it is the goal towards which mankind must move. In the meantime, whilst the status of work may change, its nature will be but little altered, and accordingly other devices must be adopted to render it more palatable. One method will be to enable the worker to realize that the part he carries out belongs to an organic whole. He must be educated to understand the various operations. He must have the possibility of moving from process to process, thus being able to survey the final result from different vantage points and not living under the feeling that his lot in life is permanently to fasten a few bolts as the piece moves along the belt. In addition, it will be necessary directly to link his life outside the factory with his daily work. He must appreciate the immediate connection between his work and his leisure hours.

Two courses, supplementing each other, are open for achieving this end. In a true democracy an enormous proportion of the people will share in the administrative and social work. Organization and administration will not be left in the hands of a small minority: the social pressure exerted will give to each man a sense of duty that he should play his part. Such service will tend to become as obligatory as earning one's bread and will accordingly constitute a direct attack on the division which exists to-day between work and leisure.

The other and complementing measures which can be taken are to make the work-place itself directly associated with recreational facilities. A club, a library, a cinema, sports grounds, all can be attached to the place of work so that those who work together can spend their leisure together. Moreover, if the increased provision of such amenities is dependent directly upon the efforts of those working in the office or factory, this will bring fresh incentives to bear on the performance of work. The act of turning a lathe, winding a spool or registering an entry will then form a direct link with the world outside of work.

To-day, similar attempts to attach people to their place of employment consistently fail. It has been found that the failure is due to the hierarchy amongst the staff being imported into the recreational activities. If such methods are to succeed, therefore, equality of status must exist between those engaged in work. This does not mean that in the factory, workshop or office there will not be some who give orders for others to obey. But it does mean that the right to give the orders will be based on efficiency to do so and that outside of the work-place the equal humanity of all will be recognized. They will be prepared to mingle and to appreciate each other as human beings. Thus the ideals they follow in their leisure and their culture can evolve spontaneously, just as the folk-songs and country dances arose from the people in earlier times. The things counted valuable, the standards of behaviour, the mode of dress, will not, as now, be copied from the few who occupy the leading social positions, but will be created by the people taking charge of their own lives.

APPENDIX TO CHAPTER V

POWERS OF LOCAL AUTHORITIES TO PROVIDE FACILITIES FOR RECREATION, WITH THE RELEVANT ACT GRANTING THE POWERS.

1. *Concerts.*

Power to provide or contribute towards band in a public park: to provide limited entertainment which must not include stage plays, anything in nature of variety entertainment, or any films (except on health topics). Expenditure is limited to the proceeds of a one-penny rate unless an increase to twopence is sanctioned by the Ministry of Health.

Public Health Act, 1925, Section 56.

2. *Public Libraries and Museums.*

General powers to provide public libraries and museums.

Public Libraries Act, 1919, Sections 1 and 9.

3. *Parks, Pleasure Grounds, Recreation Grounds; Sports Pitches and Gymnasia; Holiday Camps.*

General powers to acquire land and to set aside a portion for games; to allow the use of school gymnasia in the evening by voluntary organizations or to provide separate gymnasia; to provide and equip holiday camps and camping sites.

Physical Training and Recreation Act, 1937, Section 4.

4. *Play Centres, Vacation Schools.*

General powers to provide these in schools and in other suitable buildings.

Education Act, 1921, Section 22.

5. *Community Centres.*

General powers to provide or contribute towards a Community Centre for the use of clubs, societies or organizations having athletic, social or educational objects. The Centre "or any portion thereof may be let at a nominal or other rent to any person, club, society or organization."

>Education Act, 1921, Section 86, as amended by the Physical Training and Recreation Act, 1937, Sections 4 and 6.

6. *Swimming Baths.*

General powers to provide swimming baths which may be let in winter for such purposes as dances.

>Public Health Acts, 1936.

7. *Theatres, Opera Houses.*

No general powers have been granted.

Local Education Authorities have extensive powers to provide instruction, in their Evening Institutes, in dramatics, art, singing, violin playing and similar cultural pursuits.

A Local Authority may petition either to remove the existing limits of expenditure, as fixed for concerts, or to be enabled to provide cultural and recreational services which at the moment are not within their powers.

A SELECT BIBLIOGRAPHY

HISTORICAL

Dibelius, Wilhelm: *England,* London, Jonathan Cape, 1929, Chap. V, "Industry and Population."

Halévy, Élie: *History of the English People,* London, 1924 and 1937 (Pelican Books): Book I, Chap. I, "Local Justice and Local Government"; Book II, Chap. I, "Agriculture"; Book III, Chap. II, "Fine Arts, Literature, Science."

Hammond, J. L. and B.: *The Bleak Age,* Longmans, Green & Co., London, 1934 (with short bibliography). *The Growth of Common Enjoyment,* Oxford University Press, 1935.

Marshall, T. H.: "Les noblesses: l'aristocratie britannique: de nos jours," *Annales d'Histoire Économique et Sociale,* No. 45, May 1937.

Turnour, Edward, 6th Earl Winterton: *Pre-War,* Macmillan & Co., London, 1932.

LIVING AND WORKING CONDITIONS

Aichhorn, August, *Wayward Youth,* Putnams, London, 1937.

Bell, Mrs. Hugh: *At the Works,* Edward Arnold, London, 1907.

de Man, Hendrik: *Der Kampf um die Arbeitsfreude,* Jena, 1927.

Dreyfus, Carl: *Beruf und Ideologie der Angestellten,* Duncker und Humblot, Munich, 1933.

Freeman, Arnold: *Boy Life and Labour,* P. S. King & Son, London, 1914.

Freud, Sigmund: *Civilization and Its Discontents,* London, Hogarth Press, 1930.

Grünberg, Emil: *Der Mittelstand in der kapitalistischen Gesellschaft,* C. L. Hirschfeld, Leipzig, 1932.

Halbwachs, Maurice: *L'évolution des besoins dans les classes ouvrières,* Félix Alcan, Paris, 1933.

Hellersberg, Lisbeth Franzen: *Die jugendliche Arbeiterin: ihre Arbeitsweise und Lebensform,* J. C. B. Mohr, Tübingen, 1932.

Kracauer, S.: *Die Angestellten aus dem neuesten Deutschland,* Frankfurt a/Main, Frankfurter Societäts Druckerei, 1930.

Levenstein, Adolf: *Die Arbeiterfrage*, Ernst Reinhardt, Munich, 1912.
Mills, Charles: *Vacations for Industrial Workers*, Ronald Press Coy., New York, 1927.
Nevinson, H. W.: *The English*, London, Kegan Paul, 1934.
Ogburn, William F., editor for President's Research Committee: *Recent Social Trends in the United States*, 2 vols., McGraw-Hill, New York, 1933.
Paterson, Alexander: *Across the Bridges*, Edward Arnold, London, 1915.
Rössiger, Max: *Der Angestellte von 1930*, Sieben Stäbe Verlag, Berlin, 1930.

General Works on Leisure

Burns, C. Delisle: *Leisure in the Modern World*, London, Allen & Unwin Ltd., 1932.
Boyd, Wm., and Ogilvie, W.: *The Challenge of Leisure*, New Education Fellowship, London, 1936.
C.O.P.E.C.: *Leisure*, Longmans, London, 1924.
Cutten, G. B.: *The Threat of Leisure*, Yale University Press, New Haven, 1926.
Dark, Sidney: *After Working Hours*, Hodder & Stoughton, London, 1929.
Gill, Eric: *Work and Leisure*, Faber & Faber, 1935.
Joad, C. E. M.: *Diogenes; or the Future of Leisure*, Kegan Paul & Co., London, 1928.
Missen, Leslie R.: *The Employment of Leisure*, Exeter, Wheaton & Co. Ltd., 1935.
Rives, Paul: *La Corvée de Joie*, Les Presses universitaires de France, Paris, 1924.
Spurr, Frederic C.: *The Christian Use of Leisure*, Kingsgate Press, London, 1928.
Veblen, T.: *The Theory of the Leisure Class*, Allen & Unwin Ltd., London, 1922.

Articles on General Aspects of Leisure and Work

Brown, A. Barret: "The Leisure Problem," in *Hibbert Journal*, Vol. xxviii, 1929-30.
Craven, Ida: "Leisure," *Encyclopedia of the Social Sciences*, ix, Macmillan & Co., London, 1933. (See also "Amusements, Public," and other cross-references.)

Harding, Denys W.: "Adult Education and Adult Entertainment," *Adult Education*, London, Sept. 1934. "The Place of Entertainment in Social Life," *The Sociological Review*, London, Vol. xxvi, 1934. "Variety of Work and Leisure," *Occupational Psychology*, Vol. 12, No. 2.

Mannheim, Karl: "Der Sinn des wirtschaftlichen Erfolgstrebens," *Archiv für Sozialwissenschaft*, Vol. 63.

New Aspects of the Problem of Work, International Association for Social Progress, Report of the British Section, 1934, London.

Pangburn, Weaver: "The Worker's Leisure and his Individuality," *American Journal of Sociology*, Vol. xxvii, 1921-22.

Plant, J. S.: "Sociological Factors Challenging the Practice of Psychiatry in a Metropolitan Community," *American Journal of Psychiatry*, Vol. viii, January 1929. "Social Factors in Personality Integration," *American Journal of Psychiatry*, Vol. ix, July 1929.

Sinclair, Robert: *Metropolitan Man*, Chapter "Playtime," Allen & Unwin Ltd., London, 1937.

Sternheim, Andries: "Zum Problem der Freizeitgestaltung," *Zeitschrift für Sozialforschung*, Jahrgang 1, p. 336. "Leisure in the Totalitarian State," *The Sociological Review*, Vol. xxx, 1938.

Stewart, Herbert L.: "The Ethics of Luxury and Leisure," *American Journal of Sociology*, Vol. xxiv, 1918-19.

Williams, Hubert, editor: *Man and the Machine*, Chapter "The Future of Leisure," by Bowden, Sir Harold, Routledge & Co., London, 1935.

Winterstein, Alfred: "Zur Psychologie der Arbeit," *Imago*, Band xviii, Heft 2.

ENQUIRIES INTO LEISURE

Adams, Margarete: *Ausnutzung der Freizeit des Arbeiters*, Inaugural-Dissertation, Cologne, 1929.

Bouthoul, Gaston: *La durée du travail et l'utilisation des loisirs*, Paris, 1924.

Dépasse, Ch. and André A.: *L'organisation des loisirs du travailleur en Belgique et à l'étranger*, Libraire Valois, 1931.

Destrée, Jules: "De l'utilisation des arts populaires dans les loisirs ouvrières," *Revue Internationale de Travail*, February 1933.

Étienne, Mme Gaston: *L'utilisation de loisirs des travailleurs*, Eug. Belin, Paris, 1935.
Institut International de Coopération Intellectuelle, *Enquête sur l'utilisation des arts populaires pour les loisirs ouvriers*, Paris, 1932.
Institut International de Coopération Intellectuelle, *Enquête sur l'utilisation des bibliothèques populaires pour les loisirs ouvriers*, Paris, 1932.
International Congress of Workers' Leisure, Liège, 1931. With bibliography.
Jones, D. Caradog: *The Social Survey of Merseyside*, Vol. iii, Chapter "Leisure," Hodder & Stoughton, London, 1934.
"Leisure of the Adult Student: A Sample Investigation in London," *Adult Education*, March 1937.
Liverpool Council of Voluntary Aid, *Report on the Uses of Leisure in Liverpool*, 1923.
L'organisation des loisirs ouvriers, Comité National d'Études Sociales et Politiques. Session, 2nd March 1931.
Lundbergh, George A.: *Leisure: A Suburban Study*, Columbia University Press, 1934. With bibliography.
Lynd, Robert S. and Helen M.: *Middletown*, Chapter XIX, "The Organisation of Leisure," Constable & Co., London, 1930. *Middletown in Transition*, Chapter "Spending Leisure," Constable & Co., London, 1937.
Massey, Philip: *Portrait of a Mining Village*, Chapter "Leisure Activities," Fact, Ltd., London, 1937.
May, Herbert L., and Petgen, Dorothy: *Leisure and its Use: Some International Observations*, A. S. Barnes & Co., Inc., New York, 1928.
Mein Arbeitstag—mein Wochenend, 150 Berichte von Textilarbeiterinnen, herausgegeben vom Textilarbeiterverband, Verlag Textilpraxis, Berlin, 1930.
National Conference on the *Leisure of the People*, Manchester, Nov. 1919.
Neumeyer, M. H. and E. S.: *Leisure and Recreation*, A. S. Barnes & Co., Inc., New York, 1936. Contains references at end of each chapter.
Steiner, Jesse F.: *Americans at Play*, McGraw-Hill, New York, 1933. *Research Memorandum on Recreation in the Depression*, Social Science Research Council, New York, 1937.

The New Survey of London Life and Labour, Vol. ix, "Life and Leisure," London, P. S. King & Co. Ltd., 1935.
Publications of the International Labour Office on the use of leisure among the working classes:
Holidays With Pay, International Labour Conference, 19th Session, Report V, Geneva, 1935.
Holidays With Pay, International Labour Conference, 20th Session, Report II, Geneva, 1936.
Report on the Use of Leisure among the Working Classes, Geneva, 1924.
Reports of the Director of the Conference, 1925-1929, 1932.
Supplementary Report, 2nd Supplementary Report—
International Labour Review, June 1924.
      ,,   ,,   ,,   Nov. 1934.
      ,,   ,,   ,,   April 1935.
The I.L.O. Year Book, 1930 onwards.

CINEMA

Altenloh, Emilie: *Zur Soziologie des Kinos*, Eugen Diederichs, Jena, 1914.
Betts, Ernest: *Heraclitus*, Kegan Paul, London, 1928.
Commission on Educational and Cultural Films, *The Cinema in National Life*, Allen & Unwin Ltd., London, 1932.
Forman, Henry James: *Our Movie-made Children*, Macmillan Co., New York, 1933.
Funk, Aloys: *Film und Jugend*, Ernst Reinhardt, Munich, 1934.
Gregor, Joseph: *Das Zeitalter des Films*, Vienna-Leipzig, 1932.
League of Nations, International Institute of Intellectual Co-operation, *Le rôle intellectuel du cinéma*, Paris, 1937.
Lewis, Cecil Day, editor: Chapter "The Film Industry," Calder-Marshall, in *The Mind in Chains*, Frederick Muller Ltd., London, 1937.
Liverpool Quarterly, "Young People and the Films," Liverpool, January 1933.
London County Council: *The School Child and the Cinema*, Report No. 2890. *Report the Experiments in the Use of the Cinema in Schools*, 1937.
Mitchell, Alice M.: *Children and Movies*, University of Chicago Press, Chicago, 1929.

Motion Pictures and Youth, The Payne Fund Studies, Eight volumes, The Macmillan Company, New York.

(Reference should be made especially to: Blumer, Herbert, *Movies and Conduct*; Blumer, Herbert, and Hauser, Philip M., *Movies, Delinquency and Crime*; Dale, Edgar, *Children's Attendances at Motion Pictures, The Contents of Motion Pictures*.)

National Council of Public Morals: *The Cinema*, London, 1917. *The Cinema in Education*, London, 1925.

Periodicals: *Sight and Sound*, London (Quarterly). *World Film News*, London (Monthly).

Quigley, Martin: *Decency in Motion Pictures*, Macmillan Co., New York, 1937.

Rotha, Paul: *Celluloid*, Longmans & Co., London, 1931. *Movie Parade*, Studio, London, 1936.

The Kinematograph Year Book, Diary and Directory, London.

West, Rebecca: "New Secular Forms of Old Religious Ideas," *The Realist*, Vol. 1, No. 3, London, 1929.

Betting

Hilton, John: *Why I go in for the Pools*, London, Allen & Unwin Ltd., 1935. *The Public and the Football Pools: An Enquiry*, "Daily Telegraph," 1938 (pamphlet).

Rowntree, B. S.: *Betting and Gambling*, Macmillan & Co., London, 1905.

Royal Commission on Lotteries and Betting, Cmd. 4234, 4341.

Select Committee, House of Commons, on Gaming, 1844 (297) VI, 1.

Select Committee, House of Lords, on Gaming, 1844 (468, 544, 604), VI, 281.

Select Committee, House of Lords, on Betting, 1901 (370), V, 347.

Select Committee, House of Lords, on Betting, 1902 (389), V, 445.

Select Committee, House of Commons, on Betting Duty, 1923 (139), V, 1.

Leisure Organizations

No general account exists. Each Association publishes literature dealing with its work: references are to be found throughout Chapter IV.

Henriques, I. O.: *A Citizen's Guide to Social Service*, Allen & Unwin Ltd., London, 1938.
National Association of Boys' Clubs, *Principles and Aims of the Boys' Club Movement*.
Owen, A. D. K.: *Juvenile Employment and Welfare in Sheffield*. Social Survey Committee, 1933 (pamphlet).
Rooff, Madeline: *Youth and Leisure*, U.K. Carnegie Trust, Edinburgh, 1934.
Russell, C. E. B., and Lilian, M.: *Lads' Clubs*, A. & C. Black Ltd., London, 1932.
Stovin, Harold: *Totem: the Exploitation of Youth*, Methuen & Co. Ltd., London, 1935.
Wickwar, W. Hardy, and K. M.: *The Social Services: a historical study*, London, Cobden-Sanderson, 1936.

Adult Education

Hansome, Marius: *World Workers' Educational Movements: their Social Significance*, Columbia University Press, New York, 1931.
Hodgen, Margaret T.: *Workers' Education in England and the United States*, Kegan Paul, London, 1925.
Martin, G. Currie: *The Adult School Movement*, Nat. Adult School Union, London, 1934.
Peers, Robert, editor: *Adult Education in Practice*, Macmillan & Co., London, 1934.
Stanley, Oliver, editor: *The Way Out*, Oxford University Press, 1923. With comprehensive bibliography.
Williams, W. E.: *Auxiliaries of Adult Education*, British Institute of Adult Education, London, 1934.
Williams, W. E., and Heath, A. E.: *Learn and Live*, London, Methuen, 1936.
World Conference on Adult Education, 1929, London, 1930.

INDEX OF NAMES

Aichhorn, August, 101-2, 103, 104
Balchin, Nigel, 22 n.
Baldwin, Earl, 13
Beaudemoulin, Jean, 232
Bell, Valentine, 12 n., 105
Beveridge, Sir William, 22
Bisland, Elizabeth, 24
Blumer, Herbert, 120, 138, 139, 140
Burt, Cyril, 135

Carr-Saunders, A. M., 13
Catton, J. A. H., 153
Craven, Ida, 1 n.

Dale, Edgar, 113, 114 n., 116, 117, 123-4, 125, 127, 128, 130, 141, 142, 149
Dreyfus, Carl, 59, 64

Farson, Negley, 57
Ford, P., 77
Freeman, Arnold, 4, 84
Freud, Sigmund, 23, 100, 101
Funk, A., 135

Gallup, Dr. George, 118 n.
Glass, David, 51
Gorell, Lord, 34 n.
Gray, J. L., 13

Halbwachs, M., 79
Hammond, J. L. and B. J., 11, 41, 189, 190, 194
Harris, Constance, 4
Hauser, Philip Morris, 138, 140
Hellersberg, Lisbeth Franzen, 86 n., 89, 90, 91
Hitchcock, Alfred, 44, 127
Hilton, John, 183 n., 184

Joad, C. E. M., 2 n.
Jones, D. Caradog, 113, 161

Keynes, J. M., 182

Lang, Fritz, 143
Laski, Harold J., 17, 53
Levenstein, Adolf, 80
Loveday, A., 24
Lundbergh, G. A., 39, 52
Lynd, Robt. and M., 6, 39, 51, 117

Massey, Philip, 95 n.
Masterman, C. F. C., 174
May, Herbert, 2 n., 45, 53
Mess, Henry A., 87, 105
Mitchell, Alice, 116, 139
Moshinsky, Pearl, 13

Neumeyer, M. H., 105 n., 114
Nevinson, H. W., 87, 88

Passos, John dos, 24
Paterson, Alexander, 4, 30, 110
Pearse, Innes H., and Williamson, G. Scott, 109
Peers, Robert, 244
Petgen, Dorothy M., 45 n., 53
Plant, J. S., 14 n., 59, 90

Rooff, Madeline, 77, 221, 222, 227, 236
Rotha, Paul, 124 n., 147
Rowntree, B. S., 161, 172, 177
Russell, C. E. B., 193-6, 199, 206, 207, 208, 211, 219, 228

Sheean, Vincent, 57
Silex, Karl, 19
Smith, Adam, 9-10
Spurr, Frederic, 2 n.

Ure, Andrew, 29

Vajkai, J. F., 9

Watson, Professor J. A. S., 226
Wesley, John, 159
West, Mae, 146

Wilde, Oscar, 42
Winterton, Earl, 20, 38 n., 42 n.

Young, Terence, 85, 228

Zeitler, Dr., 107 n.

INDEX OF SUBJECTS

Adult education, 242-7
Adult Schools, 242
Amateur football, Association, 153 ; number of games played, 229
Amenities, lack of, during nineteenth century, 189-94 ; in London, 29
American Institute of Public Opinion, 118 n.
Aristocracy, and country-houses, 40-1 ; and films, 44 ; and philanthropy, 35, 37, 45

Bermondsey Bookshop, 252
Betting, attempted restriction in amounts staked, 163 ; Gaming Act (1845), 167-9 ; Governments and, 163-4, 166-8, 178-179 ; by football pools, 179-187 ; and greyhound racing, 175-6 ; growth in, 159-62 ; impetus given by increased facilities in, 173, 177 ; and pin-tables, 176 ; and Press, 173-5 ; profits from bookmaking, 177 ; Stock Exchange and, 165-6, 170-2 ; total amount annually expended in, 159-60
Boys' Clubs, and delinquency, 210 ; distribution of, 211 ; and fitness, 204-5, 217 ; and gangs, 199-200 ; organization of, 207-209 ; and Public Schools, 199-204 ; and religion, 196 ; social composition of, 216 ; team spirit in, 199, 201 ; as voluntary organizations, 206-10, 217
Boy Scouts, distribution of, 211, 215 ; origin of, 213 ; and Public Schools, 216 ; social composition of, 215

Brigade, Boys', 195-6, 212-13 ; Church Lads', 213 ; social composition of, 215
British Drama League, 236
British Institute of Public Opinion, 118, 123

Camping Club of Great Britain, 231
Cinema (see also Films), boys attend more than girls, 116-117 ; children's attendances at, 114-16 ; day-dreaming and, 120 ; men's attendances at, 117-19 ; juveniles and, 132-4 ; statistics of attendance, 111-114.; social composition of audiences, 120-3 ; women's attendances at, 117-19
Clerical work, impact of, 62-7
Community and leisure, 15-16
Community Centres, 240, 254
Competition and leisure, 38-9
Competitive emulation, 58-60
Cyclists' Touring Club, 231

Daydreaming, and cinema, 120 ; by factory girls, 90
Dead End, 143
Democratization of leisure, 38
Depersonalization, and films, 148; and work, 13-14

Education and leisure, 3-4
Emigration, 12

Factory girls, 86-94
Family, and leisure, 15 ; average size of, 51 ; rôle of, in working class, 84-6
Farewell Again, 129
Films (see also Cinema), and depersonalization, 148 ; children

274

and, 131-2 ; classification of, 124-5 ; crime in, 130 ; delinquency and, 134-7 ; formal dress in, 127 ; heroes in, impecuniosity of, 149 ; libraries in, 127-8 ; luxury and, 139, 149 ; motives of film characters, 126-7 ; news-reels, contents of, 141-2 ; occupations of film characters, 128 ; politics in, 147 ; realism, need of, 144-5 ; settings in, 127 ; social mobility in, 149
Football, Association, 152, 153 ; attendances at matches, 154-155 ; number of professionals, 154
Football pools, extent of, 181 ; and Government, 180 ; motives for entering, 182-5
Frederick the Great, and *Hamlet*, 129
Fury, 143

Gambling : see Betting
Germany, leisure in, as compared with Britain, 45-47
Girls' Clubs, membership of, 222-3, 224; organization of, 221 ; and religion, 221-2
Girls in factories, 89-94 ; upbringing in working class, 86-89

Holidays with pay, 231-2

I'm No Angel, 146
Industrial Welfare Society, 240-242
Institute of Leisure, 254
Inventions, impact on leisure, 256

Juveniles, numbers in organizations, 227

Leisure, and the Cinema, 19-20 ; democratization of, 38 ; and economic depression, 30 ; and education, 3-4 ; inventions, impact upon, 256 ; of members of professions, 249 ; new forms of, 256-7 ; official control attempted, 162 ; and the Press, 19 ; relationship of supply and demand, 24-6 ; religion and, 16-17 ; rôle of, 18, 26 ; and sex, 22-3 ; of skilled workers, 249 ; similarity in different countries, 52-4 ; and work, 1, 30-1, 48-9, 258-62
Library, circulating, institution by miners in 1741, 82
Local Authorities as providers of recreation facilities, 252-5
Loneliness, 55, 109

Mobility, social, 12-13 ; and films, 149

National Playing Fields Association, 229-30
New housing estates, 55-6

Opera, absence of subsidized, in Britain, 44

Poverty, 77-8
Press, and betting, 173-5 ; contents of, 188
Professions, members of, leisure of, 249-50
Public-houses, 95-7

Racing, greyhound, and betting, 175-7 ; horse, attendances at meetings, 169 ; and betting, 170
Recreation : see Leisure
Religion, and Boys' Clubs, 196 ; and leisure, 16-17
Rotary, 237
Rugby League, 152 ; attendances at, 156 ; number of matches played, 230
Rugby Union, 152 ; attendances at, 156-7 ; number of matches played, 230
Skilled workers, leisure of, 249

Sports grounds, disappearance of, 230
Standards of value, conflict in, 92-3, 140, 140 n.

Toc H, 219-20
Townswomen's Guilds, 239
Toynbee Hall, 237-8, 247
Trades Unions as providers of recreation facilities, 255

Unemployed and leisure, 4-5, 98-108
Urban culture in England, problem of, 43-4, 190-4

Women's Clubs, in America, in England, 54; in middle classes 50-62
Women's Institutes, 238-9

Work, and depersonalization, 13-14; hours of, 72-5; incentive to, 6-9; lack of energy after, 79; and leisure, 1, 30-1, 48-9, 258-62; as topic of conversation, 110
Workers' Educational Association, 245-7

Young Farmers' Clubs, 225
Y.M.C.A., 218-19
Young People's Adult Schools, 225
Youth Hostels Association, 230
Y.W.C.A., 220

For Product Safety Concerns and Information please contact our EU
representative GPSR@taylorandfrancis.com
Taylor & Francis Verlag GmbH, Kaufingerstraße 24, 80331 München, Germany

www.ingramcontent.com/pod-product-compliance
Lightning Source LLC
Chambersburg PA
CBHW071810300426
44116CB00009B/1259